JEWS
IN BLACK
PERSPECTIVES

JEWS
IN BLACK
PERSPECTIVES
A Dialogue

Edited with an Introduction
by Joseph R. Washington, Jr.

Rutherford ● Madison ● Teaneck
Fairleigh Dickinson University Press
London and Toronto: Associated University Presses

Associated University Presses
440 Forsgate Drive
Cranbury, NJ 08512

Associated University Presses
25 Sicilian Avenue
London WC1A 2QH, England

Associated University Presses
2133 Royal Windsor Drive
Unit 1
Mississauga, Ontario
Canada L5J 1K5

Library of Congress Cataloging in Publication Data
Main entry under title:

Jews in Black perspectives.

Contents: African diaspora and Jewish diaspora / John
Gibbs St. Clair Drake—A Black nineteenth-century
response to Jews and Zionism / Hollis R. Lynch—
Jews and the enigma of the Pan-African Congress of
1919 / Robert A. Hill—[etc.]
  1. Afro-Americans—Relations with Jews—Addresses,
essays, lectures. 2. Jews—United States—Politics and
government—Addresses, essays, lectures. 3. United
States—Race relations—Addresses, essays, lectures.
I. Washington, Joseph R.
E185.61.J48 1984   305.8′924′073   83-49270
ISBN 0-8386-3209-2

To
Sophia Washington
who illuminated brilliantly
why a legitimate claim is a
value—frequently enhanced
by volunteering not to exercise
a right—rather than a virtue,
which takes no holiday

Printed in the United States of America

Contents

Acknowledgments

A symposium on "Jews in the Afro-American Perspective: A Dialogue" was held on the campus of the University of Pennsylvania, March 25–27, 1982, under the auspices of the University's Afro-American Studies Program. The symposium was made possible by a grant from the Pennsylvania Humanities Council and Meyer and Rosaline Feinstein Foundation. This book is not the verbatim proceedings of the symposium, but is the edited version of selected papers delivered at this conference.

Joseph R. Washington, Jr.

Notes on Contributors

DR. CLAYBOURNE CARSON, JR., is Associate Professor of History at Stanford University. He is the author of *In Struggle: SNCC, Black Awakening of the 1960's,* and numerous articles. He is a member of the American Historical Association and the Association for the Study of Afro-American Life and History.

DR. NAOMI CHAZAN is a Lecturer in the Department of Political Science and African Studies and coordinator, African Research Unit, The Hebrew University of Jerusalem. She is the author of *Decolonization in West Africa* and *The Human Factor in the Israeli Technical Assistance Program in Africa.*

DR. JOHN GIBBS ST. CLAIR DRAKE is Emeritus Professor of Sociology and Anthropology, at Stanford University. He is the author of *Black Religion & Redemption of Africa, Race Relations in a Time of Rapid Social Change,* and coauthor of *Black Metropolis.* He was the 1973 recipient of the Dubois-Johnson-Frazier Award of the American Sociological Association.

DR. NATHAN GLAZER is professor of Education and Sociology, at Harvard University. He is the author of *Affirmative Discrimination: Ethnic Inequality and Public Policy, American Judaism,* coauthor of *Beyond the Melting Pot,* and coeditor of *The Public Interest.*

DR. HERBERT GUTMAN is Distinguished Professor of History, Graduate School of the City University of New York. He is the author of *The Black Family in Slavery and Freedom, 1750–1925, Work, Culture and Society in Industrializing America,* and *Slavery and the Numbers Game: A Critique of Time on the Cross.*

MR. ROBERT A. HILL is Assistant Professor of History at the University of California at Los Angeles and the editor of "The Marcus Garvey Papers." He is the author of numerous articles including "Black Nationalism in Crisis: A rejoinder to Martin Kilson," and "Afro-

9

American Linkages with Africa in Transnational Perspective." He is a member of the Association of Documentary Editing and the Association of Caribbean Historians.

DR. MATTHEW HOLDEN, JR., is Henry L. and Grace M. Doherty Professor of Government and Foreign Affairs, University of Virginia. He is the author of *The Politics of the Black Nation, The White Man's Burden, Variety of Political Conservatism,* and coauthor of *What Government Does.* He is a former commissioner of the Federal Regulatory Commission.

DR. DAVID LEVERING LEWIS is Professor of History at the University of California at San Diego. He is the author of *When Harlem was in Vogue, Prisoners of Honor: The Dreyfus Affair,* and *King: A Critical Biography.* He is a member of the American Historical Association and the Authors Guild, Inc.

DR. HOLLIS R. LYNCH is Professor of History at Columbia University. He is the author of *Selected Letters of Edward Wilmot Blyden, 1832–1912, Pan-Negro Patriot, The Black Urban Condition, 1866–1971; A Documentary History,* and *Black Africa.* He is a member of the American Historical Association and of the Caribbean Studies Association.

DR. RICHARD L. SKLAR, is Professor of Political Science at the University of California at Los Angeles. He is the author of *Nigerian Political Parties, Corporate Power in an African State,* and *Toward a Humanistic Science of Politics: Essays in Honor of Francis Dunham Wormuth.* He is president of the African Studies Association.

DR. JOSEPH R. WASHINGTON, JR., is Professor of Religious Studies and Afro-American Studies at the University of Pennsylvania. Among his books are *Black Religion: The Negro and Christianity in the United States, Marriage in Black and White, Black Sects and Cults,* and *Anti-Blackness in English Religion, 1500–1800.*

Introduction

Africans and Jews embraced graciously and clashed abrasively as Negro and Semitic peoples under the umbrageous umbrella of oppressive Egyptian slavery (ca. 1800–1500 B.C.). During the half-century, 1450–1400 B.C. (or a century later, depending upon a given scholar's interpretation of a specialist's critical imposition upon the current state of empirical evidence), Moses led his Aramaic-speaking people out of bondage; and, after wandering for many years in the desert wilderness, the nomadic Aramaean tribes took the Promised Land of Canaan (the son of Ham for whom the Canaanites were named) or Palestine by conquest (ca. 1300 B.C.). The outcome of this event was the transformation of this Aramaic ethnic group into an agricultural, Hebrew-speaking people. This monotheistic group established the religion and state or Kingdom of Israel, beginning with the Judges (ca. 1300–1030 B.C.) and advancing in the united monarchy (1020–922 B.C.) whose first king was Saul (ca. 1020–1004 B.C.).[1]

The Israelites' oral literature, which transmitted variations of this clash of cultures, originated as early as the divided Kingdom (922–586 B.C.). It developed a body of writings known as the Hebrew Bible, whose highly selective and theologically finely combed scriptures rabbis fashioned as the canon (ca. 100) Christians restrictively adopted and adapted as their Old Testament, correlating it with their New testament (ca. 50–150).

No equally universal or general and influential African or Negro testament of this Israelite-Canaanite encounter of Negro-Semitic counter-cultures is known to exist or is comparable to the statement in the Ham-Canaan myth produced by Jews and recorded in the permanent Old Testament that Christians proclaim as part and parcel of the Word of God or Holy Bible.

Pernicious Western Christian repression of Jews alternately waxed and waned but continued through pogroms of the Crusades and Spanish Inquisition beyond the fifteenth century, when the Roman Catholic Church and body politics, followed by Protestant churches and states

11

in their turn, shifted the primary focus of human oppression to Africans. In the seventeenth century, previously expelled Jews were welcomed back to England, to resuscitate the severely depressed economy resulting from the English Civil War, by the Presbyterian-Puritan Lord Protectorate Oliver Cromwell (to whose anti-Quaker, anti-Catholic, and anti-Anglican Protectorate the quintessential Puritan John Milton was entirely devoted, and who was adored by the complete millennialist and consensus Puritan "Saint" John Eliot in Boston, concurrently believing he had found the 721 B.C. Ten Lost Tribes of Israel among the Native Americans whom he was energetically transforming into Indian Jews for Jesus). Thus Jews escaped the Continent and found liberty in former Anglican and Baptist clergyman Roger Williams's Rhode Island. They journeyed to freedom in America when Puritan-Anglicans, in *Old* and *New* England and the royal-proprietory colonies, with the Protestant Bible as their ultimate defense and offense or authority, were beginning (in church- and state-united England, Massachusetts, and Virginia) to challenge the Roman Catholic Church-State, specifically competing for Christian dominance of the world and for the hegemony of both the slavetrade and the "peculiar institution."

Persecuted Jews, like Quakers (who refused the Calvinist and Anglican establishment religions and who first enjoyed unprecedented personal liberty and freedom of religion outside of New Jersey and Pennsylvania in Rhode Island), singularly contributed to the growth and development of the American economy and effectively excluded the black race from their religious societies. This policy of patented ethnic polity, shared essentially by observant Jews and Quakers, differed sharply and dramatically from that of their mercantilist-capitalist competitors and religious adversaries, the Evangelical-Calvinist Puritan-Yankees who demanded that blacks be included (in segregated status) within their churches. Unlike blacks, Jews and Quakers were not only people of enterprise, but they also comprised two religious minorities whose members profitably engaged in both the white ethnic Protestant-dominated international and domestic slavetrade and in slaveholding after the birth of democracy and slavocracy—which, invariably, proslavocrats treated as identical twins. Prior to 1776, Quakers very nearly succeeded in standardizing as a categorical imperative non-involvement in the slavery system (at any level) as the consensus criterion for good standing in the Religious Society of Friends, and thus eclipsed every other American religious institution—notwithstanding individual Quakers, who asserted their equally sincere intentions or conscience and serious purpose demonstrated in their proslavery actions.

Somewhat similar to the statistically insignificant and unrepresentative minority of relatively powerless and comparatively uninfluential black slavemasters, who were prompted by the intrinsically malevolent (or anti-Black race)[2] system (in a more imaginatively defensive than egregiously offensive manipulation of evil that good might abound) to own slaves—who were often their relatives—as the best means to shield the vulnerable from the arbitrary, Jews were frequently and chiefly commended by fugitives and freedmen as (virtually without exception) the least brutal slavemasters of the slavocracy. (This meant that the high praise earned by Afro-American and Jewish slavemasters was balanced on the backs of slaves and canceled by the essence of their existence as victims rather than beneficiaries of the system; conversely, the humane actions of the praiseworthy automatically produced blameworthy consequences).

Jews contributed the Bible and the Christian Master to Puritan-Anglicans, the inestimably mutually fertile authority they appropriated and therewith gave fundamental shape and foundational form to American culture, and (equally involuntarily but inexorably) blacks contributed their bodies: the critical capital formation of North America. In spite of the fact that Jews, unlike Afro-Americans (whom the English—largely—severed from their multi-ethnic, multi-lingual African heritage, and thus transformed the deethnicized and deculturalized American black race-specific peoplehood), share with all other American groups a distinctive ethnicity (one that is viable as a relative whole and, like other normative dynamic ethnicities, whose approach to a total way of life is distinctly aided by a vital living language, and that attracts as well as repels the positively negated black race with whom it shares slave-religion created spirituals, blues, jazz, and gospel music).[3] The further difference between Jews and Afro-Americans comprises a decisive distinction: Jews in the main resist the command to conform and become Christians (which, incidentally, is the crucial fact about John Eliot's descendants in the Moral Majority whose resolute defense of the state of Israel rests upon this ultimate objective), and therewith the whole body suffers (irrespective of individual exceptions and achievements or outside admiration of the group). But blacks are predominantly Christians who were preempted of a real alternative and choice and who demand to be citizens, but who are refused unconditional equality because the race is unacceptable to the standard of values known as the Americanization of virtue—a pervasive rejection by which each individual is bound until the race prevails.[4]

It is, therefore, no less true for being more paradoxical than ironic: Afro-Americans and Jews are among the most formidable peoples poetically shaping and forming the national superstructure and infrastructure as well as the American character, although they differ in a number of crucial ways, including the definite capacity of the one to identify with the white ethnic majority (or to be so identified), as a matter of freedom of choice or personal privilege. In spite of their different historical, social, economic, and political experiences, Afro-Americans and Jews have, as individuals, shared values (even religious ones). As involuntary and voluntary constituents of distinct disasporas, they have experienced discrimination, segregation, persecution, and rejection in what is euphemistically called the American mainstream.

In their struggle to achieve equal status and acceptance by making the American dream the American mainstream, Afro-Americans and Jews created democratic organs such as the American Jewish Congress, the National Association for the Advancement of Colored People, the Jewish Congress, the National Urban League, B'nai B'rith, and the Southern Christian Leadership Conference as means to the "preservation of the security and constitutional rights" of all Americans. In a pattern that distinguished these two from nearly all the minorities in America, Afro-Americans and Jews developed organizational alliances whose moral and financial interaction resulted in American judicial, educational, political, and bureaucratic reform.

In recent years, this traditional alliance among leadership organizations has been insufficient to stem the tide of disquieting conflict generated by the general populace. The litigation turning on affirmative action and equal opportunity legislation, particularly in the aftermath of the *Bakke* and *Webber* decisions, has sometimes exhausted the goodwill between Afro-Americans and Jews, the two harbingers of our American experiment in unity through diversity. The rising level of nationalism within each group, especially the concern with Israel by the one and the concern with the independence of Africa (focused on the dispute over the appropriate American relationship with South Africa) of the other, drives a deep wedge of resentment between Jews and Afro-Americans. The national implications of this rift are unsettling, and they hardly contribute to healthy international prospects.[5]

The impetus for this symposium emerged from these recent national issues. Humanists, particularly those who have engaged in the scholarly study of history, religion, ethics, and philosophy, are uniquely equipped to address this conflict of rights and values in a judicious manner.

This multidisciplinary exploration of Afro-American and Jewish relations will be useful because the knowledge it imparts is not only interesting and perceptive, but the practical value of the information is remarkable as well. The humanities function to increase the critical faculties, whereby knowledge of the self and the world is creatively combined to generate correctly prioritized values, coordinated for personal development and the authentic public interest for the enrichment of society. Humanists, who contribute relevant, reliable empirical data and solid ideas, steeped in compelling virtues, and who also offer sound judgment on a range of questions that relate to these demanding issues of moral and social history (that are problems and opportunities at once), must be called upon to stem the tide of fear and ignorance that abounds in minority relations, particularly the special and peculiar but most significant relationship between Afro-Americans and Jews.

The national mood of conservatism directed against these two traditional models of unity—who in the past functioned as pacesetters for liberating ideals, social justice, and political activism for all minorities—makes apparent the need for this study. With the emergence of the New Right and the resurgence of the Ku Klux Klan and the American Nazi Party, Afro-Americans and Jews can ill afford to be embroiled in illogical and specious arguments based upon propaganda and media sensationalism.

Every issue has at least two sides. Thus the Afro-American and Jewish humanist-social scientists that appear here have been selected in fair and representative numbers, based upon their sense of fairness and scholarly wisdom, which leads them to respect rational differences in intentions and purposes and to avoid taking comfort in the cold statistics of the sincere and serious (whether naive and imperceptive or also deceptive) that may be dangerous. At the same time that they are aware of the human inclination to promote power interests that are not necessarily valuable because they are valued, or desirable because they are desired, and demanded (as if flaunted enlightened self-interest successfully buried the primordial urge to flout the obligatory public interest), these scholars are acutely conscious of their role as facilitators of the academic vistas of communication in what is a most volatile issue. The reality principle, to which operative standard of moral excellence they rise, is that the challenge to be right (beyond merely correct or sheerly accurate) and good (excellent and therefore obligatory) persists between inevitable conflict of interest and the uncertainty of conciliation.[6]

The symposium (set in the aftereffects of *Bakke, Webber,* Andrew Young, and the Palestine Liberation Organization, the possible revocation of the Voting Rights Act, and the continuing debate over Israeli foreign policy in the Middle East and South Africa, after Jesse Jackson's 1979 religious-secular mission to Israel and Syria but prior to his positive 1983 moral-humanitarian appeal and response in Syria) represents an attempt to engender a logical analysis of national and international events that are threatening not only Afro-American–Jewish relations but also the relationship between world minorities. The essayists make a timely contribution to harmonizing the coordinates of consciousness-raising and conscience-bearing and thereby raise the level of civility (replete with urgency) for the advancement of the human species through the improvement of its social relations. They effectively alert us to the seductive reality of dogmatic American pragmatism and of satisfaction incurred by deference to or preference for the convenient or expedient that may seem to be relevant and useful but that is neither necessary nor the best (possible or good). The best good (or possible) is undergirded by these contributors, for they show that rational thought and action along with correctly prioritized values can both correct and overturn previous error as well as produce the equally accurate and good desire, value, interest, preference, and demand.[7]

Humanist-scholars were not asked to solve the dilemma of this currently more-diverging or less-converging life-enhancing relationship between Afro-Americans and Jews. However, through reviewing and analyzing the threads of historical similarity and diversity, as well as by examining the uniquely positive role and qualitative effect this alliance has had on the social, political, legislative, educational, and economic trends in twentieth-century America, these social scientists, as humanists, simultaneously improve our comprehension of these realities and our understanding of what individuals and communities can or should do to effect redeeming social change in order to benefit the public.

Joseph R. Washington, Jr.

Notes

1. Throughout this constricted construction I am relying upon the accurate and objective critical commentaries of the twenty-two towering biblical scholars whose essays are developed in *The Interpreter's Bible,* 12 vols. (Nashville: Abingdon-Cokesbury Press, 1952), 1:3–438.

2. My elucidation of anti-black race interest, emerging in the English roots and American Puritan-Anglican branches, is set forth in *Anti-Blackness in English Religion 1500–1800* (Lewiston, New York: Edwin Mellen Press, 1984).

3. Joseph R. Washington, Jr., *Black Religion: The Negro and Christianity in the United States* (Boston: Beacon Press, 1964), pp. 95–220; Lanham, Md.: University Press of America, 1984.

4. Joseph R. Washington, Jr., *The Politics of God* (Boston: Beacon Press, 1967), pp. 30–150.

5. Joseph R. Washington, Jr., *Black and White Power Subreption* (Boston: Beacon Press, 1969), pp. 19–115.

6. Joseph R. Washington, Jr., *Marriage in Black and White* (Boston: Beacon Press, 1970), pp. 1–148.

7. Joseph R. Washington, Jr., *Black Sects and Cults* (New York: Doubleday & Company, 1972; Lanham, Md.: University Press of America, 1984), pp. 11, 16, 132–35, 155, 163.

JEWS
IN BLACK
PERSPECTIVES

African Diaspora and Jewish Diaspora: Convergence and Divergence

John Gibbs St. Clair Drake

I have been asked to discuss "The Afro-American Journey" as it relates to our larger topic of "African Diaspora and Jewish Diaspora." It is only since the mid-1960s that the black experience has been conceptualized by scholars and publicists as analogous enough to the Jewish experience in one of its aspects to warrant the use of the term *diaspora* to refer to it. Some students of what are broadly defined as emigrationist movements began to speak of The Return (with capital *T* and capital *R*) as a dominant theme in some social movements that stressed Africa as a Homeland from which black people had been exiled into a Western Hemisphere diaspora. Some aspects of Marcus Garvey's Universal Negro Improvement Association, for instance, were referred to in the literature as embodying a doctrine of Black Zionism. Whether as metaphor or research tool, the diaspora concept has been useful in broadening and deepening our understanding of the black experience. In 1975 I contributed an article to *The Black Scholar* on "The Black Diaspora in Pan-African Perspective" in which I suggested studies of other dispersions out of sub-Sahara Africa that carried black people into Asia, the Middle East, and Europe prior to the westward dispersal across the Atlantic.

The diaspora into the Western Hemisphere was only the latest of several black diasporas spread out over four millennia. In both the Jewish diasporas and those of the African peoples, an unknown portion of those who were dispersed were "lost" so to speak through the combined interaction of two processes: cultural assimilation as the end point of the acculturation process, and amalgamation or biological absorption due to miscegenation. One of the most fascinating discoveries made by Africanists has been the extent to which the genes and fragments of Jewish culture are scattered about West Africa as opposed to the persistence in the East African Jewish diaspora of a large group of black Jews, the so-called Falashas. Herodotus discovered a colony of blacks living on the shores of the Black Sea in what is now the USSR. Blacks have been found that far afield in more recent times, too, and all Russians are aware of Pushkin's Ethiopian great-grandfather though probably only a few Americans know about a Georgia collective farm whose residents all share an obscure origin.

Of the Jews who found themselves in Asia, the last organized group, in China, in Kaifeng, was forced to close their synagogue when the Revolution came. *Encyclopedia Judaica* includes pictures and comments on several Jewish communities varied in racial type. They have persisted despite miscegenation because they defied complete acculturation. However strange their customs may sometimes seem to some of the Western orthodox when they appear in Israel, African and Oriental Jews are recognized as Jews. To use a modern black ghetto expression, "They've kept the faith." Both Africans and Jews, in their various diasporas have had to exert deliberate collective pressure to keep at least a remnant of the group together, although in the North American black diaspora a rigid caste system has prevented the Afro-American community from disappearing. In Mexico, on the other hand, the Africans were, except for a few spots in Vera Cruz and Guerrero, absorbed. The story of the worldwide wanderings of both groups, of the factors in their persistence where they have survived and in their disappearance where they did not, is fascinating. But this subject has an esoteric and exotic quality that is appropriate when I'm among my fellow anthropologists, though perhaps out of place at this particular conference.

While the scholars studying Africans have only recently begun to use the term *diaspora,* I think it should be emphasized that from the landing of the first Africans in the Americas in the sixteenth century, there were some who (like a segment of the exiled Hebrew community in Babylon) fitted the paradigm. They refused to make sport for their captors and hanged their harps on the willow tree, asking "How can I sing the Lord's songs in a strange land?" And there were always some who thought of Africa as the Jewish people did of Jerusalem, "If I forget thee . . . may my tongue cling to the roof of my mouth." We in North America are apt to forget this, for the areas where this nostalgia for the Homeland has been deepest and most persistent have been elsewhere—in certain portions of the Caribbean and South America. Parallels with the Jewish experience must not be pushed too far, however, for there has been no single religion binding the far-flung fragments of Africa's population together as there has been among the even more far-flung Jewish people—both groups, incidentally, made up of several races—nor has there been a belief in descent from a common ancestor with a common patrimony, and rituals related to The Return such as the Passover. Indeed, it is not parallels that I wish to emphasize but, rather, something else; namely, the historic intersections of pathways on the two great journeys through time and space, to see "what we can learn" about relations between the Jewish people and black people; and second, the extent to which, in the North American black diaspora, the Jewish journey has had special implications for the black journey.

From the twenties until the mid-sixties, there was a tendency within Afro-American communities to say that the Jewish people "understood" the plight of black people because they had suffered greatly themselves in the past and were even linked with blacks as "the enemy" by the Ku Klux Klan that said it was against "*K*oons, *K*ikes, and *K*atholics." The Jewish leaders and organizations were considered to be what were sometimes called "natural allies" in the struggle against bigotry. Throughout the twenties, the activities of a single individual did more to focus attention upon Jews as friends of Afro-Americans than anything else. That was the work of the philanthropist Julius Rosenwald who helped blacks to build schoolhouses in the South where local governments had neglected to do so. The Rosenwald plan provided for joint contributions by the Rosenwald Fund, the local black and white citizens, and the school board, which used tax funds and assumed future responsibility for the school and its teachers.

During the thirties, other Jewish individuals in liberal and left-wing circles became known to middle-class Afro-Americans: the Spingarn brothers who were supporters of the National Association for the Advancement of Colored People, and one of whom inaugurated the Spingarn awards to stimulate creativity in the arts and literature; the Stern family, allied to the Rosenwalds, who became known for gifts to black education; a Jewish scholar, Franz Boas, who was given credit for moving American anthropology into a firm antiracist direction, and Melville Herskovits, one of his students, for focusing attention upon the contributions of Africa to world culture. Among the masses, however, it was names occurring in newspapers, names of people they knew or suspected to be Jewish and who ran in communist and socialist circles, who attracted attention, who carried the banner of full racial equality, and who crusaded for total black liberation. Among these, Liebowitz who defended the Scottsboro Boys stood at the top of the list. When an anti-Fascist front was put together to resist Hitlerism, a large number of black Americans found themselves working side by side with Jewish individuals in a common cause. Lasting personal relationships sometimes developed.

When this so-called natural alliance persisted into the postwar years, it was gradually merged into what came to be called the "grand coalition": liberal trade unions, committees of church people, leaders of Jewish organizations, the NAACP, the Urban League, the American Civil Liberties Union, the American Friends Service Committee, and numerous other organizations that supported the civil right movement between 1955 and 1965. It is no accident that this movement assumed its first organizational expression through a Southern Christian Leadership conference and that a young black preacher was its leader. The preacher-in-politics or the preacher-as-leader-of- protest is a historic constant in Afro-American history. It was no surprise to black Americans that a Baptist preacher, Martin Luther King, became a leader of both the churched and the unchurched.

King's 1973 speech about the Dream to over 200,000 people at the Lincoln Memorial signalized the high-water mark of dedicated concerted, cooperative effort that knew no lines of race, color, or religion. It represented the kind of unity in a struggle for justice that must be restored if the gains for which many have suffered and some have died are not to be frittered and whittled away by the not-so-benign neglect of those who now sit in high places, and by the doubts, timidity, and indifference, as well as honest disagreement on tactics, of many who once fought that good fight. Reading the *New York Times* yesterday led me to alter my prepared remarks somewhat and to interpolate something here that may relate some of my wandering remarks to the current scene.

I can imagine the dismay with which some of my friends and former students read this article about the National Conference of Christians and Jews honoring the nation's president as a man who exhibits great compassion. I am inclined to interpret the action as the expression of a hope that he will develop that virtue, now that he has received the award, rather than as a statement of their sincere conviction that he has already "attained it" given some of his statements about why the poor are poor and his economic theories about alleviating their plight. I can understand those who say, "If Martin Luther King were living he and those rabbis who marched with him down South would have been in the crowd of ten thousand who protested the award outside, not on the platform inside." And so I suspect they would. And there were a few invited ministers and rabbis who did refuse to attend. Many people see a moral and ethical issue here, not just politics, and would say that any unity between Christians and Jews should occur upon a more principled basis than this meeting of the National Conference displayed.

Two other newspaper stories also caught my eye today. One was about a debate in the Israeli Knesset over issues involving the land that Begin insists upon calling "Judea and Samaria" and the Arabs insist upon calling "occupied Palestine." The other one was a short biography of our new ambassador to South Africa who recently announced that because his mother was a Jew (although he grew up in Nazi Germany and served in the United States Army) he could be counted upon to oppose apartheid. This was not a convincing argument to the NAACP which opposed his appointment. South Africa is a very sensitive point to Afro-Americans, just as Israel is with the Jewish people. I offer these remarks about the Israel article and the South African article to provide some additional context for matters to be discussed by your panel of experts later.

I want to speak briefly about a phenomenon that characterizes the Afro-American journey. It is that the recent intensification of what might be called political Pan-Africanism, which is at least one hundred years old, equally stresses common origins and common mutual responsibilities involving Africans in The Homeland and people of African descent in the West Hemisphere diaspora. This unity is not on the same intense level as the international solidarity of Jews that derives from identification with a history traceable back to an ancestor whose covenant with Jehovah defined a special people and is ritualized in a ceremony that marks the casting off of bondage, the building and destruction of a kingdom, enforced dispersal, and the hope of the ultimate gathering in of the exiles. Nevertheless, Pan-Africanism is an attitude of psychological unity that is real, full of meaning, and has historic implications.

The Need to Understand Pan-Africanism

The sentiments surrounding political Pan-Africanism began when the slaves revolted on the island of Hispaniola in 1791 and then, in 1804, established the second independent nation in the New World, Haiti. The greatest of its kings, Christophe, set aside funds for a ship to bring North American free Negroes to Haiti as settlers and actually brought Africans from Dahomey to help him administer his state. In 1847 a second black nation, Liberia, was founded, this time, in Africa.

During my early youth over sixty years ago I was trained (in my home church and I still observe the discipline) to contribute in the weekly foreign missions offering financial support for several schools and hospitals that black American National Baptists established and sustained in Liberia. In 1900, three years after the international Zionist movement began among the Jewish people, a group of black intellectuals formalized the Pan-African Congress in London, and between 1919 and 1930 William Edward Burghardt Du Bois was the catalytic agency that generated four Pan-African Congresses and, the host in himself, in 1945, presided over a fifth in England. The Sixth Pan-

African Congress met in Tanzania in 1974. Throughout the 1920s, Marcus Garvey's Universal Negro Improvement Association functioned as a mass movement giving expression to Pan-African ideas. The presence of over fifty independent African states has heightened Pan-African consciousness throughout the world.

Now, back to those *New York Times* articles. The ones on the Arabs and South Africa have Pan-African significance. If we are to fully understand why (since 1956) there has been a tendency for some politically conscious black people everywhere to sympathize with Egypt when it is disputing with Israel, we must be aware that one of the triumphs of African and Afro-American scholarship during the last thirty years has been to reclaim the history of Egypt for the black world: to remind us of what struck French scholars so forcibly when they first gazed at the Sphinx in the eighteenth century, namely, that the image is that of a Negro not a Caucasian. Today, neither Egyptologists nor laymen dispute the point. I doubt that either Aetna or the Prudential Life Insurance Company has thought seriously about this.

Previous to repeated invasions, the Egyptian people were decidedly more Negroid than they are currently. This is a more or less telling point ably argued in Cheikh Anta Diop's readily accessible paperback book, *African Origin of Civilization: Myth or Reality*. The deep-seated belief that Egypt is a part of the black world that Europeans are repeatedly trying to "whiten" reinforced political Pan-Africanism. But even without any emphasis upon its blackness, the fact that Egypt is in Africa has made it a crucial Pan-African symbol. Israel attacked Egypt in 1955 and then joined France and Britain in further attacks. Africans have never forgotten these preemptive strikes.

During the anticolonial upsurge after World War II, as new African nations emerged their slogan became "The Sahara no longer divides us; it unites us." In 1963 when the Organization of African Unity (OAU) was formed, Egypt had a large operational air force; therefore, it was assigned a key role in any future defense of the continent and the black states against Rhodesia and/or South Africa. When the Egyptian air force was decimated during the 1967 war by the Israelis, politically conscious Africans considered this devastation a mortal blow to the military resources of the OAU. When the OAU supported Egypt in the United Nations and called for the return of occupied lands, the action was the action neither of a Machiavellian Arab plot nor of superior Arab diplomacy. It was the inevitable consequence of the post war Pan-African upsurge! When Afro-Americans supported (in opposition to Israel) African political initiatives, it was simply another facet of Pan-Africanism expressing itself. Furthermore, withdrawal of support for Israel was sometimes done with reluctance and sadness.

The Republic of South Africa, whose racist minority regime oppresses its black, Colored, and Asian minority, has been receiving military aid and advice from Israel. Even Afro-Americans who do not support the militant Pan-African demand for a Palestinian state are opposed to those who give aid and comfort to the government of South Africa in any way; unless they happen to be certain nearby African states whose survival, at this moment in history, depends upon some economic relations with the racist republic. They cannot understand, however, why Israel sees any such necessity or is willing to go farther and give military assistance. These feelings go deeper than political Pan-Africanism. Black churches, since the late nineteenth century, have been deeply involved in South Africa through missionaries they have sent there, students they have trained in church schools here, and personal ties with individuals that have developed.

Since the mid-sixties, disagreements on these issues have been a psychological barrier to the kind of cooperation between Jewish organizations and the Afro-American community that once existed. Also, the tilt toward the Arabs of some Afro-American leaders was the reaction to an attempt by some Jewish organizations and individuals to "punish" the black community by actually withdrawing their financial support of selected institutions. This policy created widespread resentment.

These international extensions of our two community's interests and loyalties have created difficulties that could not be avoided. I have stressed the need to understand Pan-Africanisms because I want to emphasize that it is not something contrived and artificial. It is one result of the diaspora into the Western Hemisphere that created consciousness among people of diverse languages and cultures, and even differing physical types, of being *African* as opposed to being members of specific tribal groups. The modern upsurge in Africa of a continent-wide consciousness has merged with the diaspora-born aspect of Pan-African ideology.

I see that the issues that I have just broached are being addressed courageously in these sessions so I shall drop them now, with only one additional comment. *We must find a way to rebuild the grand coalition for dealing with pressing domestic concerns despite inevitable disagreement over some of the results of Pan-Africanism and Zionism in the Middle East and Africa.* We can do so only if both groups understand these aspects of our respective journeys, and refrain from charges of racism hurled by one side or anti-Semitism by the other when honest disagreements arise about these overseas situations, as important to us as they are. The more widely the knowledge about our respective journeys is disseminated, the easier this task of rebuilding confidence will become.

The implications of our theme are global and extend far back into time. If I wander far afield from the specific part of the journey upon which our conference is concentrating—the contemporary United States—you must, in your own minds, constantly try to relate what I am saying to present responsibilities. The historical and comparative context are of *some* relevance, I think, although I readily admit anthropologists are apt to overdo it.

The metaphor of the journey has been selected for our two opening presentations concerning the fate of two widely dispersed branches of humankind—one bound together by a body of beliefs about themselves and their role in history that has been carefully conserved for many millenia; the other united by common experiences of oppression during the past five hundred years—experiences that have led to a reevaluation of the group's past that stretches back many millenia upon the vast continent of Africa. The road for both groups has been long and torture-ridden.

From Africa into the Diaspora

During the three hundred years between 1500 and 1800, incalculable millions of men, women, and children were dragged from the cities, villages, and chattel camps of the vast African continent and marched toward coastal trading posts for eventual shipment across the Atlantic Ocean, bound in chains, to be sold as slaves. Hundreds of thousands were killed in the raids and sometimes deliberately engineered into intertribal wars that produced black bodies for the march to the sea—during which many more died—where the ships for the Middle Passage were waiting. Of those placed aboard, at least a third died of disease, mistreatment, and malaise. Perhaps ten or twelve million were eventually landed in what Europeans (ironically from an African perspective) called "The New World." Similarities to the experiences of the Jewish people during the first hundred years after the Roman outrages following 70 C.E. come immediately to mind.

For over a hundred years, these kidnapped sons and daughters of Africa and their children and grandchildren were forced to toil on the plantations and in the mines, on public works and as domestic servants, throughout Latin America and the West Indies, before the first of them were landed in the British colonies of North America in 1619. Then, for nearly two hundred and fifty years, they formed as domestic servants the basic labor supply in the tobacco-, cotton-, and rice-producing colonies. They brought their craftsmanship in working metals as well as skill in hoe agriculture and cattle culture. By means of these skills and instruments they helped to develop this segment of the New World, whose indigenous Indian population was raped of the land

and relentlessly forced westward, first to the northern plains, and then to the southwest.

Everywhere in the Western Hemisphere, black people were in the ambiguous situation of being defined legally as property—as chattels—while they were obviously also treated as persons, especially in the planters' bedrooms. African males, confronted by a shortage of available mates due to the premium placed upon the capture and export of males from Africa, had to watch the constant increase of mulattoes, quadroons, and octoroons produced by concubinage of slave women by dominant white males. Insurrections were frequent and ruthlessly suppressed as they were in the North African and Mediterranean Jewish disaporas during the first century C.E.

Everywhere the fact that the slaves brought directly from Africa were un-Christian when captured was used as an excuse for having snatched them away from their kith and kin. Thus pious alibi closed the mouths of some who might have otherwise protested against the African slave trade: "Enslavement increased their chance of conversion and their souls' salvation." The Biblical story of Noah's curse on his son Ham and his descendants were distorted by North American apologists for slavery to justify retaining the presumed black descendants in bondage on the grounds that they were the "sons of Ham."

Later, a theory of inborn biological inferiority was elaborated to supplement, or substitute for, the theological justification. It was made clear that a profession of Christianity was no passport to freedom, no cause for manumission. White racism—doctrinal and institutional—arose to defend the existence of the African slave trade and the system of chattel slavery. Something new, that might be called *racial* slavery, had emerged in history; a previously unknown type of slavery, where all masters were expected to be of one race and the slaves of another. Slavery was abolished in the Americas between 1838 and 1888. Still, the white racism remained. It was an entrenched, integral part of the fabric of life in the North as well as in the South. The journey of the Jewish people from eastern Europe to America brought them from a system where white racism was unknown, into one where it was institutionalized and taken for granted as a "normal" fact of life. Had they resisted conformity to the racist norms and values they would have been stigmatized as un-American! Some of their intellectuals and labor activists willingly accepted that stigma many years later.

All similarities between the experiences of the Jewish people and the African people in North America pale into insignificance in the face of this fact of white racism; for it carries with it built-in privileges and access to opportunities for one denied to the other. No matter how severe anti-Semitism has been in the United States at times, it did not deny access to some, positions of power and privilege in the total society, (not just within the Jewish ethnic group). Fate put this part of the Jewish journey into an area and an era characterized by white racism; and this racism had as its origin a transatlantic slave trade for which a segment of the Spanish, Portugese, French, Dutch, Danish, and English nations were responsible, and who thereby from which they had reaped vast profits. The existence of white racism, therefore, cannot be blamed upon the Jewish people. And to have expected individual Jews not to have maximized opportunities open to people of their race in the United States would have been completely unrealistic. On the other hand, for some Afro-Americans not to have built up resentment about Jews taking advantage of them—as they did toward all of the foreigners who came and "got ahead" while they were slavery-bound or caste-bound certainly would be to demand the unusual.

In other times and other places, segments of the Jewish and black populations have met and interacted without the corrupting influence of white racism being present in the environment. Even a casual reading of Kings and Chronicles, Isaiah and Jeremiah, reveals a situation in which Hebrew kings and Ethiopian/Egyptian pharaohs were dealing with each other as equals and allies who needed each other. The prophets who objected did not resort to racial slurs or pejorative color abuse. In Josephus's *Antiquities of the Jews,* he gives us a picture of a black Queen of Sheba visiting Soloman and of a youthful Moses making a dynastic marriage with an Ethiopian princess.

In sharp contrast with this Biblical acceptance of blacks is the legend handed down by Jews in the Mesopotamian diaspora: those who compiled the Babylonian Talmud after 400 B.C., wrote of black skin color being a curse for Ham's sexual sins on the Ark. In India we even find castes: black Jews, brown Jews, and white Jews. Yet, in the Ethiopian highlands, no such division seems to have existed and Falashas or black Jews are there today to remind us that once a Jewish kingdom ruled Abyssinia. What racism can do when it goes into reverse is seen in Israel today where black migrants from Chicago, claiming to be descendants of the original Israelites, and claiming that the original Hebrews were black and that Arabs and Polish/Russian Jews suppress that fact, look with scorn on white Jews who, they say, are usurpers of the original black patrimony.

While the presence of ancient black kingdoms having power and prestige is a well-attested fact, by 1500, European traders had persuaded some African petty rulers to become their partners in a transatlantic slave trade. So traumatic was the process of capture, transatlantic transportation, and the sale of Africans on the auction block, that those who endured it preferred not to transmit the details of the ordeal to their children and children's children in either story or song. Rather, they seem to have suppressed the memories of the horrors of the manhunts and the Middle Passage and to have passed on instead more pleasant retrospective and prospective myths. They handed down tales of the joys and wonders of the Homeland that they called "Guinea"; as well as skills ranging from craftsmanship in metals to the curing of the ailments of the body with herbs and folk psychiatry. They expressed their faith that when they died, their spirits would journey back to "Guinea," to join the ancestral dead who watch constantly over the living in the land of the ancestral shrines. Some of their descendants cherished this tradition; some did not.

Virtually all of the first-generation Africans landed in this hemisphere over that long span of years—including a few Muslims—were members of cultures in which the individual was firmly anchored in an extended family and lineage composed of the living, the dead, and those not yet born. They were all in spiritual communion with one another through rites and ceremonies, that had been created by a High God who was over all and who was concerned with everything from cosmic matters of prayers about mundane matters to the ancestral dead of the lineage and the family, to matters concerning the village and larger political units. In some areas from which the slaves came, gods dealing with many specialized cosmic duties had their priests and priesteses and specialized ceremonials. Some cults involved long years of preparation for devotees as well as leaders. This rich fabric of religion and kinship intertwined was ripped asunder by the indiscriminate mixing of Africans without regard to kinship or tribe as they were distributed to owners in the Americas. And for all Africans, the African shrines were too far away across the seas for regular observances of prayer and sacrifices, celebration of periodic holy days and seasons, or pilgrimages to sacred spots. Karl Marx allegedly said of capitalism that in its impact, "all that is holy is profaned. All that is solid melts into thin air." This was certainly as true of the process of African enslavement as it was of European proletarianization—both facets of the same process of early capitalist development.

After the first generation of slaves had been introduced into any section of the Americas, a new Afro-American culture into which children were inducted began to grow. It drew upon the experiences and environment of the new milieu as well as the African heritage. New myths about the past and the future grew up; subsequently, potent new symbolic meanings became attached to old songs, dance movements, and to African folktales. Elements of African languages became fused with European tongues to form Creoles and pidgins. Two new types of spiritual paths were trod in the New World to replace the great highway of tradition that the peoples of Africa had walked for many millennia. These were new pathways for pursuing the journey in the diaspora. One was the Latin Catholic pathway, the other the Anglo-Dutch Protestant pathway. Our emphasis is upon the latter path, but we shall say a few words about the other one first.

Religion in the Latin-Catholic Diaspora

One of the new paths for pursuing the journey on the diaspora was walked by those who were landed first in the Western Hemisphere from Africa. The earliest cargoes were composed largely of people from the great Congo river basin that includes Angola and the modern state of Zaire. Great numbers of Nigerians, Muslim and non-Muslims, joined them later. Slavery existed in the West Indies and Central and South Africa, as well as in Mexico for 115 years before the first settlement at Jamestown in Virginia. Within slave communities of Catholic-America—(French Santo Domingo, Martinique, and Guadeloupe; Portuguese Brazil; and a multitude of Spanish settlements)—African individual and collective beliefs about man and his destiny became fused in such a way as to partially knit together the severed links with ancestral cults.

Catholicism was able to accommodate syncretisms in which West African gods were given the names of saints, as their followers became familiar with another group of beings who inhabited the other world. Some African ceremonies or partly African ceremonies were allowed to grow up alongside the Catholic orders of baptism, the mass, and the confessional. Drumes were named and baptized; not destroyed as instruments of the devil as Protestants were wont to do. So it is that even today an African from Dahomey can visit Haiti and recognize many features of his own worship in *vodoun,* and Yorubas from Nigeria can find lineal descendants of their own gods being worshipped in Brazil in the *candomble* cult houses of Bahia and in the Macumba shrines of Rio de Janeiro. An African-derived religion that has absorbed both Christian and American Indian elements, *umbanda,* is sometimes referred to as the religion of San Paulo's lower-class people of all races. In Trinidad a very attentuated African ceremony directed toward the thunder god, Shango, attracts even some well-adjusted middle-class people, while in Cuba, Shango as well as other Yoruba gods have presented a problem for those who wish to keep the Marxism of the revolution pure.

Religion in the Protestant North American Diaspora

The Anglican and Free church settlers in North America never tolerated the kind of African-Christian syncretisms in religion that the Latin catholic cultures accepted. "Papist idolatry" (images of saints) was anathema; African heathen idols were doubly so. An attempt to use selected biblical texts to justify holding Africans in slavery was accompanied by teaching slaves enough about the Bible to try to get them to accept these biblical sanctions for their degraded state. Then, during the late eighteenth century, less than a hundred years after the first Africans landed at Jamestown, many people of color in Maryland, Virginia, and North Carolina were caught up in the revivalism of the First (1740) and Second Great Awakenings. Some became members of racially mixed Baptist and Methodist congregations. Usually, they were forced to sit "Jim Crow" while, ironically, black preachers occasionally preached to the integrated congregations.

In other instances they formed congregations of their own and laid the foundations of the black church in the United States. Individual congregations frequently combined the word *African* with a biblical name to designate their place of worship: such was the First African Shiloh Baptist Church. One of the first large national denominations was the African Methodist Episcopal Zion Church. Cut off from ancestral roots in Africa, but not accepted as citizens in this country, even free Negroes proudly called themselves "African" to establish an identity well into the nineteenth century. However the worship inside any of these churches that called themselves African differed only slightly from that of white churches of the same denomination—no drums, no invocation of African gods, no syncretisms. A bit more soul was added to Baptist and Methodist forms of worship; and sometimes as well, a touch of the African heritage as in the "ring shouts" or hand clapping that substituted for the drums.

In theology, the black churches did not differ at all. They did, however, apply the general eschatological and apocalyptic emphases to their own history and destiny. When possession took place, it was explained as the outpouring of the Holy Spirit, not as an African god or goddess—an *orisha* or *loa*—"entering the head" or "riding" his devotee as a horse. Differences in theological interpretation had social and political significance. The Protestant path, like the Catholic one, had a strong this-worldly orientation. Prayers for success and health and for welfare of loved ones, existed side by side with charms to aid in situations where chance prevailed. Conjuring brought all New World blacks close to Africa with some sense of the Obeah religion in the West Indies, but less of the *conjur'* woman or *conjur'* man in North America. Attempts to influence masters by supernatural means—sometimes aided with overt action—were widespread. Slave rebellions—individual and collective—drew upon Christian sources in North America—as in the case of rebellion leader Nat Turner who saw visions in the sky—while they more often had an African idiom in the Caribbean.

By the time of the Second Great Awakening (1787–1812), hundreds of slaves knew how to read and write and could pass on their interpretation of what the Bible said to others. So-called Free Churches gave wide latitude to both laymen and preachers to interpret the Bible and for sects and denominations to proliferate. At the same time, a traditional eschatological framework based upon the Old and the New Testament forms a common core around which doctrinal variations fluctuate. All sorts of permutations and commutations of the assumed prophecies and events, sometimes with abstruse mathematical calculations, have arisen since the break in the Catholic consensus in the sixteenth century. But the point I want to make is that Afro-Americans received this apocalyptic eschatological scheme as a part of their legacy when they adopted Christianity and it influenced the imagery that went into the creation of their hymns and sermons. A favorite prophecy was found in the Psalms: "Princes shall come out of Egypt; Ethiopia shall soon stretch forth her hands unto God."

Sitting segregated, and listening to the exhortations of white ministers, it is likely that some of the slaves heard sermons in which the Jewish people were denounced for not having accepted Jesus as the Messiah and were said to be suffering for this "sin." But being God's chosen people they would eventually regain the Promised Land and would then accept Jesus at the second coming just before the Millennial Reign. However, there was nothing in Protestant Christianity similar to the religious anti-Semitism that led to pogroms in Eastern Europe, and Jews were so few in the South that a contemporary referent would have been hard to visualize. I doubt if these theological disquisitions about the fate of the ancient Jews meant much to the slaves. As to the question of guilt for the crucifixion, I think I was brought up on the usual Afro-American assessment, namely, that a group of corrupt money changers who got driven out of the Temple persuaded the Romans—including a reluctant Pilate—to crucify Jesus and to release Barabbas. They paid off the crowd to scream their choice of the latter. They'd never heard of Karl Marx but they made a class analysis of the matter!

Afro-Americans were only forty-five years out of slavery when I was born. They had experienced a brief period of substantial equality during Reconstruction and then suffered the furious reaction spearheaded by the Ku Klux Klan. The year before I was born, a renewed joint commitment of idealistic Northern whites and militant young blacks had just been made when they organized the National Association for the Advancement of Colored People. A new movement was just beginning to surface in Protestant Christianity, the Social Gospel. While its leaders did not crusade for justice to the Negro they did call for justice to all of the poor. My father, who was a young preacher, along with most of those who secured theological training during his generation, accepted the view that the Judaeo-Christian ethic had been obscured and even perverted. They felt it needed proclaiming anew with special reference to the fate of persecuted black people, at a time when lynchings in the Bible Belt of the South were at an all-time high.

In Pittsburgh where I then lived, while I heard occasional pejorative references to Jewish merchants, these were offset by praise for Jews who were friendly to recent migrants from the South. Young people of my generation (World War I and its aftermath) were brought up on the idea that Jesus accepted his Jewishness; that He said He came to fulfill the Law and not to destroy it; and most importantly, that "the common people heard him gladly." All my life I was to hear black preachers, and especially those who adhered to the Social Gospel in one form or another, preach with eloquent emphasis the story that the Gospel according to Luke (4:14–20) gives of the first sermon of Jesus after His baptism in the river Jordan. He had been tempted for forty days in the wilderness and then came to Jerusalem where he had again to fight off Satan:

And Jesus returned in the power of the Spirit into Galilee, and a report concerning him went out through all the surrounding country. And he taught in their synagogues, being glorified by all.

And he came to Nazareth, where he had been brought up; and he went to the synagogue, as his custom was, on the sabbath day. And he stood up to read; and there was given him the book of the prophet Isaiah. He opened the book of the prophet and found the place where it was written, "The spirit of the Lord is upon me, because he has anointed me to preach good news to the poor. He hath sent me to proclaim release to the captives and recovering of sight to the blind, to set at liberty those who are oppressed, to proclaim the acceptable year of the Lord."

And he closed the book.

Admittedly, a rather hot argument is said to have ensued after the reading about his personal role in the divine plan; so He left, going on to a number of other cities, teaching and healing. It is from the episode at Nazareth that the expression comes "No prophet is accepted in his own country."

It was inevitable that the slaves on North American plantations would see in Jewish history of the periods referred to in the Bible, some parallels to their own. Their yearning for emancipation from slavery led them to incorporate the story of the Exodus (but not this episode alone) into sermons and songs. Biblical figures peopled their imagination and served as examples to be emulated and of behavior to be avoided. The folktales of Africa were obliterated, except as some of them appear transformed in Uncle Remus Stories. Biblical tales replaced them. The "Hebrew children" were substituted for African tribesmen in their own past histories.

Symbols of Deliverance in Slave Religion

Congregational worship of the "low church" type that was adopted by both slaves and free Negroes—the former, surreptitiously in many cases—was conducive to innovations in preaching style, singing, and motor expression. For those slaves on the plantation who found religious worship a congenial form in which to express their fears and hopes, their sense of alienation, and their anguish, as well as a milieu of fictional kinsmen to replace the African lineage of "brothers" and sisters," the congregations became a milieu out of which a body of music came that we know as the spirituals. The world was dichotomized into saints and sinners, the saved and the unsaved, and there is some reason to believe that the sinners, the unsaved, were in the majority on most plantations.

The metaphor of the journey appears frequently in the group of spirituals that have survived the editing, censorship, and rewriting by well-meaning New England educators who came South after the Civil War, and that were preserved in the Deep South by the ex-slaves themselves. Some, thinking of them as "slave songs," preferred to forget them, and to adopt the most measured hymns of the British and Methodist hymnbooks, investing them with swing and soul. There is a sense of the painful dragging of tired bodies in the somewhat doleful: "I'm a tramping/I'm a tramping/Trying to make Heaven my home." But the journey has a purpose. Discipline and devotion here, to insure bliss after death. There is a somewhat rollicking Spiritual that answers in another mood, "Let us cheer the weary traveler! Let us cheer the weary traveler! Let us cheer the weary traveler! Along the heavenly way." And there is an ebullient outburst when everybody sings "I'm a rolling/I'm a rolling! I'm a rolling through this unfriendly world."

But "making it" demands both divine and human aid so the Spiritual continues, "Oh sister wont you help me? Oh sister wont you help me to pray? Oh sister won't you help me? Help me in the service of the Lord!" From the little I know of how the Hasidim worship and experience the joys of worship that involves some motor activity, I glimpse a bit of that same Hasidic spirit, born of East European ghettoization, in the ring shouts and lively spiritual singing of the plantations in the past—and of the store-front church with its gospel singing today. Similar situations produce similar responses.

Sometimes the journey is marked by a prayer struggle to renew faith and it is no accident that Ebenezer, the spot where Jacob struggled with the angel, appears so often in the naming of churches, or that this spiritual was popular:

> We are climbing Jacob's ladder,
> We are climbing Jacob's ladder,
> We are climbing Jacob's ladder,
> Soldiers of the cross!

Black Christians found no difficulty in combining the symbols of Jacob's ladder and the cross in a single metaphoric statement.

In "trying to make heaven my home," the ultimate destination was often symbolized by the Holy City (in contrast to wicked cities like Babylon and Sodom and Gomorrah). But most often the hymns that bore the name of Zion or Jerusalem came from another tradition of hymnody than their own; one that black worshippers accepted and modified—Fundamentalist white Christianity. For example, there are "We're marching to Zion, Beautiful beautiful Zion/We're marching upward to Zion, the City of our God," and "Jerusalem the Golden." But these stately measured tributes to Zion did not always suffice to express the vivacious élan of the spiritual journey, so we have the stirring spiritual that Louis Armstrong turned into his secular signature song:

> When the saints go marching in—
> Oh, when the saints go marching in; Lord,
> I want to be in that number,
> When the saints go marching in.

This spiritual signaled a boisterous *collective* entry into heaven at the end of the journey that for each had been an *individual* path. Some were far from joyous. As one haunting spiritual put it, "Look down, look down that lonesome road, before you travel home." And another sobering reflection: "You gotta walk it for yourself / Nobody else can walk it for you / You gotta walk it for yourself."

These spirituals reflected the sentiments of the "saved." They still do. However, many people who consider themselves in that category use a very different idiom of expression today. Also, the sinners then, as now, had *their* music—and then, in contradistinction to now—the two genres did not interpenetrate and fuse, as Charles Keil has so vividly demonstrated in his book *Urban Blues,* they do today. The blues and the field hollers in those early years were characteristic of the world of sin in which the saved were always diligently trying to "snatch brands from the burning"—often their own close kinsmen. And there was the ever-present danger of "backsliding."

There are many people in the black world for whom this spiritual journey is still a living reality and it still takes innovative forms of folk expression. The more sophisticated middle and upper classes must not think that their paradigms and styles prevail everywhere. I have witnessed an authentic folk pageant called "Heaven Bound," presented in a black church in Chicago, that was similar to a medieval mystery play. The prancing and cavorting Devil was the most popular character, as he used playing cards, whiskey, and pretty women to try to divert the struggling Christian from the straight and narrow path—a church aisle leading to the choir loft behind the pulpit. As the choir sang "Coming home, never more to roam," the pilgrim traveled on. When he was almost there, Satan turned him aside toward the "mouth of hell" constructed near the pulpit. Someone in the choir threw out a real life buoy connected to a rope. Several angels hauled him through the gate as St. Peter watched and choir and congregation sang the hymn, "Throw out the lifeline." The celestial coast guard had saved him from Satan. This was urban folk religion, a far cry from *Green Pastures.*

As I mull over the spirituals, I am struck by the fact that there were others that had a universal appeal; and that the "unsaved" as well as the "saved" could enjoy them because of their dramatic appeal, even if their life journey was along a different path. A surprisingly large number of these had Old Testament themes. There is the exuberant "Joshua fit de battle of Jericho and the walls came a-tumbling down." Ezekiel's mysterious wheel moving about in the middle of the air with the big wheel running by faith and the little wheeel running by the grace of god; a spiritual about the Hebrew children in the fiery furnace and Jonah in the belly of the whale, all equally under the care of the Almighty. One, of inimitable beauty, that must have appealed to children was "Little David play on your harp, Hallelu." Both adults and children liked the spiritual about Noah and the flood, "The Old Ark's a-movering, there's room for many a more"—that speaks of the animals going in one by one and two by two. The fascination of that ark for the slaves must have been similar to its fascination millennia ago, for the Jewish folktales contain a number of stories about those animals and the people on the ark and their "goings on," some being explanatory myths and not all being tales for the ears of children. The story of Samson and Delilah appealed to the imagination and carried with it several pointed morals. All of these stories and many more were reworked in eloquent sermons as well as in folk songs.

Some of the most significant spirituals expressed the ethnic group experience and I suspect that when they were sung at church and camp meetings, they bound saved and unsaved together in the consciousness that they were one kidnapped and transported people, traveling the same rocky road and seeking the same end on earth whatever their destinations might be after life ended. As Albert Raboteau, in his book *Slave Religion* has demonstrated, symbols from the Exodus were key symbols in what E. Franklin Frazier called the "invisible church" of the plantation, since slaves were often compelled to worship clandestinely if no whites were present. It takes no wild stretch of the imagination to emphathize with slaves hearing a song leader cry out "Go down Moses, Way down in Egypt Land and tell Ol'Pharaoh to let my people go." And verse after verse tells the dramatic story of how Jehovah showed his strength to free his abused chosen people. In dealing with this phase of Jewish history, the sentiments of the black religius community were always with the Hebrew children as the underdogs not with the Egyptian oppressors.

The story of Moses as the liberator from slavery became so much a part of Afro-American culture that popular dialect poet, Paul Laurence Dunbar, evoked a responsive chord with his "Antebellum Sermon":

Oh' paraoh down in Egypt was the wust man eval bo'n.
He had those Hebrew chillum down there wukkin in his corn. . . .
The Lord got tired of his foolin' and said,
I'll make him rue the houah
I'll empty down upon him all the vials of my powah.
An' he did.
An' pharaoh's army wan't worth a half a dime.
You can trust the Lord my chillum,
He'll do it evah time.

I'm not sure the originators of the Exodus songs knew that Egypt was in Africa. In any event it wouldn't have mattered to them. "Crossing over Jordan into Canaan" was symbolic of the triumph of the oppressed people. Later the Jordan River, as the stream where John baptized Jesus and also as the last barrier to be crossed before reaching heaven, came to have additional levels of symbolism: "Jordan waters are chilly and cold," as was the Ohio River, the last barrier to be crossed when fleeing North on the Underground Railroad.

Ethiopianism: Ideology of Free Negroes

The "Exodus" and "Crossing Over Jordan" dominated the imagery of the preachers and congregations on plantations where the folk produced the spirituals. However, my own limited research leads me to conclude that other key symbols became salient during the period of slavery, in those urban churches that were pastored by free Negroes many of whom were well-read and took a keen interest in politics. In these circles an eschatological myth developed that various scholars have recognized and named "Ethiopianism." It expressed a conviction that something they called "African redemption" would eventually take place as the Psalms had prophesied: "Princes shall come out of Egypt and Ethiopia shall soon stretch forth her hand unto God." After slavery was abolished the otherworldly referents of Zion—Jordan and Jerusalem remained, but the this-worldly goals had been retained.

Onward and Upward

"Deep in my heart, I do believe, We shall overcome . . ." The civil rights movement of the sixties contributed this song of optimistic faith in the future to the worldwide struggle for social justice. Other American movements took it as their own. It became a theme song in the Irish civil rights movement. Anti–nuclear-war protesters have been singing it as they march through the streets in Europe. This is an example of a contribution by one racial group—as opposed to a contribution by some individual within a racial group to the ongoing stream of world culture. People as diverse as Malcolm X and W. E. B. Du Bois on one hand and Booker Taliferro Washington and Martin Luther King, Jr., on the other have insisted that the suffering of black people had a meaning that, if understood, could benefit humanity—as blacks are not just here, they are here for something and have a mission. King said black suffering has "redemptive value"; that it can change the hearts of their oppressors.

The black Marxists said their suffering had so sensitized and steeled them that they would supply the leadership in the fight for socialism in America that no one could expect from white workers. DuBois carried the black "mission" a step further. After he became a Communist he wrote a long poem in which he said that the new African nations would teach the world how to build socialism suffused with "soul." This idea that black people have special traits of spirituality and peacefulness as compared with other races of mankind—particularly Anglo-Saxons—is at the heart of the doctrine of *negritude* as taught by Leopold Senghor, the poet-politician in Senegal.

Not all Jews have cherished the idea that they were a chosen people with a special mission; similarly, many black people reject the idea of a black mission. It persists, however, and gives meaning to the existence of many among both groups who believe.

The unsophisticated folk did not ponder the question of whether God would eventually free them so they could serve mankind. They exulted only in the fact that they did "overcome" and they elaborated a spiritual about "How I got over / Oh my Lord." Near the turn of the century, a lawyer-school teacher, James Weldon Johnson, with a gift for writing poetry as well as briefs, collaborated with his brother, J. Rosamund Johnson, a pianist, and composer, to produce a more sophisticated version of the same theme. It soon won wide acceptance as what became known as the "National Negro Anthem" or the "National Negro Hymn." It begins with a summons, "Lift every voice and sing / Till earth and heaven ring / Ring with the harmonies of liberty." At one point it evokes reminders of past tragedies: "Stony the road we trod / Bitter the Chastening Rod / Felt in the days when hope, unborn, had died." It details the torments of the journeys: "We have come / Over a way that with tears has been watered. / We have come / Treading our path through the blood of the slaughtered; / Out of the gloomy past / Till now we stand at last / Where the white beam / of our bright star is cast /." The anthem ends with a plea; "God of Our Weary Years / God of Our Silent Tears / Thou Who hast brought us thus far on the way / Thou who hast by thy might / Led us into the Light / Keep us forever in the path; we pray." It ends with a pledge to be . . . "true to our God; true to our nativeland."

Just before his assassination, Martin Luther King, Jr., reminded us that being true to our native land might at times demand aggressive action against unjust laws; that it must involve compassion for the poor—of all races—and refusal to continue the raining down of death upon peasant villages in Asia.

The Afro-American Studies Program at Stanford sponsored a memorial service to Martin Luther King, Jr., on his birthday in 1982. An advertisement in the school newspaper welcomed everybody. This was evidence to me of a striking change in black student attitudes since the mid-seventies. A large number of white students, a few faculty members, and the university president and his wife came. They no longer felt as they once did that black students wanted them to keep their distance on an occasion like this. Time had softened bitterness and resentment. The main speaker stressed the point that King had died for values all Americans say they cherish—peace and abolition of poverty, as well as equality of opportunity for all men and respect for them as persons regardless of their race or color. The words to James Weldon Johnson's "Lift Every Voice and Sing" were printed on the program so we could all end by pledging to be true to our God and "true to our native land." Then, someone remembered that we hadn't sung "We shall Overcome," and this we did. The younger people had to be coached about holding hands and swaying by the veterans of the sixties. Whether this ceremony marked a new stage on the black student journey or is something peculiar to the Stanford milieu, I cannot say.

In my conclusion I shall restrict my focus to North America, although I have spoken of other Western Hemisphere situations. The meaning of the journey has always been conveyed better by those who use metaphor and simile, and who write in such a way as to touch the heart, than by those who deal in charts, graphs, and statistics and who employ social science jargon. Many rich metaphors have been employed. I am sure that some of us have already read volume one of

Vincent Harding's projected trilogy, *There is a River,* in which, as he writes Afro-American history, he eloquently paints a picture of the unceasing flow of energy rippling through the years, powering a determination among black Americans to be free, and, in doing so constantly merging with, and giving renewed impulse to, other streams of progressive American thought and action. Harding believes that what makes the Afro-American component distinctive is the fact that the significant social actions of black individuals and groups have always been suffused with religious faith. Not everyone agrees with this interpretation, but the symbol of the river remains a powerful one without it. There is, of course, Paul Robeson singing of *Ole Man River* "who jes' goes rollin' along." I have already spoken of what the Jordan meant during slavery days. I am sure we have not heard the last of the river symbolizing some aspect of the black experience.

Then there is the simile of the *climb.* I have already spoken of the fascination that Jacob's Ladder had for a generation that expressed its highest values through the spirituals. This concept of climbing onward and upward—striving forward—is a part of the American Weltanschauung, and it appears constantly in a secularized form. In the days of slavery, the "climb" symbolized a spiritual struggle whose aim was to "make heaven my home," but sometimes it meant struggling above the inward torture of day-by-day waiting for the day of Jubilee that would someday come on earth. Sometimes it meant wandering through woods and swamps, across creeks and rivers, heading toward the North Star with the North or Canada as a destination. After slavery the climb, in its secularized form, was apparent when old folks urged youngsters to "make something out of yourself," and leaders spoke continuously of "advancing the Race." Booker T. Washington preached: "Get a basic education; Work and Save; Get money; Get land; Go into Business," while W. E. B. Du Bois was saying, "All of this, yes, but cultivate a Talented Tenth, too, to supply leadership to the recently emancipated race." The doctrine of self-improvement was preached as assiduously in churches as was the gospel of Jesus Christ.

During the twenties, Langston Hughes wrote a popular poem that presented the upward climb in a more this-worldly form than the Jacob's Ladder of which the spiritual sings. When I was in high school and college, my generation found the poem particularly relevant to our experience. Since the machismo of the early days of the contemporary Black Rebellion has given way to renewed emphasis upon the nurturing role of black women, I suspect many modern youths would appreciate the *poem's* sentiments while rejecting some of the language and imagery. Hughes called the poem, with the memorable line "Life for me ain't been no crystal stair," "Mother to Son."

The present generation would have no problem at all with another of

Langston Hughe's poems, a sort of response to the one about the mother. He called the poem "Youth" and meant it to be a reply on behalf of all the sons and daughters who were climbing stairs. He changed the symbolism. Now it is the journey along a road. It is an optimistic youthful reaction facing forward from James Weldon Johnson's "stony road we trod." It has universal appeal despite the age-specific title. He ends the poem with two words, "We march," and sets a theme for us that all the weary travelers are impelled to embrace. The most single-minded and courageous Afro-American will certainly "march" whether "friends desert us" or "turn against us" and in countermeasure to their cautious counsel of standpattism.

Even though clever dialecticians try to confuse us, WE March! And while we march, we are confident that those who are honestly pursuing the same goal that we are, even though they be journeying by different paths, will join us again, somewhere someday down the road, even if they cannot march with us now.

Some years ago I wrote a bit of doggerel about those inspired individuals who refuse to deviate from a straight march toward the dawn, and who become prophets and sometimes martyrs. They will of course always be few. But some of them will always be on the road with us saying:

> In us some surging elemental power—
> We focus Freedom's rays into a beam
> Illuminate the Destined Hour
> and justify the Dreamer's Dream.

A Black Nineteenth-Century Response to Jews and Zionism: The Case of Edward Wilmot Blyden, 1832–1912

Hollis R. Lynch

In retrospect, 1862 was a landmark in the history of both Pan-Africanism and Zionism. In that year, Edward Wilmot Blyden, a thirty-year-old West Indian born Liberian who was to become the leading Pan-African intellectual of his time, published in New York his first major book, *Liberia's Offering;* and Moses Hess, a fifty-year-old assimilated German Jew, published *Rome and Jerusalem*, the first reasoned and mature rationale for political Zionism.[1]

Neither book attracted much attention and neither man was aware of the parallel efforts of the other on behalf of his own people. But their books were based on similar assumptions and called for a similar solution. They both assumed that "race" not class was primal in human existence. They both argued that members of their "race" in the West, even when they were culturally fully assimilated, lived precariously, subject to discrimination, persecution, and even violent death. Each called for the establishment of a "nationality" that would gather up his people and provide an opportunity for the flowering of his people's genius. They both recognized that a major obstacle to the realization of the proposed nationality came from assimilated members of the diaspora who persisted, on limited evidence, in taking a hopeful view of the future. But let me offer you the words of these racial prophets themselves. Hess wrote:

The "new" Jew who denies the existence of the Jewish nationality is not only a deserter in the religious sense but is a traitor to his people, his race and even his family. If it were true that Jewish emancipation in exile is incompatible with Jewish nationality, then it is the duty of Jews to sacrifice the former for the latter.[2]

And Blyden lamented about Afro-Americans:

All other people feel a pride in their ancestral land, and do everything in their power to create for it, if it has not already, an honorable name. But many of the descendants of Africa, on the contrary, speak disparagingly of their country; are ashamed to acknowledge any connection with that land, and would turn indignantly upon any who would bid them go up and take possession of the land of their fathers.

And then admonished:

An African nationality is our great need. . . . We shall never receive the respect of other races until we establish a powerful nationality. We should not content ourselves with living among other races, simply by their permission or their endurance. . . . We must build Negro states. . . . Nationality is an ordinance of Nature. The heart of every true Negro yearns after a distinct and separate nationality.[3]

Clearly, had Blyden known of Hess's Zionist ideas, he would have endorsed them. For from childhood, and throughout his life—he died in 1912—Blyden held a strong and special interest in Jews. He had early concluded that there was and ought to be a close affinity between blacks and Jews, stemming from the persecution they both suffered, and what he claimed to be their high spiritual nature. Indeed, as we shall see, he had both peoples sharing in providing moral and spiritual leadership in the future world civilization.

Blyden's initial interest in Jews was natural. He was born and lived in a predominantly Jewish community in Charlotte Amalie, the capital of St. Thomas, Virgin Islands. He wrote feelingly of this experience:

For years, the next door neighbors of my parents were Jews. I played with Jewish boys, and looked forward as eagerly as they did to the annual festivals and fasts of their Church. I always went to the Synagogue on the solemn Day of Atonement—not inside. I took up an outside position from which I could witness the proceedings of the worshippers, hear the prayers and the reading, the singing and the sermon. The Synagogue stood on the side of a hill; and, from a terrace immediately above it, we Christian boys who were interested could look down upon the mysterious assembly, which we did in breathless silence, with an awe and a reverence which have followed me all the days of my life.[4]

There were reasons other than the religions to make Blyden aware of Jews. The Jewish population of four hundred during Blyden's boyhood made up an overwhelming proportion of nonblacks on the island. They suffered no disability and thus played a dominant role in the commercial, intellectual, and social life of the island. Indeed, Virgin Island Jews, most of whom lived in St. Thomas, produced at least three internationally known figures in the nineteenth century: Judah P. Benjamin, 1811–84, eminent jurist and major Confederate politician; Camille Pissarro, world-renowned painter and "father of French Impressionism;" and Jacob Mendes da Costa, an outstanding American physician and author.[5] Pissarro, da Costa, and Blyden were born in the early 1830s within three years of each other in the same community in Charlotte Amalie.

It seems certain that Blyden's acquaintance with local Jewish intellectuals was one of the early spurs to his bookish interests. In particular, young Blyden struck up a fast friendship with David Cardoze, eight years his senior and then studying for the rabbinate. It was from Cardoze's obsession with reading the Bible in its original language that Blyden first developed his keen interest in studying Hebrew and in examining for himself those parts of the Old Testament that referred to or were purported to refer to black people.[6] Incidentally, Cardoze was to serve as rabbi of the St. Thomas congregation from the late 1860s until his death in 1914.

Naturally enough, Blyden's interest in Hebrew could only be sustained by continuing communication with Jewish scholars. And so we find the young Liberian corresponding with "that distinguished Hebrew scholar and divine," Dr. Marcus Moritz Kalisch (1828–85), who sent Blyden "his Hebrew Grammar, with the Key and his Commentaries on Exodus and Genesis" that the African scholar found to be "a wonderful storehouse of philological, historical and even theological information."[7] His interest in Hebrew was symptomatic of his genius as a linguist: he was to master Greek and Latin and became fluent in French, Spanish, German, and Arabic.

For, in truth, Hebrew was mastered only by a small Jewish elite; it was the language of prayer, of sacred scholarship, and of official documents; it had remained unaltered for more than three thousand years. It was not a language fitted for everyday use, for secular scholarship, for commerce and science. But through the enormous and intolerant exertions of one man, Eliezer Ben-Yehuda, this was to change. An East European who became fully Westernized in Paris, Ben-Yehuda not only supported a Jewish return to Palestine but advocated the highly controversial and seemingly impractical idea that the return be accompanied by the introduction of Hebrew as the spoken language of the reconstituted nation. Acting on his conviction, Ben-Yehuda and his wife emigrated to Jaffa in 1881 and by spoken example, teaching, writings, translations, and above all by his prodigious efforts towards compiling a Hebrew dictionary did bequeath to Israel a modern and flexible

Hebrew language.[8] Thus had a Zionist patriot answered the thorny question of what appropriate language for the new nationality. Blyden gives no indication that he was aware of the patriotic linguistic exertions of Ben-Yehuda, but, as we shall see, he too addressed the language problem.

Just as for Hess the Jewish "nationality" had to be established in the original homeland—the Holy Land—so, too, with Blyden, only in Africa could a major modern black nation be established. And Blyden at first saw Liberia, settled since 1822 by Afro-Americans and independent as a black republic since 1847, as the nucleus of such a nation. He had purposefully emigrated there in 1851. In Monrovia he was trained and served as a high school teacher and Presbyterian clergyman, and through his writings, sermons, and public lectures rapidly became the leading intellectual in Liberia. Thus between 1856 and 1861, in addition to newspaper and journal writings, he authored five pamphlets seeking to demonstrate the blacks had a worthy past and could again be major actors on the historical stage. He also advocated selective repatriation as a means of building Liberia into a modern nation.

Indeed Blyden's visit to the United States in 1862 and the publication of his book, *Liberia's Offering,* were intended to stimulate emigration to Liberia. Partly toward this same end, as well as to visit his mother, he revisited St. Thomas in August 1862. The St. Thomas press had carried stories on the growing literacy and academic reputation of Blyden, including the fact that in 1861 he was named Professor of Greek and Latin at the newly established Liberia College—the black republic's first institution of higher learning. Not surprisingly, the Jewish community of St. Thomas gave Blyden a warm and lavish welcome on his 1862 visit.[9]

Blyden's solution to the problem of what language or languages for the new "nationality" was different from that of Ben-Yehuda. he had no quarrel with English as Liberia's official language; indeed he considered the black republic fortunate to have inherited a language so rich, so flexible, so widespread. Nonetheless, Blyden wished to see Arabic play an important role in Liberia and, consequently, took steps to have its study introduced at Liberia College. Blyden's interest in Arabic was based on the knowledge that Islam, through jihads as well as peaceful conversions had, since the late eighteenth century, spread rapidly in West Africa, particularly in the savanna belt. Blyden calculated that Liberia's expansion into the interior would certainly be facilitated if members of its elite knew Arabic and respected Islam.

It was a combination of his preoccupation with improving his Arabic, his keen interest in the pyramids, and "his desire to visit the original homeland of the Jews" that led to his three-month visit, in the summer of 1866, to Egypt and the Middle East—Syria, Lebanon, and

Palestine. After careful study, Blyden had concluded that the flourish-
ing early Egyptian civilization was the product predominantly of Africans, and the pyramids particularly appealed to his racial pride. Here
are his words:

> This, thought I, was the work of my African progenitors. . . . Feel-
> ings came over me far different from those I have ever felt when
> looking at the mighty works of European genius. I felt that I had a
> peculiar heritage in the Great Pyramid built . . . by the enterprising
> sons of Ham, from which I was descended. The blood seemed to
> flow faster through my veins. I seemed to hear the echo of those
> illustrious Africans. I seemed to feel the impulse from those stirring
> characters who sent civilization to Greece. . . . I felt lifted out of the
> commonplace grandeur of modern times; and, could my voice have
> reached every African in the world, I would have earnestly ad-
> dressed him . . . : "Retake your Fame."[10]

Blyden's first sight of Jerusalem, where he spent five days, evoked
similar emotions, although these were of a religious nature. He wrote:

> The sun was just peeping up from behind the blue hills of Moab when
> I caught my first view of the "City of the Great King." I stopped my
> horse to take a good view. . . . The view was in every respect
> refreshing. I forgot the fatigue of the long and weary night's ride—all
> the dreams of the past seemed to be realized. A new class of feelings
> was excited in my bosom, different from those which I had experi-
> enced at the pyramids.[11]

On this visit, Blyden made it clear that he was in favor of Jewish
resettlement of Palestine; he did not consider this incompatible with
local Arab interests. He made one dubious assertion—there existed a
general consensus that "Jews are to be restored to the land of their
fathers." He mildly admonished "the Jews [who] are away in exile from
the land which God gave unto Abraham their father . . . ," a neglect all
the more reprehensible because of "the misrule of the Turks."[12] He
noted that Jerusalem had a large Jewish population and vividly described Jewish worship at the Wailing Wall:

> Winding through some narrow, crooked lanes, we reached another
> most interesting section of the wall of the ancient Temple—the wail-
> ing place of the Jews. . . . No sight in Jerusalem affected me more
> than that which presented itself in this retired spot, beneath the
> massive remains of that ancient building. . . . I had the opportunity of
> seeing Jews of both sexes, of nearly all ages, from various parts of
> the earth, lifting up a united cry of lamentation over a desolated and
> dishonoured sanctuary. . . . It was indeed a touching scene.[13]

It does not appear that Blyden was acquainted with the limited Zionist efforts in Palestine, which centered on establishing modest settle-

ments and agricultural projects. Thus, the French Jews, through the Alliance Israelite Universelle, had set up an agricultural training school at Mikveh Israel, near Jaffa.[14] Hess himself had been partially instrumental in establishing this project—his lone, small, practical step toward the realization of his large dream. Although Blyden visited Jaffa, he showed no awareness of this project.

Blyden's experiences and reflections on his 1866 trip were published in his book, *From West Africa to Palestine* (1873), which he reported was "generously received" by the Jews of St. Thomas.[15]

Between his visit to Palestine and the publication, in 1898, of his pamphlet, *The Jewish Question,* the much-traveled Blyden continued to number Jews in Britain and America among his friends and correspondents. Thus on a visit to New York in 1880, he was a guest of Joseph Seligman, the banker, and the recipient of his philanthropy—one hundred dollars that he solicited to purchase agricultural equipment for prospective Liberian emigrants.[16] And on that same visit to the United States, in a lecture subsequently published as "Africa's Service to the World," Blyden explicitly compared the history of service to humanity of both people:

> Africa is distinguished as having *served* and *suffered* [original italics]. In this her lot was not unlike that of God's ancient people, the Hebrews who were known among the Egyptians as the servants of all; and among the Romans in later times, they were numbered by Cicero with the "nations born to servitude" and were protected, in the midst of a haughty population, only "by the contempt which they inspired."[17]

Blyden's independently published lecture was reprinted in his brilliant collection of essays, *Christianity, Islam and the Negro Race* (1887). This book, Blyden's magnum opus and a controversial landmark in Pan-African literature, attracted widespread attention in the English-speaking ecclesiastical and literary world. Five years earlier, in 1882, a similar landmark in Zionist literature appeared: *AutoEmancipation,* by Leo Pinsker, a Jewish-Russian physician who, like Hess, made a reasoned case for the establishment of a Jewish nation, although he was skeptical that this could be done in Palestine.[18] Although published in German in Berlin, Pinsker's book received little notice outside of Russia and certainly did not come to Blyden's attention.

Indeed, it was not until 1897, when the Zionist movement began to take a major organizational form under Theodore Herzl, that Blyden began to pay close attention to it. Herzl, like Hess and Pinsker, was responding to endemic anti-Semitism in backward Eastern Europe and enlightened Western Europe alike. A Hungarian-born, Viennese-educated lawyer, Herzl was an assimilated Jew and a highly successful journalist based in Paris. But he had come to realize, as he put it, that "we are a people living perpetually in enemy territory."[19] For Herzl, the final proof of this was the humiliating Dreyfus affair that fanned the flames of anti-Semitism in France. He was goaded into action. Within a few months, ignorant of the Zionist works of Hess and Pinsker, Herzl produced *Judenstaat,* his own blueprint for a Zionist state, which was published in Vienna in 1896. But unlike his predecessors, and heedless of the enormous obstacles to its realization, Herzl was determined to act urgently on his plans. A man of majestic and inspiring presence, he convened and dominated the first Zionist Congress, which met in Basle, Switzerland, in late August and was attended by some two hundred delegates. The Congress met annually thereafter, attracting an increasing number of delegates. When Herzl died in 1904, the Zionist movement, though still in its weak infancy, had been irreversibly launched.[20] Herzl's book, together with his feverish rounds of diplomatic, journalistic, and organizational efforts had given widespread publicity and currency to Zionism, a term that was first used in 1892.[21] Not surprisingly, Herzl and Zionism had quickly come to the attention of Blyden, who had long remained conversant with major developments in Europe.

But before we look at Blyden's response to Herzlian Zionism, it would be illuminating to briefly examine his own efforts at fostering repatriation of Afro-Americans to Africa. His personal effort in 1862 had not been successful, partly because Afro-Americans were primarily concerned with using the opportunity provided by the Civil War to bring an end to slavery. Up to the 1880s Blyden had continued to hold the belief that black Americans had a significant role to play in the establishment of one or more major black modern nations in Africa. He himself had continued to support selective repatriation. His own belief that the destiny of black Americans lay with Africa was reinforced by their pariah status in the post–Civil War decades. Of course, there was the aberration, of several years' duration, Radical Reconstruction, during which blacks were granted and exercised their basic political and civil rights.[22] But the status of blacks quickly declined thereafter, and for the rest of Blyden's lifetime was characterized by economic discrimination, peonage, political disfranchisement, social discrimination, Jim Crowism, lynchings, and other forms of white mob violence against blacks—often accomplished with the connivance and support of law-enforcement agencies.[23]

Equally endemic, not surprisingly, was the desire on the part of a significant proportion of Afro-Americans to return to Africa. This had been couraged by Henry McNeal Turner, the ebullient and tart-tongued Bishop of the A.M.E. Church: the leading Afro-American proponent of repatriation and Pan-Africanism in Blyden's lifetime.[24]

But there were serious obstacles in the way of translating this desire for Africa into a historic modern nation-building movement on the continent. Afro-Americans themselves did not possess the financial resources and requisite skills for organizing such a movement. White Americans, for the most part, did not seem to want to lose this abundant supply of cheap labor and/or source of an easy sense of superiority. Obviously, Liberia was neither ready nor able to accommodate such a mass repatriation. Concomitantly, in the mid-1880s, virtually all of black Africa had been brought under European colonial rule. Further, because of intragroup conflict, largely based on color, both in Liberia and Afro-America, Blyden, who prided himself on being a "pure Negro," reached the controversial conclusion that mulattoes did not belong to the black race. In his judgment, therefore, they were ineligible to emigrate to Africa.

After 1862, Blyden made five additional visits to the United States— in 1874, 1880, 1882, 1889, and 1895—where he lectured and preached extensively among Afro-Americans. His exhortations to his listeners were characteristically more full of pathos and romance than of reality, as indicated by the following typical selection:

> There are Negroes enough in this country to join in the return— descendants of Africa enough, who are faithful to the instincts of the race and who realize their duty to the fatherland. I rejoice to know that here where the teachings of generations have been to disparage the race, there are men and women who will go, who have a restless sense of homelessness which will never be appeased until they stand in the great land where their forefathers lived; until they catch the glimpse of the old sun, and moon and stars, which still shine in their pristine brilliancy upon that vast domain; until from the deck of the ship which bears them back home they see visions of the hill rising from the white margin of the continent, and listen to the breaking music of the waves—the exhilarating laughter of the sea as it dashes against the beach.[25]

He began to dream of a black Moses who would lead an exodus of blacks from America to Africa. He wrote:

> The Negro leader of the exodus, who will succeed, will be a Negro of Negroes, like Moses was a Hebrew of the Hebrews—even if brought up in Pharaoh's palace he will be found—no half-Hebrew and half-Egyptian will do the work—he will have brass and assurance enough—for this work heart, soul and faith are needed.[26]

Blyden's prediction was almost fulfilled in the remarkable career of Marcus Mosiah Garvey, the charismatic Jamaican black who in the half a dozen years after World War I organized the first genuine Afro-American mass movement, one of whose professed goals was a return

to Africa.[27] Yet, from the mid-1880s, Blyden simultaneously continued
to maintain that an Afro-American exodus would take place and yet
abandoned his own efforts to encourage it. Paradoxically and contro-
versially, Blyden came to view European colonial rule, which he predicted would be short-lived, as an unwitting agent of modern nation
building and Pan-African unity in Africa.

It was predictable that Blyden would be delighted by the discovery
of the parallel efforts of Herzl on behalf of his own people. Here is his
own rationale for his interest in "that marvellous movement called
Zionism":

> The question, in some of the aspects, is similar to that which at this
> moment agitates thousands of the descendants of Africa in America,
> anxious to return to the land of their fathers. It has been for many
> years my privilege and my duty to study the question from the Afri-
> can standpoint. And as the history of the African race—their en-
> slavement, persecution, proscription, and sufferings—closely
> resembles that of the Jews, I have been led by a natural process of
> thought and by a fellow feeling to study the great question now
> uppermost in the minds of thousands, if not millions of Jews.

The speedy publication of his response to Zionism was made possible
by a Jewish friend of long standing from Liverpool, Louis Solomon. He
had been a trader on the West African coast since the 1860s and in the
early 1880s became a partner in Lionel Hart and Company, whose
trading interests centered in West Africa.[28] Solomon's Company under-
wrote the publication of Blyden's pamphlet, which the African dedicated to the Jew with the hope that "members of the two suffering
races . . . who read these pages may have a somewhat clearer understanding and a deeper sympathy with each other."

Blyden expressed clear sympathy for the Zionist goal of a Palestine
located Jewish nation, "if the conditions were favourable," or elsewhere if necessary. Like most British Zionists, he no longer believed
literally in the biblical prophecy of a return to the original Jewish
homeland. Blyden further related why he enthusiastically agreed with
those contemporary Jewish thinkers who proclaimed "the Jew has a
higher and nobler work to accomplish for humanity than establishing a
political power in one corner of the world."[29] He continued:

> They believe that their race have been qualified by the unspeakable
> suffering of ages to be the leaders not in politics but in religion; that
> to them has been entrusted the spiritual hegemony of mankind; that
> it is they who are to bring about the practical brotherhood of human-
> ity by establishing, or, rather, propagating the international religion
> in whose cult men of all races, climes, and countries will call upon
> the one Lord under one Name.[30]

He conceded that the "persecution of ages" have driven Jews "to an almost exclusive . . . consideration of their own internal affairs," and advised them to overcome their "timidity" in order to assume their lofty mission as spiritual saviors of the world.

Elsewhere, Blyden had assigned to blacks a similar role for similar reasons. Like the Jews, the suffering and persecution of blacks, he felt, had fitted them to be spiritual leaders. There is to be found in the character of the African, averred Blyden, "the softer aspects of human nature": cheerfulness, sympathy, willingness to serve. The special contribution of the African to world civilization, he had insisted, would be a spiritual one. He envisioned Africa as the "spiritual conservatory of the world"; playing the role of peacemaker among European nations, and of consoler when the destructive scientific inventions of white men led to a crisis in their civilization.[31]

With this assumption of a spiritual role shared between the two peoples, Blyden invited Jews to regard tropical Africa as an important field for their activities. "They would," he wrote, "find there religious and spiritual aspirations kindred to their own, and they would recognize the existence in the people of large possibilities for the higher work of humanity. . . ." Blyden's response and advice, mystical and romantic as they were, had no practical outcome. But it is interesting to note that his goodwill invitation to Jews (it was no more than this as he had no political authority to make it) predated by five years the offer made by the British Government in 1903 to the Zionist Movement of six thousand square miles on the uninhabited Guas Ngishu plateau of Uganda for the establishment of an autonomous settlement. Herzl was disposed to accept it. It was, however, turned down due to the opposition of orthodox Zionists who regarded Palestine as the only homeland.[32]

Blyden himself played no role in organized Pan-Africanism. But it is instructive to note that it began not long after organized Zionism. On September 14, 1897, two weeks after the first Zionist Congress had met, Henry Sylvester Williams, a barrister-at-law from Trinidad, founded in London the African Association, whose membership was restricted to blacks and one of whose goals was to convene a conference to be attended by representatives of "the African race from all parts of the world."[33] This first Pan-African Conference, which gave currency to the term *Pan-Africanism* was held in London, July 23 to 25, 1900 and was attended by some thirty delegates from the West Indies, the United States, and Europe.

It is thus not an unreasonable speculation that Herzl's Zionist movement was one of the stimuli that led to organized Pan-Africanism. But the latter did not show the same vigor or sense of urgency as the former. The African Association quickly became moribund, and it was not until after World War I that organized Pan-Africanism again manifested itself in the form of the elite conferences organized by W. E. B. Du Bois, who had been a prominent participant in the 1900 conference, and Garvey's mass-based transnational Universal Negro Improvement Association. Blyden did not attend the 1900 Pan-African Conference and there is no evidence of his attitude to it. He might have boycotted it because of anticipated mulatto participation, and/or because he felt such a meeting should have been held on African soil.

After 1898, though Blyden did not write explicitly on Jews or Zionism, his views on both remained unchanged for the rest of his life. It is symbolic of his warm relationship with Jews that a Jew, Leo Weinthal, was among four Englishmen who contributed funds for the most significant Blyden memorial anywhere: an imposing bust of Blyden erected on Water Street, Freetown, Sierra Leone.[34]

In sum, Blyden's response to Jews derived in large part from his childhood experiences, his continued intellectual relationship with members of their elite, his deep religious knowledge, and his romantic and mystical nature. It owed little to West African circumstances, as there was in 1898 not, to quote Blyden himself, "a single synagogue in West Africa, along three thousand miles of coast, and probably not two dozen representatives of God's chosen people in that whole extent of country."[35] It was only in the United States that there was a significant interaction between Afro-Americans and Jews. And, as Blyden might well have been aware, by the first decade of the twentieth century there was a growing cooperation, motivated by mutual interests, between the two groups. Thus Booker T. Washington, foremost black leader of his time, had close links with Julius Rosenwald, the Jewish Chicago merchant prince and philanthropist.[36] And among the founders and early influential officers of the NAACP (1910) were such Jews as Henry Moskovits and Joel Springarn.

But nowhere did black-Jewish relationship bear any resemblance to the idealized state of cooperation of which Blyden dreamed. In the United States, the relationship was hardly conducted on a basis of equality and was, indeed, a "bitter-sweet encounter."[37] Doubtless Blyden would have rationalized that such cooperation as existed between Afro-Americans and Jews, imperfect though it was, represented the slow working of their religious natures toward giving moral content to American society, and thus bringing it closer to its own democratic ideal. But, truth to tell, Blyden's career is more instructive in pointing to parallels between Zionism and Pan-Africanism than in actually illuminating the group relations between blacks and Jews.

Notes

1. For Blyden see Hollis R. Lynch, *Edward Wilmot Blyden, Pan-Negro Patriot, 1832–1912* (New York: Oxford University Press, 1967); Hollis R. Lynch, ed., *Black Spokesman: Selected Published Writings of Edward Wilmot Blyden* (London: Frank Gass, 1971); and Hollis R. Lynch, ed., *Selected Letters of Edward Wilmot Blyden*, KTO Press, 1978; for Hess, see Sir Isaiah Berlin, *Life and Opinions of Moses Hess* (London: Cambridge University Press, 1959).

2. Quoted in Barnet Litvinoff, *To the House of their Fathers: A History of Zionism* (New York: Praeger, 1965), p. 33.

3. Lynch, *Black Spokesman*, pp. 25 and 29.

4. Edward W. Blyden, *The Jewish Question* (Liverpool, England: Lionel Hart & Co., 1898), p. 5.

5. Isidor Paiewonsky, *Jewish Historical Development in the Virgin Islands* (1959), no pagination.

6. See Isidor Paiewonsky, "History Corner," *Daily News* (St. Thomas), 18 May 1981.

7. Blyden, *Jewish Question*, p. 7.

8. Litvinoff, *To the House of their Fathers*, chap. 2.

9. *St. Thomas Tidende*, 23, 27, 28 August 1862.

10. Edward W. Blyden, *From West Africa to Palestine* (Freetown, Manchester, and London: 1873), p. 112.

11. Ibid., p. 157.

12. Ibid., pp. 192–99.

13. Ibid., pp. 180–82.

14. Walter Laquer, *A History of Zionism* (New York: Holt, Rinehart & Winston, 1972), p. 55.

15. Blyden, *Jewish Question*, p. 6.

16. *Monrovia Observia*, 14 October 1880.

17. Edward W. Blyden, *Christianity, Islam and the Negro Race* (London: W. B. Whittingham, 1887), p. 120.

18. Laquer, *History of Zionism*, pp. 70–75.

19. Quoted in Litvinoff, *To the House of their Fathers*, p. 63.

20. Laquer, *History of Zionism*, chap. 3.

21. Ibid., p. xiii.

22. See E. L. Thornborough, *Black Reconstructionists* (Englewood Cliffs, N.J.: Prentice-Hall, 1972); and W. E. B. Du Bois, *Black Reconstruction in America* (1935; reprint ed. New York: Atheneum, 1969).

23. See Rayford Logan, *The Betrayal of the Negro* (New York: Collier Books, 1965).

24. Edwin Redkey, *Black Exodus: Black Nationalism and Back-to-Africa Movements, 1890–1910* (New Haven: Yale University Press, 1969), chap. 2.

25. Blyden, *Christianity, Islam and the Negro Race*, p. 109.

26. Quoted in Lynch, *Edward W. Blyden*, p. 121.

27. See Tony Martin, *Race First: The Ideological and Organizational Struggles of Marcus Garvey and the Universal Negro Improvement Association* (Westport, Conn.: Greenwood Press 1976).

28. Christopher Fyfe, *A History of Sierra Leone* (New York: Oxford University Press, 1962), p. 444.

29. In his pamphlet he cites and quotes from Herman Adler, Felix Adler, Israel Abrahams, Israel Zangwill, Oswald John Simons, and I. Singer.

30. Blyden, *Jewish Question*, p. 8.

31. Lynch, *Edward W. Blyden*, p. 62.

32. See Robert G. Weisbord, *African Zion: The Attempt to Establish a Jewish Colony in the East African Protectorate*. Jewish Publication Society of America, Philadelphia, 1968.

33. See Owen Mathurin, *Henry Sylvester Williams and the Origins of the Pan-African Movement* (Westport, Conn.: Greenwood Press, 1976), chaps. 4 and 5; also Immanuel

Geiss, *The Pan-African Movement: A History of Pan-Africanism in America, Europe and Africa* (New York: Holmes & Meier, 1976), chap. 12.

34. Lynch, *Edward W. Blyden*, pp. 161 and 246.

35. Blyden, *Jewish Question*, p. 16.

36. Lenora E. Berson, *The Negroes and the Jews* (New York: Random House, 1971), chap. 4.

37. See Robert G. Weisbord and Arthur Stein, *Bittersweet Encounter: The Afro-American and the American Jew* (Westport, Conn.: Negro Universities Press, 1970).

Jews and the Enigma of the Pan-African Congress of 1919

Robert A. Hill

> We black folk easily drift into intellectual provincial-
> ism. We know our problem and tend to radical thought
> in its solution, but do we strive to know the problems
> of other forward forging groups whose difficulties are
> inevitably intertwined with ours?
>
> W. E. B. Du Bois,
The Crisis,
September 1919

The question could rightly be asked—why should the frequently
glossed over First Pan-African Congress of 1919 be deemed worthy of
further attention? This understandable concern caused one recent authority to complain about the placing of "so much emphasis on the
ritual of the Du Boisian Congresses between 1919 and 1927." The
reason for this state of affairs, it was adduced, derived from the fact
that "histories of the Pan-African movement have usually depended so
heavily on the partisan accounts of Du Bois and [George] Padmore."[1]
And much the same view has been also echoed by Imanuel Geiss,
another authority on the Pan-African movement, but his main lamenta-
tion has been "the unsatisfactory state of the sources."[2]

Despite the extensive body of commentary that has grown up around
what Geiss refers to as "the Pan-African Congress movement between
1919 and 1927," the movement's political substance still remains for
the most part undisclosed. However, what the comments of the two
scholarly authorities point up is a remarkable irony: the tendency on
the part of many, on the one hand, to reduce the Pan-African movement to more or less a scenario of the Du Boisian congresses, and on
the other hand to adduce the premise that the sources are either too

obscure and inadequate or too unavailable for any meaningful interpretation of the historiography to be evaluated or validated.

The force of this revisionist criticism of the Du Boisian Pan-African congresses is at first sight persuasive. J. Ayodele Langley, the first critic mentioned above, has certainly made an immense contribution by helping to shift the conceptual axis of the field toward the study of "some of the less-known influences in the complex history of Pan-Africanism."[3] Moreover, Geiss claims that this shift in focus "diminishes the importance of Du Bois's Pan-African congresses, and also of Du Bois himself and his contribution to Pan-Africanism."[4] Thus, if one is not to succumb to the revisionist arguments, it becomes necessary to prove that both the traditional commentators as well as the revisionists themselves have glossed over matters in such a way as to obscure certain instructive connections that go beyond the prevailing history of the Pan-African congresses. The purpose of this chapter is to attempt to elucidate one important aspect of these connections in relation to the First Pan-African Congress of February 19–21, 1919.

The immediate idea for the holding of the congress arose out of Du Bois's reflection upon the loss suffered by Germany (in the course of the 1914–18 War) of her former African colonies. Writing from Paris on December 14, 1918, Du Bois pointed out that it was "the question of the reapportionment of this vast number of human beings (estimated at 13,420,000) which has started the Pan-African movement."[5] Du Bois's thinking on the subject, however, was first evidenced in his essay on "The Negro's Fatherland" published in the *Survey* on 10 November 1917 (vol. 39, p. 141). Du Bois began the piece by declaring "The future of Africa is one of the most important questions to be solved after this war, and will be, he added, a consequence of "the freeing of Africa through this war." This could be accomplished, he said, if Europe, in recognition of its indebtedness to black soldiers, would "see that a great free central African state is erected out of German East Africa and the Belgian Congo."

This demand went beyond the proposal that had been contained in Du Bois's 1900 declaration "To the Nation of the World," through the Pan-African Conference, which called for the creation of the Congo Free State and its development as "a great central Negro State of the world." The effect of the establishment of such a state in the aftermath of the Great War, first "upon the millions of Africa and them upon the descendants throughout the world," Du Bois thought "would be tremendous": the spiritual effect of this "new Africa" would be "a new beginning of culture for the Negro race," since blacks in the West Indies and North America "need[ed] only such encouragement as just treatment of their fatherland" would supply in their "struggle for self-expression."

The publication date of Du Bois's statement was significant. It was issued November 9, one day after the public release of the now famous Balfour Declaration, which expressed official British sympathy with Jewish aspirations for "the establishment in Palestine of a national home for the Jewish people" and promised "to facilitate the achievement of this object."[6] The impact of the impact of the Balfour Declaration in America was very considerable,[7] as Chaim Weizmann later pointed out, "in the mobilization of Jewish public opinion," where "by far the greatest emphasis was placed on America." The aftereffects were active over several months, particularly after July of that decisive year. The impending declaration had been a matter of common knowledge. In fact, in his speech on May 20, 1917, Weizmann assured the English Zionist Federation "that the Zionists could rely upon British support and protection during their progress towards their final aim, 'the creation of a Jewish Commonwealth in Palestine.'"[9] After Weizmann's disclosure, the only remaining uncertainties were the exact date of the official British declaration and the precise limit that it would set on the scope of Zionist rights in Palestine.

Du Bois first became "aware of the Jewish problem of the modern world and something of its history" in 1893, while he was a student at the University of Berlin. In recounting this experience, he was revealing: "I was astonished; because race problems at the time were to me purely problems of color, and principally of slavery in the United States and near-slavery in Africa." It was when Du Bois went on his 1893 summer vacation to visit with his schoolmate, Stanislaus Ritter von Estreicher, that he was also told for the first time "about the problem of the Poles and particularly of that part of them who were included in the German empire." On his way to Cracow in Poland, Du Bois reminisced:

> I was traveling from Budapest through Hungary to a small town in Galicia, where I planned to spend the night. The cabman looked at me and asked if I wanted to stop "unter die Juden." I was a little puzzled, but told him "Yes." So we went to a little Jewish hotel on a small, out-of-the-way street. There I realized another problem of race or religion. I did not know which, which had to do with the treatment and segregation of large numbers of human beings. I went on to Krakow, becoming more and more aware of two problems of human groups, and then came back to the university, not a little puzzled as to my own race problem and its place in the world.

Upon returning to Berlin, he was further "astonished" as he experienced firsthand the "Jewish problem," which he found was "continually obtruding, but being suppressed and seldom mentioned." This exposure to German and Polish anti-Semitism was exactly why he "went further to investigate this new phenomenon."[10]

The theoretical inflection of his deepened awareness of the problematics of race as a phenomenon that was worldwide in scope, and not confined to white American racism, was channeled, in March 1897, in Du Bois's poignant essay, "The Conservation of Races," which appeared as Occasional Paper No. 2 of the recently formed American Negro Academy.[11] In this essay Du Bois attempted to discover the teaching of "the law of race development" in order to apply it to the needs of "the rising Negro people." But in making his analysis, it is clear that Du Bois fell back upon the combination of the Germanic racial theory and his direct experience with and indirect comprehension of the problem of Central European Jewry—particularly as articulated in the Jewish debate over assimilation v. autonomy.[12] Moreover, the racial prognosis that Du Bois outlined in 1897 can be seen to possess the same character as the theoretical inventions advanced by Otto Bauer, Karl Renner, and Max Adler (within the school of Austro-Marxism)[13] on the subject of nationalism and cultural autonomy.

What Du Bois was struggling to express in 1897 was not the problematics of "cultural pluralism," but this is what certain commentators have unfortunately misread his essay to mean.[14] It was rather an attempt to translate into American terms what has since become a staple in the historiography of the Austro-Hapsburg empire, namely, the idea of cultural and national autonomy for racial-cum-national minorities. Perhaps the best way to understand the problematics that were present in "The Conservation of Races" is to compare it with the then current struggles of Jews and other minorities in East-Central Europe. After World War I, the various successor states, and particularly the entire movement for Jewish autonomy in the Ukraine, would bring this entire problem of national minorities very starkly to world attention.[15] From this vantage point Jonathan Frankel's statement [15] in his recent study of the radicalism of Russian Jewry, *Prophecy and Politics: Socialism, Nationalism, and the Russian Jews, 1862–1917* (1981), carries with it a special significance for our purposes: "To find a parallel one has, perhaps, to turn to black history in the United States which likewise has been torn between integration and separatism, territorialism and cultural autonomism, organized emigration and violent opposition to the state" (p. 4).

In turn, it is significant that in explaining the objective of his revised program of autonomy or self-segregation in 1933–34, Du Bois did not hesitate to make use of the Jewish parallel. "If the Negro in America is successful in welding a mass or large proportion of his people into groups working for their own betterment and uplift," he argued, "they will certainly, like the Jews, be suspected of sinister designs and inner plotting; and their very success in cultural advance be held against them and used for further and perhaps fatal segregation."[16]

His published essay, "The Negro's Fatherland" represented the start of Du Bois's Pan-African design for an independent African state. "This war ought to result in the establishment of an independent Negro Central African State," he wrote (January 1918), one "composed, at least, of the Belgian Congo and German East Africa and, if possible, of Uganda, French Equatorial Africa, German Southwest Africa, and the Portuguese territories of Angola and Mozambique." However, regarding state governance, it "should be under international guarantees and control."[17] This was his identical approach to the British Labor party's program for postwar reconstruction. The program was drafted (August 1917) and published as "Labor and the New Social Order" in *The New Republic* (December), reprinted in a special supplement (vol. 14, no. 16 [February 1918]), and became available as a committee document of the Labor party in January 1918.[18] Du Bois wrote to congratulate the framers on their inclusion of the section that dealt with "Colonies in Tropical Africa," but he nonetheless felt obliged to draw their attention to "one unfortunate phrase." The program stated that "no one ever expects Africa to rule itself," which sparked Du Bois to issue a firm rejoinder:

> This is not only unfortunate but untrue. Twenty-five million persons of African descent in North and South America and the West Indies, added to a good many civilized Negroes in Africa not only expect but are determined that in time Africa shall be for the Africans and shall escape not only the domination and exploitation but the guardianship of white nations.[19]

On 28 August 1918, Du Bois wrote the Georgia-born philanthropist George Foster Peabody, then in Boston, requesting advice about a proposal he wished to make for the disposition of the ex-German African colonies. Du Bois preferred their disposition to rest on "the demand of the people affected," the "Negroes of German Africa" who, however indirectly, also "are the Negroes everywhere." When Du Bois informed Peabody of his approach, the obvious parallel to the Zionist strategy of seeking official sanction for a Jewish national home in Palestine under a British protectorate was apparent:

> The question comes, then, how can this demand of the Negroes be voiced. I am sure that by convention or signed petition I can get the adherence of every Negro American of prominence to a demand that German colonies be not restored. To this it would be very easy to add the assent of West Indian Negroes and the Negroes of West and South Africa. With co-operation on the part of the allied govern-

ments, Negroes of intelligence everywhere would, I am sure, join us. Would not this be in the hands of the Allies an effective weapon and on the other hand would it not be a heartening thing for Negroes to feel that they are being thus consulted and their wishes taken account of?[20]

A practical example of how this process of consultation worked in the case of American Zionists was soon forthcoming. On 5 September 1918, the *New York Times* carried the text of the letter President Wilson sent on the eve of the Jewish New Year (31 August) to his friend Rabbi Stephen S. Wise, former president of the Provisional Zionist Committee. The communication to Rabbi Wise reaffirmed the president's support of the Zionist movement and expressed Wilson's satisfaction with its progress. In his memoirs, Wise exclaimed with pleasure: "No more joyous greeting for the New Year could have come to American Jewry and the Jews of the world than the utterance of the President."[21]

Within a few days of the publication of the president's letter, Du Bois informed the NAACP board (meeting on 9 September) that "it is necessary for us immediately to take steps concerning the future of Africa." He disclosed that he was currently "seeking to get in touch with the Government in order that at the Peace Conference some recognition of the rights of the Negro race in Africa may be recognized."[22] At the 11 November NAACP board meeting, Du Bois read "a memorandum affecting the African colonies and their status at the Peace Conference" which he reported he had "put in the hands of the (Colonel) House Commission through the interest of George Foster Peabody and P. W. Wilson of the London Daily News."[23] We know nothing else about Du Bois's link with this British journalist. However, we do know that Du Bois presented his memorandum to the NAACP board one week after he presided at a meeting at Carnegie Hall at which Emmett J. Scott, the special assistant to the Secretary of War for black troops, had urged the granting of self-government to Germany's former African colonies under "an appointed International Commission, upon which shall be a colored American to voice the inarticulate yearnings of that host of exploited and pillaged people."[24]

His document, "Memoranda on the Future of Africa," contained Du Bois's basic proposals for the disposition of the German colonies that he thought "must come before the Peace Conference." However, it envisaged only a partial application of the principle of self-determination in much the same manner as the Zionist idea of a Jewish National Home or a Jewish Commonwealth in Palestine was conceived as being under British protection, and from which followed the struggle at the peace conference to ensure that Britain was granted the mandate in Palestine. According to the Du Boisian memorandum, the opinion of "the thinking classes of the future Negro world" ought to represent "in the case of the former German colonies . . . the decisive voice." For their opinion to be known, however, Du Bois recommended "the calling together of a Pan-African Congress to meet in Paris sometime during the sessions of the Peace Conference." But it proposed as before that the disposition of the former German colonies should constitute the basic building block of a completely reconstructed Africa "in accordance with the wishes of the Negro race and the best interests of civilization." What was thus proposed in the memorandum was "an international Africa" composed of the "internationalized" former German colonies, and added to them Portuguese Africa and the Belgian Congo.

The reorganization of these African territories would bring them "under the guidance of organized civilization," the chief mechanism of which was to be an international commission whose governing principles were to be "modern culture-science, commerce, social reform and philanthropy." Whereas Palestine was to be under British protection, this "reorganized Africa" would be under international protection and administration.

In many respects, there was a familiar ring to Du Bois's proposal for a "Governing International Commission," particularly as it pertained to the sovernance makeup, as well as to his recommendations of specific "practical policies" to be followed in the field of education. It definitely bore marks of influence from the well-known Zionist Commission, which the British Government had appointed and sent to Palestine early in 1918 under the leadership of Chaim Weizmann.[25] Finally, the memorandum sought to end on a sage note by appealing to the presumed idealism of America's peacemakers: "We can, if we will, inaugurate on the Dark Continent a last great crusade for humanity. With Africa redeemed, Asia would be safe and Europe indeed triumphant." It was clear that Du Bois was hoping for a part in the peace crusade inaugurated by Wilson, with Africa as the direct beneficiary.

When Du Bois chose to describe in the memorandum the proposed Pan-African Congress as the body whose "wish should have weight in the future disposition of the German colonies" at the peace conference, it is possible that he might have been influenced by the parallel example of the first session of the American Jewish Congress, which would finally assemble the following month in Philadelphia, after being postponed from the fall of 1917.[26] The task of the American Jewish Congress, formed in June 1917 after an enormous fight that wracked the entire Jewish community in the United States, was likewise to formulate a post-war program for the Jewish people and to name a delegation to the peace conference in Paris. Although Du Bois would continue for a brief while to employ "Pan-African Conference" interchangeably with "Pan-African Congress," as when he informed Emmett J. Scott November 27 that George Foster Peabody agreed with him that "a Pan-African Conference in Paris during the Peace Conference is of the highest importance."[27] The nomenclature of the latter, he felt, should not only be understood as a semantic matter but should be seen primarily as reflecting substantive issues of program and organization that were operating in parallel fashion among American Zionists.

Du Bois vested leadership of the Pan-African Congress in the hands of a tiny group of "thinking" black individuals, in a manner akin to the elite wise men of the Zionist movement. He was playing a role parallel to that of Louis D. Brandeis. In his letter to Emmett Scott, Du Bois made it plain that black America should be represented by "about six carefully selected delegates of the highest type." He also wrote on the same day to the American secretary of state, Robert Lansing, requesting passports for "about six representative American Negroes, carefully selected in consultation with Dr. Moton, Mr. Peabody, Mr. Scott and others." These six men, in conjunction with their "thinking" counterparts from the black world, would represent "two hundred million of human beings" who would otherwise be "without voice."[28] At the same time, Du Bois was unsuccessful in his attempt to arrange an interview with President Wilson for his delegation to discuss Du Bois's "memorandum on the question of African colonies to be submitted to the Peace Conference." Du Bois's letter to Wilson was designed to be rather more remonstratory than diplomatic:

> Has this race not earned as much consideration as most of the smaller nations whose liberties and rights are to be safeguarded by international convention?
> In principle this is as much an international question as that of the Poles or the Yugo-Slavs who were comprised until recently within the Central Empires. In fact, the question "a people" applies with exceptional distinctness in this case. This appeal can have no rapport with class distinction or class legislation. The ideals of the Peace Congress have to do with the rights of distinctive peoples; a more distinctive people than the American Negro would be difficult to imagine when taken in his present surroundings and as compared with the other races interested which have not the distinguishing mark of color.[29]

Two days after Wilson denied his request for an interview, Du Bois was offered an opportunity to go to France as a newspaper correspondent.[30] On Sunday, 1 December 1918, he sailed on the SS *Orizaba* (the ship from which Hart Crane would jump to his death in 1932). On board ship he encountered Arthur Deerin Call, the executive director of the American Peace Society, whom he apprised of his plan to call a

Pan-African Congress in Paris, and provided him with a copy of his memorandum, which Call published in the January 1919 issue of the society's organ, *Advocate of Peace*. Shortly after his arrival, on 14 December 1918, Du Bois sent back an editorial to the *Crisis* that showed the track on which his thoughts had been moving. The editorial, which was headed "Not 'Separatism,'" declared:

> The African movement means to us what the Zionist movement must mean to the Jews, the centralization of race effort and the recognition of a racial fount. To help bear the burden of Africa does not mean any lessening of effort in our own problem at home. Rather it means increased interest. For any ebullition of action and feeling that results in an amelioration of the lot of Africa tends to ameliorate the condition of colored peoples throughout the world.[31]

Du Bois was effectively responding to criticism engendered by his scheme. The plan, he reiterated, looked toward eventual creation in Africa, of "an autonomous state" that, he hoped, would be founded after a period of development "under the guidance of organized civilization."[32]

Thus there is no room for doubt concerning the objective of Du Bois's plan upon his arrival in France. To date, however, only one commentator, Imanuel Geiss, has recognized that the resolutions emerging out of the Pan-African Congress were "tantamount to a retreat from the principle of self-government."[33] The reason why Geiss has perceived the discrepancy between what Du Bois brought with him to Paris and what issued from his efforts—something that Du Bois himself never admitted or understood—is not difficult to discover. As a historian of the Great War and German foreign policy, Geiss was able to approach the Pan-African Congress from the perspective of the peace conference, which is something that other commentators have overlooked, to the detriment of the understanding of both events.[34] By looking at the Pan-African Congress as a black phenomenon in isolation from the broader political discourse of the peace conference, one is bound to miss the salient point of contact between the two. It alone can explain the substance of the discussions that took place among the delegates to the Pan-African Congress and the true meaning of the resolutions that emerged from the deliberations. A proper understanding of the Pan-African Congress within this broader context has the additional advantage of shedding further light on the political rivalries that characterized the peace conference.

If, prior to his hurried departure, Du Bois had reason to hope he could secure official American support for his peace plan, his strategy received a rude shock immediately upon arrival in Paris. "I first went to the American Peace Commission and said frankly and openly: 'I want to call a Pan-African Congress in Paris.' The Captain to whom I spoke smiled and shook his head. 'Impossible,' he said, and added: 'The French Government would not permit it.' 'Then,' said I innocently: 'It's up to me to get French consent!' 'It is!' he answered, and he looked relieved."[35] If Du Bois had been counting on the same American support that the Zionists had succeeded so well in securing, he was now made aware that he would have to seek the support of the French government, which, according to the British diplomat, Sir Mark Sykes (cosigner of the Sykes-Picot agreement), embodied the main obstacle to the realization of Zionist aims.[36]

Shortly before Christmas, Du Bois wrote to the NAACP secretary, John R. Shillady, to inform him of where things stood: "I am to meet colored French deputies soon to plan for a Pan-African Conference in Paris during the Peace Conference. It may not be possible but plans are afoot."[37] While Du Bois was waiting to make contact with the black deputies, he urgently undertook the gathering of material for his projected war history of black Americans. He discovered to his amazement that the stories of discrimination and the shabby treatment experienced by black combatants at the hands of their white American officers that filtered back to America had hardly even scratched the surface of the reality. On the other hand, Du Bois was struck by another revelation that was just as unexpected, but it was one that caused him a transcendent emotion. "Never have I seen black folk—and I have seen many—so bitter and disillusioned at the seemingly bottomless depths of American color hatred—so uplifted at the vision of real democracy dawning on them in France." He exclaimed at what he had discovered: "all this ancient and American race hatred and insult in a purling sea of French sympathy and kindliness, of human uplift and giant endeavor, amid the mightiest crusade humanity ever saw for Justice!"[38] Du Bois also wrote later of the flood of emotion that swept over him as he witnessed the official celebration in honor of colored troops held in the Trocadero on 19 December: " 'Mine eyes have seen' and they were filled with tears." He entitled it "Vive La France!", and he succinctly expressed his feelings: "How fine a thing to be a black Frenchman in 1919—imagine such a celebration in America!"[39] This stood in sharp contrast to the attitude adopted toward him by the General Staff on the American Expeditionary Forces (AEF), whose intelligence officers were notified on 1 January 1918 to report promptly "all his moves and actions while at station of any unit."[40]

The way was now opened for Du Bois finally to disengage himself from the illusion of forthcoming American support for the Pan-African Congress. On 20 December 1918, the acting American Secretary of State, Frank L. Polk, cabled Lansing in Paris that he was "inclined to refuse passports" for the delegation of "six representative American Negroes" to the Pan-African Congress in Paris. The following day, Secretary Lansing cabled back to Washington, D.C., instructing the department that the "inclination not to grant passports is a wise one as racial questions of this nature ought not to be a subject to come before the Conference."[41] This confirmation killed the Du Boisian dream of being joined by other "representative Negroes" from the United States. The one exception, Rev. J. W. H. Jernagin representing the National Race Congress, arrived under other auspices and a day late.

Cast on his own, with a hostile government at his back, Du Bois was compelled to look for new allies. More importantly, he had to begin to rethink his strategic outlook for the Congress *within the context of France.* On 24 December 1918, he wrote a memorandum addressed to the acting NAACP chairman, Mary White Ovington, and to the chairman who was serving with the AEF in France at the time, Major Joel E. Spingarn, explaining what he felt was now required. He stated his view as follows:

> Every attempt must be made to present the case of the Darker Races of the world to the enlightened public opinion of Europe.
>
> It is of equal importance to understand and rightly interpret the general attitude and outlook of the World just not toward the social problems in which we are interested.[42]

Everything now hinged on securing permission from the French Government. This required their understanding of "the social problems in which we are interested," in a context that was quite different from the American experience.

Du Bois finally met with the black French deputies, who were led by Blaise Diagne. It is likely that Du Bois's introduction to them was arranged by the recently retired black American consul at Cognac, George H. Jackson. Diagne was the crucial link to French officialdom, for he had not only the ear of the French colonial minister but also that of Premier Clemenceau.[43] Du Bois gave this account of what then transpired: " 'Of course, we can have a Pan-African Congress,' he [Diagne] said—'I'll see Clemenceau.' "[44] What Diagne submitted for French approval, however, was the memorandum that Du Bois had prepared that contained a significant development. He added to its outline of "principles upon which the future development of the Negro race must take place," one on "Political rights for the Civilized" that headed his list of seven "principles":

> Political rights for the Civilized.
> Modern education for all children.
> Native rights to the land and natural resources.

Industrial development primarily for the benefit of the native and his country.

Development of autonomous government along lines of native custom, with the object of inaugurating gradually an Africa for Africans.

Full recognition of the independent governments of Abyssinia, Liberia, and Hayti, with their fully natural boundaries, and the development of the former German colonies under the guarantee and oversight of the League of Nations.

The cordial and sympathetic cooperation of the black, yellow and white races on terms of mutual respect and equality in the future development of the world.[45]

These principles are indicators of the fact that Du Bois had commenced to move away from his original demand for an African state to be governed by an international commission. In place of the demand for statehood, Du Bois was now embarked in a new direction that was taking the Pan-African Congress essentially toward the French colonial ideal of African assimilation.[46]

Concurrently in the United States, the NAACP proceeded quite naturally on the assumption that the original program outlined by Du Bois still held. A mass meeting was called (6 January 1919 at Carnegie Hall) to acquaint the public with the substance of the political program Du Bois had ostensibly taken to the Paris peace conference. The subject of the meeting was announced as "Africa in the World Democracy." The two featured speakers among the six prominent people who addressed the meeting were Professor Horace Meyer Kallen, speaking on "The Future of Africa and A League of Nations," and James Weldon Johnson, NAACP field secretary, whose subject was "Africa at the Peace Table and the Descendants of Africans in Our American Democracy." Both Kallen and Johnson hewed closely to the original Du Boisian line of partial self-determination for an internationalized Africa.[47] Best known as the foremost philosopher of cultural pluralism in America, Kallen was also one of the most notable Zionist leaders in the United States and an exceedingly active principal organizer of Zionist support.[48] All that Kallen and Johnson had to say, however, was soon to become moot as the events they knew little or nothing about unfolded in Paris.

Du Bois's meeting with the black French deputies took place sometime in the period between 1–4 January 1919. The shift in his political outlook, however, had begun to occur before that meeting. He had spent Christmas with Spingarn, who was his closest lifelong friend and to whose memory as a "scholar and knight" he would later dedicate his first autobiography, *Dusk of Dawn* (1940). The son of a Jewish emigrant from Austria, Spingarn was elected chairman of the NAACP board of directors in January 1914, a position that he held until he left (August

1918) for service in France with the AEF. His brother, Arthur Spingarn, was also the head of the NAACP legal committee. Hasia R. Diner has offered the view that Joel Spingarn "can be considered the most important white in the NAACP and one of the pivotal figures in the early history of the black civil rights movement."[49]

Du Bois secured Springarn's approval of the first memorandum that he sent back to the NAACP on 24 December, a communication that included details of his entire program of activities: "Before sending this I shall submit it to the judgment of our friends such as I can reach." There was also this handwritten addendum at the foot of that memorandum: "The above memo. was laid before Chairman J. E. Springarn today Dec. 25 and has his *complete approval.* For obvious reasons he does not add his signature but authorizes the above statement." But Springarn did much more than merely use his leave to spend Christmas with Du Bois. Du Bois wrote to inform the NAACP on 4 January 1919 that it was Springarn who "gave me my first introduction to French people of influence."

In the same memorandum, by way of contrast, Du Bois described his continuing effort to obtain some degree of official American endorsement: "I have got the interest of Ray Stanndard Baker of the House Commission," he informed the officials of the NAACP, "and the more guarded cooperation of Walter Lippman." Baker was a journalist who had corresponded with Du Bois in 1906 in the course of researching the series of articles that would eventually be published as *Following the Color Line: American Negro Citizenship in the Progressive Era* (1908). Baker held the Paris post of director of the press bureau for the American Commission to Negotiate Peace (ACNP).[50]

Walter Lippman had recently been reassigned from his army position as captain with the propaganda wing of American military intelligence in France to the political and economic intelligence section of the commission staff by Colonel House.[51] Du Bois was a friend of Lippman from 1913 when, shortly after his graduation from Harvard, Lippman had sought without success to have the Liberal club admit Du Bois as a member. Immediately upon his arrival in France (15 December 1918), Du Bois wrote Lippman to ask for an appointment and the following day Lippman both replied ("I should be very glad, indeed, to see you")[52] and welcomed him that afternoon. This evidence would suggest that Lippman was in fact the "captain" whom Du Bois met with on the staff of the ACNP and who told him that the holding of the Pan-African Congress would be "impossible."

The reason for Lippman's "guarded" attitude toward Du Bois in Paris, however, would thus have antedated the official American attitude of displeasure that subsequently developed toward Du Bois's presence. Du Bois was probably unaware that Lippman had resigned

and had already left France to return to the United States, when he
wrote (31 January 1919) informing him that he would be "interested to
know that Premier Clemenceau has given us permission to hold in Paris
a 'Pan-African Conference on the Protection of the Natives of Africa
and the Peoples of African Descent.'" When Du Bois's letter finally
caught up with Lippman in America, he wrote a brief congratulatory
note to Du Bois (20 February 1919): "I am very much interested in your
organization of the Pan-African Conference, and glad that Clemenceau
has made it possible. Will you send me whatever reports you may have
on the work."[53]

Du Bois made the maximum use of the access to French society that
he gained through Spingarn's contacts. Perhaps his most prestigious
association involved Mme. Calmann-Levy, the widow of France's best-
known publisher and a member of one of the most-prominent Jewish
families in France.[54] Du Bois informed the NAACP board in his
memorandum of 4 January that Mme. Calmann-Levy "has invited me
to dinner with those who will guide me to influential persons in university circles." In his autobiography, Du Bois pays her a notable tribute
by recalling her importance to the task that he had set himself in Paris:

> My greatest helper in this [Pan-African] Congress was Madame Cal-
> man-Levy, widow of the Paris publisher. This quiet, charming
> woman became enthusiastic over the idea of my Congress and
> brought together in her salon groups of interested persons including
> [Paul] Otlet and [Henri La] Fontaine of Belgium and several French
> officials.[55]

In order to fully appreciate the impact that such hospitality had upon
Du Bois, while he was trying to navigate, against considerable odds,
the politically parlous course of the Pan-African Congress's transformation in France, it is useful to view it in the context of his American experience. In a vivid testimonial that Du Bois sent back for
publication in the *Crisis,* he described the ennobling effect that Mme.
Calmann-Levy's reception had upon him:

> My God! For what am I thankful this night? For nothing. For nothing
> but the most commonplace of commonplaces; a table of gentlewo-
> men and gentlemen—soft-spoken, sweet-tempered, full of human
> sympathy, who made me, a stranger, one of them. Ours was a fellow-
> ship of common books, common knowledge, mighty aims. We could
> laugh and joke and think as friends—and the *Thing*—the hateful,
> murderous, dirty *Thing* which in America we call "Nigger-hatred"
> was not only not there—it could not even be understood. It was a
> curious monstrosity at which civilized folk laughed or looked
> puzzled. There was no elegant and elaborate condescension of—
> "We once had a colored servant"—"My father was an Abolition-
> ist"—"I've always been interested in *your people*"—there was only

the community of kindred souls, the delicate reference for the Thought that led, the quick deference to the guests you left in quiet regret, knowing they were not discussing you behind your back with lies and license. God! It was simply human decency and I had to be thankful for it because I am an American Negro and white America, with saving exceptions, is cruel to everything that has black blood— and this was Paris, in the year of salvation, 1919.

Fellow blacks, we must join the democracy in Europe.[56]

Du Bois had now experienced the sweet feeling of French assimila- tion; thus when he spoke of blacks joining "the democracy in Europe," it was the new experience of racial democracy in France that he had in mind. But if Du Bois had tasted French assimilation, it would be very accurate to say that it was provided less by French citizens at large and rather more particularly by the *French Jewish elite*. Du Bois's contact with French Jewry through Mme. Calmann-Levy's circle thus repre- sented a double case of French assimilation, a factor that increased the intensity of Du Bois's conversion to France's political outlook. But while they welcomed him, the political outlook of French Jewry ran completely counter to Du Bois's initial Pan-African program.

The deep-seated patriotism of French Jews, which made them sec- ond to none in the nation, lent strong support to France's aim of colo- nial expansion in the negotiations surrounding the peace settlement. The immediate relevance of this influence is that the elite French Jews, among whom Du Bois found support, were steadfast in their opposition to Zionism. This fact is exemplified best in the stance adopted during the peace conference toward Zionist aims in Palestine by the principal Jewish organization in France, the *Alliance Israelite Universelle,* and its leader, professor Sylvain Lévy.[57] Some illumination is provided by Walter Laqueur: "On the whole the Zionist movement struck few roots in France; the great majority of French Jews always stressed their attachment to the French nation, denying that their feelings differed from those of other Frenchmen."[58] The antinationalist French Jews, together with their English coreligionists, actually went so far as to file separate memoranda opposing national minority rights for Jews at the peace conference. This action led to a serious clash with the Jewish delegations from Central and Eastern Europe,[59] according to Paula Hy- man,

to the Alliance Israelite emancipation meant civil and political equal- ity. Any decision to accord national minority status to the Jews of Eastern Europe would, in its eyes, cast doubt on the tested solution of Western Jewry and provide ammunition to anti-Semites, who had always claimed that the Jews remained an eternally unassimilable people. During the Peace Conference the Alliance was, therefore, one of the most determined lobbyists for civil emancipation and one of the most vigorous opponents of national minority rights for Eastern European Jews.[60]

This opposition by the French Jewish elite to all forms of Jewish nationalism, whether that arising from the demand for national minority rights in Eastern Europe or for Zionism, which was seeking international recognition at the Peace Conference, provides the essential context in which to view Du Bois's relationship to the Calmann-Levy circle. For Du Bois to have been assured of the support of his French Jewish mentors, therefore, probably would have entailed a drastic attenuation in his own Pan-African Zionism.

Paul Otlet (who was one of the persons to whom Du Bois was introduced by Mme. Calmann-Levy), popularly known as "the father of the League of Nations" because of his several books on the subject, made sure to point up this Zionist dimension in the original Pan-African program in a lengthy article, "Les Noire et la Societe des Nations." The article was written for *La Patrie Belge* (19 January 1919), and Du Bois saw that reprints were distributed prior to the Pan-African Congress. Upon his return to the United States, Du Bois also presented copies at the NAACP board meeting on 14 April. In his article, Otlet said:

> The initiators of the Pan-African movement believe that there is a strong analogy between the situation of blacks and that of the Jews. The latter, like the former are dispersed and in many countries they have been persecuted or degraded, and none of them were able to establish the natural center of their national culture. The Jews thus asked that Palestine, the ancient Zion, be returned to them and have just obtained it. If there existed somewhere in Africa a black state consisting of the best elements of the race, it could rapidly become a center of civilization, autonomous, a home sending its rays towards all the other black centers; it could exert indirect political influence to gain improvement everywhere, beginning with the colonies.

This analysis reflected the original design of Du Bois's Pan-African Zion. However, Otlet's article also clarified the changed conception that Du Bois was now offering:

> Here are the blacks deciding by themselves to contribute to the elimination of racial prejudice. Those among them who talk like you and I put forward this judicious formula: "The color is nothing, the civilization is everything." Consequently let us help the blacks to get civilized, let us provide them with the means to achieve it and let us accept without ulterior motive this conclusion proposed by the Pan-African Congress: "The cordial and sympathetic cooperation of the black, yellow and white races on the basis of reciprocal consideration and quality in the future development of the world."

Here was the new basis on which plans for the Pan-African Congress now proceeded; without which it hardly would have been acceptable to the French authorities, given the assimilationist ethos of their own colonial policy. After presenting Diagne and the other black deputies with the revised program of the Pan-African Congress and the proposed agenda, Diagne, according to Du Bois's subsequent testimony, "saw Clemenceau, and there was a week's pause." After this, "Clemenceau saw Pichon [French minister of colonies] and there was another pause."[61] Du Bois did not sit idly by while waiting, however. He made his own written submission to Clemenceau (14 January), asking that he "take up with the Great Powers, looking to an exchange of views, regarding the establishing of a great independent State in Africa, to be settled and governed by Negroes." Du Bois outlined his suggestions for the territorial composition of his proposed "Independent Negro Central African State" and asked Clemenceau to respond with his views on the subject. It is nearly certain that Clemenceau would have dismissed the submission if Du Bois had not included the following penultimate paragraph: "I beg to state that I took the matter up with my own American government, and am attaching herewith copy of the reply to the same."[62]

The French now had solid evidence of the embarrassment that the presence of Du Bois and his attempt to stage the Pan-African Congress in Paris was causing the American officials. They were not slow to seize the opportunity to increase the ante in their propaganda war, which was aimed at undercutting the American posture of idealism at the peace conference.[63] Du Bois presented the French government with an excellent opportunity to gain access to a public platform from which to expose America's racism, and thereby raise questions about its moral qualifications to preach to France about the principles of mandates. Contemporaneously, France, through the effective use of its black deputies, could claim persuasively that her policy of colonial assimilation was a success and had the wholehearted support of her colonial black population. It was, in the words of Christopher M. Andrew and A. S. Kanya-Forstner, "a minor triumph for French stage-management."[64]

High stakes were now associated with the holding of the Pan-African Congress. Thus while French officials lied and fed America's representatives in Paris the illusion that they were opposed to its being held, they prepared to gain the maximum benefit from the event.[65] Eventually, the broader French propaganda campaign brought the peace conference to a crisis point. According to Colonel E. M. House, President Wilson (on 11 February) asked Ray Stannard Baker "to let the newspapers have a story to the effect that if the French continued their propaganda against the Governments assembled here, that the Conference would probably be moved elsewhere." House remarked on the futility of this approach and instead noted: "What the President and the two Prime Ministers [Lloyd George and Orlando] should have done was to have gone directly to Clemenceau and read the riot act to him."[66]

If the Americans were duped by the French, it must be admitted that Du Bois also failed to comprehend the French ploy; nowhere in his several accounts of the Pan-African Congress does there appear any hint of France's ulterior motives. What prevented Du Bois from understanding this French subversion of the Pan-African Congress? The answer to be given to this question essentially falls into two parts. The first is Du Bois's seduction by the experience of French assimilation. This allurement was so captivating he never suspected that he was a captive of French diplomatic intrigue arrayed against the Americans and the British. Correspondingly, the gratitude following upon the official French permission to hold the Congress made it equally inopportune and difficult or churlish to question France's motives. Du Bois was no more culture-bound than he was color-blind, but the intellectual moral idealist, in the spheres of pragmatic and power politics, wore blinders—so the reality escaped his awareness. In the light of his priorities, what he had seen of French treatment of its Jewish elite, and its public outpouring of gratitude for the sacrifice and heroism of black servicemen, skepticism would have been out of the question.

The second factor is that Du Bois never discerned the inner working of France's diplomatic struggle against her American and British allies at the peace conference. This can be seen most clearly in the statement made by Du Bois in his (14 January 1919) communication to the NAACP board: "Any agitation of any kind obnoxious to the French or their Allies is absolutely impossible on pain of arrest and expulsion. *C'est la guerre en France,* whatever it may be in America."[67] When later, Du Bois asked the question in his account of the event, "What could a Pan-African Congress do?", he answered it with the following important qualification: "It could not agitate the Negro problem in any particular country, except in so far as that problem could be plausibly shown to be part of the problem of the future of Africa."[68]

What these various statements demonstrate is that Du Bois viewed the Allied governments as a unified group. He thus failed to differentiate between their contending interests and deep-seated conflicts over the peace settlement. In truth, whereas the French government worked with supreme finesse to promote the Pan-African Congress precisely in order that it should "agitate the Negro problem" in the United States, Du Bois saw its approbation simply as yet further proof of France's racially benevolent attitude. The result was that it reinforced Du Bois's acceptance of the philosophy of French assimilation, to which he had been weaned by the elite members of French Jewry and by the intense warmth of the French public's gratitutde and the sympathy that it showed toward all black troops in France.

Word of French approval to hold the Pan-African Congress finally came through on 26 January 1919. A preparatory meeting to organize the details of the congress was held in early February. At that meeting, Diagne was nominated president of the provisional committee and Du Bois its secretary. The title of the memorandum discussed at this meeting contained a significant new feature: the name of the Congress was expanded into "Congress PANAFRICAIN pour la protection des Indigenes d'Afrique et les Peuples d'origine Africaine."[69] The expansion of the original title was indicative of the changed perspective now guiding the Pan-African Congress. The memorandum of the preparatory meeting contained the following declaration of the two purposes that the Pan-African Congress now set itself:

(1) At this critical moment in the history of the world, we want to demand a serious review of the rights of the Negro race and demand the end to all negotiations in regard to African colonies that do not provide for the rights and wishes of the Africans themselves.
(2) To take the first step toward unity and understanding among various groupings of peoples of African origin wherever they might be, without diminishing their loyalties as Frenchmen, Englishmen, Liberians, Haitians, or Americans; to inspire in them, as members of a great and powerful race, that they have a particular objective on earth [and] that they propose in the future to work together for the defence of their rights and the development of their genius.[70]

This statement is self-revelatory: no trace of Du Bois's earlier desire to see "partial self-determination" for Africa achieved in the settlement of peace was present. Instead of an organization committed to the creation of an autonomous African state, the Pan-African Congress underwent a qualitative change that made it in reality nothing more than the black version of the various protective bodies of native rights that it had invited to paricipate. Maurice Delafosse concluded his review of the Congress on an optimistic note, disclosing therein the identity of outlook between French colonial views and those of the Pan-African Congress:

None of the wishes expressed by the Pan-African Congress can appear as other than legitimate; none goes beyond the limits of reason nor displays exaggerated pretensions. Not only do they correspond to what the friends of the black race have ceaselessly clamoured for, but also they represent some of the claims of the colonial world as a whole. I do not think it possible for anyone interested in the future of our African colonies not to subscribe to the ideas expressed by the Pan-African Congress and not to try and realise them.

France, for her part, is very willing to implement the few parts of the program that she still has to implement. . . . [71]

The Pan-African Congress was convened in the Grand Hotel in Paris on 19, 20, and 21 February 1919. There were only three full sessions held; the first on the afternoon of the nineteenth, the second on the afternoon of the twentieth, and the third on the morning of the twenty-first. In addition, there were several committee meetings for the drafting of the resolutions. These numbered nine in all and pertained to land, capital, labor, education, medicine and hygiene, the state, culture and religion, civilized Negroes, and the League of Nations. The resolutions were couched in the form of demands presented "in the interest of justice and humanity and for the strengthening the forces of civilization."

Finding themselves outmaneuvered by their French counterparts in the art of diplomatic manipulation, the American representatives in Paris attempted to obtain reliable intelligence on the meetings of the Pan-African Congress. But as a result of their alienation from Du Bois, the American task was far from simple. It appears that the difficulty was solved, however, by the shrewd observation made by a Lt. Heath of the intelligence service of the American Commission to Negotiate Peace who said:

> We are following the meetings of the Congress, but have found that a Major Spingarn, unattached service, is very much interested in it and this Major was formerly a Professor at Columbia and offered a prize quite recently for essays on the relations towards the Negroes in America. It is not easy for the representative of the Intelligence Service to ask Major Spingarn to take any notes, but he is able to follow the proceedings very closely and if he is known at the Embassy it will be possible to ask him to make a report in the premises.
> This matter of Major Spingarn is merely a detail and I am only mentioning it because if he were known by anyone at the embassy it would make it a little more easy to get a thorough report on the proceeedings although we are covering it quite fairly. [72]

The American official who assumed responsibility for implementing the suggestion was George Louis Beer, chief of the colonial division of the American Commission to Negotiate Peace. [73] Beer was doubly well suited for this role. As professor of colonial economic history on the faculty at Columbia University, he would have been acquainted with Spingarn who was also a member of Columbia's faculty until he resigned in 1911. There was another capacity in which Beer would most certainly have known Spingarn. Before deciding to devote himself to historical study, Beer was a very successful tobacco merchant in New York (1893 and 1903). It would have been difficult for him not to have been acquainted with the Spingarn family, as it was also engaged in a prosperous tobacco trade in New York. The result was that Du Bois, on 25 February, received a rather hastily written letter from his friend Spingarn:

> I have just seen George L. Beer the historian at 4 Place de la Concorde; he is the Commission's official adviser on Africa, and is much interested in your Congress. He asks that you send him immediately a fully report of its proceedings; and I suggest that you also have a talk with him. He wants you to write a letter to Col. House about Africa (also asking for an interview) and to send a copy to him.[74]

Du Bois followed this advice and met with Beer on 1 March. According to Beer's diary, they "talked about Pan-African Congress and future of Africa." But he found Du Bois less than well informed about developments in Africa, and he claimed that "his [Du Bois's] interest is frankly in the educative native."[75] The following week, Du Bois was received by Colonel House (at 5:45 p.m. on the afternoon of March 10) in the Hotel Crillon.[76] Du Bois was ushered in to see House promptly at the appointed hour and he was out again at 5:50 p.m. House noted in his appointment book the sum and substance of this cursory exchange: "With Du Bois it was the Negro question and its relation to the Peace Conference."[77]

But if, understandably, Du Bois and House (the Texas confidant of native Virginian President Wilson) were all but congenitally conditioned by values and interests so extreme they shared none sufficiently that would have endeared them to each other, there was no lack of clarity in the memorandum that Du Bois prepared for another important engagement two days later. It was circulated to "Messrs. Diagne, Candace and Their Friends on the Future of the Pan-African Congress." This most transparent of all documents made unmistakable the explicit political calculation underpinning the entire Pan-African Congress:

> We must make France see that there are millions of intelligent persons scattered throughout the world who are her friends and allies because of her stand on the race problem and that if she refused to retreat and even advance in the recognition and uplift of the Negro race, the growing power of the Negro and colored world will everywhere swing in her favor.

The Memorandum concluded by posing a series of questions aimed at clarifying the means that would be required to implement the movement's "general principles and policies." Du Bois asked:

> 1. How can the Pan African Congress be permanent, effective and self sustaining?

2. What rapprochement can we make with France?
3. What alliance can we make with organized labor the world over?[78]

If in 1919, as he would describe it subsequently, "Pan-Africa was a phase of war";[79] and if, as we know, war is in reality the continuation of politics by other means, then what the memorandum relates is the desire to assure France that the Pan-African Congress was an important means for the continuation of French interests. Unfortunately for Du Bois, France was to adopt the view in 1921 that the Pan-African Congress was a mere variant of the anti-European agitation known as the phenomenon of Garveyism. At that point, France withdrerw its political support, and the Second Pan-African Congress was marked throughout by Blaise Diagne's unrelenting attacks against Du Bois.

Upon his return to the United States from the first Congress (in 1919), Du Bois wrote that of the nine resolutions passed, two especially possessed "tremendous significance to us"; these focused upon the "Civilized Negroes" and the League of Nations:

> 8. Wherever persons of African descent are civilized and able to meet the tests of surrounding culture, they shall be accorded the same rights as their fellow citizens; they shall not be denied on account of race or color a voice in their own government, justice before the courts and economic and social equality according to ability and desert.
> 9. Whenever it is proven that African natives are not receiving just treatment at the hands of any State or that any State deliberately excludes its civilized citizens or subjects of Negro descent from its body politic and cultural, it shall be the duty of the League of Nations to bring the matter to the attention of the civilized World.

In Du Bois's view, "Precisely the same principles are being demanded today by the Jews and the Japanese."[80] To the degree that the resolutions ventured beyond the position adhered to by the antinationalist Jews in France, they displayed evidence of the unsuccessful efforts waged at the peace conference to secure, through the protection of the League Covenant, the rights of *minorities;* among whom, of course, were numbered the Jews of Eastern Europe.[81]

What this suggests is that Du Bois's thinking had settled finally within the ideological and juridicial framework of Jewish minority rights. The shift from his earlier evaluation of Africa's claims, squarely based, in my view, on his knowledge of the recognition of the case for a national Jewish homeland in Palestine, was thenceforth toward a similar conception of the protection of black rights based on the identification of blacks and Jews as minorities.

While Du Bois's position was subject to change, the factor that remained constant throughout was his evaluation of the black political future through the prism of the Jewish dilemma. If the catalyst for his original African conception was the political success of the American Zionist movement, the mediating agency of his subsequent shift toward assimilation was the cultural success of the Jewish elite in France. And behind both halves of the divergent Jewish strategy stood the tremendous weight respectively of the American state and the French state: the former postulated support for Jewish Zionism, while the latter postulated support for French imperialism.

The structural requirement of Du Bois's parallel conception of an African Zion, which he valiantly tried to secure, would have been the support of the American state. His failure drove him to seek the support of the French state, with the consequence that the original Pan-African idea experienced an unexpected rebirth that accommodated itself within the legitimating ideology of French assimilation. However, in Du Bois's view, this would not have been seen as accommodation; rather it was a case of protection extended by a state whose power was its civilization.

In the broadest sense, these questons of the state, racial allegiance, and cultural identity are ones that black people, like Jews, are today still trying to sort out.

Notes

1. Ayodele Langley, *Pan-Africanism and Nationalism in West Africa, 1900–1945* (Oxford: Clarendon Press, 1973), p. 286.

2. Imanuel Geiss, *The Pan-African Movement: A History of Pan-Africanism in America, Europe and Africa,* trans. Ann Keep (New York: Africana, 1974), p. 233. The only sustained published account to date of the First Pan-African Congress has been Clarence G. Contee, "Du Bois, the NAACP, and the Pan-African Congress of 1919," *Journal of Negro History* 57 (January 1972): 13–28; see also Clarence G. Contee, ed., "The Worley Report on the Pan-African Congress of 1919," ibid., 55 (April 1970): 140–43. An extensive treatment of the subject is to be found in the present writer's still unpublished work, "The First Pan-African Congress of 1919—Myth and Reality: A Documentary Analysis."

3. Langley, *Pan-Africanism,* p. 325.

4. Geiss, *The Pan-African Movement,* p. 233.

5. "Africa," *Crisis* 17 (February 1919): 165.

6. The declaration was communicated by letter to Lord Rothschild by Arthur James Balfour in his capacity as foreign secretary on 2 November, but it was not relased for publication until 9 November; see Leonard Stein, *The Balfour Declaration* (New York: Simon & Schuster, 1961); also Isaiah Friedman, *The Question of Palestine, 1914–1918* (New York: Schocken Books, 1973).

7. Charles Israel Goldblatt, "The Impact of the Balfour Declaration in America, *American Jewish Historical Quarterly* 57 (June 1968): 455–515; Melvin I. Urofsky, *American Zionism from Herzl to the Holocaust* (Garden City, N.Y.: Anchor Press/ Doubleday, 1975), pp. 202–20.

8. Chaim Weizmann, *Trial and Error: The Autobiography of Chaim Weizmann* (1949 reprint ed., New York: Schocken Books, 1966), p. 193.

9. *The Letters and Papers of Chaim Weizmann,* vol. 7, series A, ed. Leonard Stein (London: Oxford University Press; Jerusalem: Israel Universities Press, 1975), "Introduction," p. xxix.

10. "The Negro and the Warsaw Ghetto," *Jewish Life* 6 (May 1952): 14–15. The issue is incorrectly dated April 1952 (Paul G. Partington, *W. E. B. Du Bois: A Bibliography of His Published Writings* [n.p., 1977], p. 152).

11. Alfred A. Moss, Jr., *The American Negro Academy: Voice of the Talented Tenth* (Baton Rouge, La.: Louisiana State University Press, 1981), pp. 54–61, 94–96.

12. Cf., A. Norman Klein, Introduction to *The Suppression of the African Slave Trade*, by W. E. B. Du Bois (1896; reprint ed., New York: Schocken, 1969), p. xiv; see also *The Autobiography of W. E. B. Du Bois* (New York: International Publishers, 1968), pp. 162–65.

13. Tom Bottomore and Patrick Goode, eds., *Austro-Marxism* (Oxford: Clarendon Press, 1978), pp. 102–35; Michael Lowy, "Marxists and the National Question," *New Left Review* 96 (March–April 1976): 92–94; Robert A. Kann, *The Multinational Empire: Nationalism and National Reform in the Habsburg Monarchy, 1848–1918*, Vol. II (1950; reprint ed., New York: Octagon Books 1964), vol. 2, chap. 20.

14. Ernest Kaiser, Introduction to *The American Negro Academy Occasional Papers* 1–22 (New York: Arno Press, 1969), p. iv; this interpretation of Du Bois in terms of cultural pluralism is followed by William Toll, *The Resurgence of Race: Black Social Theory from Reconstruction to the Pan-African Conferences* (Philadelphia: Temple University Press, 1979), pp. 168–73.

15. Oscar I. Janowsky, *The Jews and Minority Rights, 1898–1919* (New York: Columbia University Press, 1933), and *Nationalities and National Minorities (with special reference to East-Central Europe)* (New York: Macmillan, 1945); Solomon I. Goldelman, Jewish *National Autonomy in the Ukraine, 1917–20* (Chicago: The University of Chicago Press, 1968).

16. W. E. B. Du Bois, *Dusk of Dawn: An Essay Toward An Autobiography of A Race Concept* (1940; reprint ed., New York: Schocken Books, 1968), p. 215; cf. E. Franklin Frazier, "The Du Bois Program in the Present Crisis," *Race* 1 (Winter 1935–36): 11–13.

17. *Crisis* 15 (January 1918): 114.

18. Paul F. Bourke, "The Status of Politics 1909–1919: *The New Republic,* Randolph Bourne and Van Wyck Brooks," *Journal of American Studies* 8 (August 1974): 173–75.

19. W. E. B. Du Bois Papers, "Memorandum to the Labor Party of England on the American Negro," 21 February 1918, Microfilm Reel 6, Frame 724, University of Massachusetts Library, Amherst, Mass. (hereafter referred to as the Du Bois Papers).

20. Ibid., Reel 6, Frame 1096.

21. *Challenging Years: The Autobiography of Stephen Wise* (New York: G. P. Putnam's Sons, 1949), pp. 194–95.

22. Records of the NAACP, Manuscript Division, Library of Congress, Washington, D.C. (Hereafter DLC.)

23. Ibid., NAACP Board Minutes, 11 November 1918. The memorandum was later expanded upon by Du Bois in the chapter, "The Hands of Ethiopia," in *Darkwater: Voices from Within the Veil* (New York: Harcourt, Brace and Howe, 1920), in which he elaborates on his "conception of a new African World State" (p. 65).

24. Scott to Moton, 5 November 1918, Emmett J. Scott Papers, Soper Library, Morgan State University, Baltimore, Md. The text of Scott's address was released to the press on 8 November 1918.

25. Weizmann, *Trial and Error,* pp. 212–39.

26. Urofsky, *American Zionism,* chap. 5; Naomi W. Cohen, *Not Free to Desist: The American Jewish Committee, 1906–1966* (Philadelphia: The Jewish Publication Society of America, 1972), pp. 91–98; Wise, *Challenging Years,* chap. 12. See also Stephen S. Wise, *A Jewish Conference or Congress: Which and Why?* (New York: Free Synogogue Pulpit, September 1915), no. 7.

27. Du Bois Papers, Reel 7, Frame 89.

28. Du Bois Papers, Reel 7, Frame 88.

29. Du Bois to President Woodrow Wilson, 27 November 1918, Woodrow Wilson Papers, DLC.

30. Two different accounts of the circumstances making possible Du Bois's departure are available: Major W. H. Loving to Colonel Masteller, Memorandum, 28 March 1919,

Record Group 165, File 10218-279/12, National Archives and Records Service, Washington, D.C. (Hereafter DNA); and Richard R. Wright, Jr., *87 Years Behind the Black Curtain: An Autobiography* (Philadelphia: Rare Book Co., 1965), pp. 203–4.

31. *Crisis* 17 (February 1919): 166.

32. "Reconstruction and Africa," ibid., p. 165.

33. Geiss, *The Pan-African Movement*, p. 239.

34. Imanuel Geiss, ed., *July 1914–The Outbreak of the First World War: Selected Documents* (London: Batsford, 1967), and *German Foreign Policy, 1871–1914* (Boston: Routledge & Kegan Paul, 1976).

35. "My Mission," *Crisis* 18 (May 1919): 8.

36. Walter Laqueur, *A History of Zionism* (New York: Schocken Books, 1976), p. 192.

37. "Bulletin #3," ca. 19–24 December 1918, NAACP Records, DLC.

38. W. E. B. Du Bois, "An Essay toward a History of the Black Man in the Great War," *Crisis* 18 (June 1919): 63.

39. *Crisis* 17 (March 1919): 215.

40. Major F. P. Schoomaker, General Staff, H/Q 92nd Div., AEF, to Intelligence Officers, Secret, 1 January 1919; copy in Du Bois Papers, Reel 8, Frame 286; published also in "Our Success and Failure," *Crisis* 18 (July 1919): 128–29.

41. Correspondence of the American Embassy, Paris, Vol. 64 (1919), File 540.1, RG 84, DNA.

42. NAACP Records, Box C-385, DLC.

43. Diagne's official title as a member of Clemenceau's cabinet was "Commissaire general charge du controle des militaires francais d'origine coloniale et des militaires et travailleurs indigenes originaires des possessions africaines dependant du Ministere des Colonies." For a recent study of the military aspects of Diagne's role, see Charles John Balesi, *From Adversaires to Comrades-in-Arms: West Africans and the French Military, 1885–1918* (Waltham, Mass.: Crossroads Press, 1979); see also G. Wesley Johnson, *The Emergence of Black Politics in Senegal,* (Stanford, Calif.: Stanford University Press, 1971), chaps. 9–12.

44. "My Mission," *Crisis*, p. 8.

45. Copy of the original in Du Bois Papers, Reel 8, Frame 45; also published in the *Crisis* 17 (March 1919): 224–25.

46. Martin Deming Lewis, "One Hundred Million Frenchmen: The 'Assimilation' Theory in French Colonial Policy," *Comparative Studies in Society and History* 4 (January 1962): 129–53.

47. The speeches were printed and distributed in pamphlet form by the NAACP under the title *Africa in the World Democracy;* also reprinted in it was Du Bois's November Memorandum ("The Future of Africa–A Platform") prefaced with an approving introduction by Mary White Ovington, acting chairman of the NAACP. A full report of the proceedings was published along with the resolutions passed, under the same title in the *Crisis* 17 (February 1919): 173–76.

48. For Kallen's contributions to Jewish Zionism, see Arthur Hertzberg, ed., *The Zionist Idea* (New York: Atheneum, 1971), pp. 525–33; see also Kallen's *Zionism and World Politics: A Study in History and Social Psychology* (Garden City, N.Y.: Doubleday, Page & Co., 1921), and *"Of them which say they are Jews," and Other Essays on the Jewish Struggle for Survival* (New York: Bloch Publishing Co., 1954). Details of Kallen's active role as a key leader of the American Zionist movement can be found in Urofsky, *American Zionism.*

49. *In the Almost Promised Land: American Jews and Blacks, 1915–1935* (Westport, Conn.: Greenwood Press, 1978), p. 120. See Spingarn's letter from France to Du Bois in October 1918 in the *Crisis* 17 (December 1918): 60–61.

50. *American Chronicle: The Autobiography of Ray Stannard Baker* (New York: Charles Scribner's Sons, 1945) makes no mention of a conversation with Du Bois in Paris, nor does it make any mention, for that matter, of the subject of Afro-Americans.

51. Ronald Steel, *Walter Lippman and the American Century* (Boston: Little, Brown Co., 1980), pp. 148–54; see also Stephen Vaughn, "Walter Lippman, World War I and the Writing of Public Opinion" (Paper presented at the seventy-fourth annual meeting of the American Historical Association, Pacific Coast Branch, Eugene, Oregon, 1981).

52. Selected Correspondence, 1906–1930, Walter Lippman Papers, Box 8, Folder 346, Yale University Library.

53. Du Bois Papers, Reel 7, Frame 1055. There has recently been controversy over this Lippman letter. In a review of Herbert Aptheker's edition of *The Correspondence of W. E. B. Du Bois: Selections, 1877–1934*, vol. I (Amherst, Mass.: University of Massachusetts Press, 1973), Elliott Rudwick took the position that Aptheker failed to "shed any light on anything when he reprints a 1919 Walter Lippman letter requesting 'whatever reports' Du Bois had on the [Pan-African] movement." (*Journal of Negro History* 61 [1976]: 403). A rejoinder from Sterling Stuckey was also published, in which he reasoned: "Very few people are conscious of the fact that the Pan-African movement by 1919 had gained the attention of journalists of the importance of an editor of the *New Republic*. . . . In any case, the Lippman request for 'whatever reports' Du Bois had on Pan-Africanism was an unusual one for 1919" ("Communication," *Journal of Negro History* 62 [1977]: 408). Before his military intelligence commission with the army in June 1918, Lippman had served from June to October 1917 as special assistant to the secretary of war to handle relations between the War Department and organized labor; and in September 1917 he was appointed secretary of the commission directed by E. M. House to prepare data for the peace conference (see Steel, *Walter Lippman and the American Century*, chaps. 10–12; Lawrence E. Gelfand, *The Inquiry: American Preparations for Peace, 1917–1919* [New Haven: Yale University Press, 1963]).

54. The brothers Michel, Alexandre-Nathan, and Calmann Levy founded their publishing enterprise in Paris in 1842; as Michel Levy Freres, they eventually built up one of France's largest firms of publishers, who were the first to publish the works of Anatole France. They also published works of writers such as Balzac, Dumas, and Renan. After the death of Michel Levy in 1875, the business was continued by Calmann Levy (1819–91). It was at that point that it became known as Calmann-Levy. Calmann's sons, Paul, Gaston, and Georges Levy, took over the management of the firm on the passing of their father. See N. Stern, "The Brothers Calmann and Michel Levy in Paris," *Ha-tzofe* (Tel-aviv), 4 April 1958, pp. 7–8

55. *Dusk of Dawn*, p. 262. Otlet and La Fontaine were later described by Du Bois as "the Belgian leaders of internationalism [who] welcomed the [Second] Congress warmly to Belgium" in 1921 (*The World and Africa* [New York: Viking Press, 1947], p. 237). In addition to being an organizer of international life, Otlet also was the inventor of microfilming and an outstanding bibliographer and organizer of international documentation. Henri La Fontaine (1854–1943) was an influential Belgian senator from 1894–1932 and sometime vice-president of the Belgian Senate; also professor of International Law and cosecretary with Otlett of the Palais Mondial; Nobel Peace Prizeman in 1913; Belgian delegate to the League of Nations, 1920–21; member of the Inter-Parliamentary Council, 1927–32; president of the International Peace Bureau; secretary-general of the Union of International Associations; and secretary of the International Institute of Bibliography, through which he coauthored with Otlet several important works in the field of bibliography and documentation.

56. "For What?", *Crisis* 17 (April 1919): 268.

57. Andre Chouraqui, *Cent ans D'Histoire: L'Alliance Israelite Universelle et la Renaissance Juive Contemporaine, 1860–1960* (Paris: Presses Universitaires de France, 1965), pp. 203–30; *The Letters and Papers of Chaim Weizmann*, vol. IX, series A, edited by Jehuda Reinharz (New Brunswick, N.J.: Transaction Books, 1977), p. xxi. Weizmann declared, "France and the French Jews are against us . . ." (p. 99); Lévi's "betrayal" is also described by Weizmann in *Trial and Error*, pp. 244–45.

58. *A History of Zionism*, p. 35; see also Michael R. Marrus, *The Politics of Assimilation: A Study of the French Jewish Community at the Time of the Dreyfus Affair* (Oxford: Clarendon Press, 1971); and Paula Hyman, *From Dreyfus to Cichy: The Remaking of French Jewry, 1906–1939* (New York: Columbia University Press, 1979).

59. The position of the AIU on Jewish rights in Eastern Europe was set forth in its pamphlet, *La question juive devant la conference de la paix* (Paris, 1919).

60. *From Dreyfus to Vichy*, p. 60.

61. "My Mission," *Crisis*, p. 8.

62. Du Bois Papers, Reel 6, Frame 402.

63. George Bernard Noble, *Policies and Opinion at Paris, 1919: Wilsonian Diplomacy, the Versailles Peace, and French Public Opinion* (New York: Howard Fertig, 1968); David Stevenson, "French War Aims and the American Challenge, 1914–1918," *The Historical Journal* 22 (1979): 877–94.

64. *The Climax of French Imperial Expansion, 1914–1924* (Stanford, Calif.: Stanford University Press, 1981), p. 185. A fuller and more detailed treatment of the objectives of French diplomacy in its use of the Pan-African Congress is offered in this author's ms., "The First Pan-African Congress of 1919." The study of the peace conference will not be complete until the Pan-African Congress is integrated into the existing accounts. For details of the African Colonial settlement, see Wm. Roger Louis, "The United States and the African Peace Settlement of 1919: The Pilgrimage of George Louis Beer," *Journal of African History* 4 (1963): 413–33), and *Great Britain and Germany's Lost Colonies, 1914–1919* (Oxford: Clarendon Press, 1967).

65. For evidence of this French deception, see Questions generales, Vol. 27, "Congres pan-Africain' Archives Diplomatiques, Ministere des Afaires Etrangeres, Africa, 1918–1940,; and DNA, RG 84, American Embassy, Paris, Vol. 64 (1919), File 540.1.

66. Colonel E. M. House Papers and Diary, Sterling Memorial Library, Yale University, New Haven, Conn.

67. Du Bois to chairman of NAACP Board of Directors, Paris, 27 January 1919, Box C-385 NAACP Papers, DLC.

68. "My Mission," *Crisis*, p. 8.

69. The original memorandum was found only in the Du Bois Papers that until last year were still in Ghana; they have now been incorporated into the Du Bois Collection at the University of Massachusetts Library. The copy of the memorandum was provided by Professor Imanuel Geiss.

70. NAACP Records, "Report of the Director of Publications and Research December 1, 1918–April 1, 1919," ca. 14 April 1919, *Crisis* files, Box F-10. The summary of the meeting held on 21 March 1919 can be found printed in *Cahier des droits de L'Homme* 19 (1919): 579–81; the meeting is also described by Henri See, *Histoire de la Ligue des Droits de L'Homme, 1898–1926* (Paris: Ligue des Droits de L'Homme, 1927), pp. 187–88.

71. M. Delafosse, "Le Congres panafricain," *l "Afrique Francoise*, nos. 3 & 4 (March-April 1919): 53–59; see also Marc Michel, "Un Programme reformiste en 1919: Maurice Delafosse et la 'politique indigene en AOF," *Cahiers d'Etudes africaines* 58, vol. 15, no. 2 (1975): 313–27. For a recent account of his career, see Louise Delafosse, *Maurice Delafosse: le Berrichon conquis par l'Afrique* (Paris: Societe Francaise d'Histoire d'Outre-Mer avec le concours de l'Academie des Sciences d'Outre-Mer, 1976).

72. File 540.1, RG 84 (1919), DNA.

73. See George Louis Beer, *African Questions at the Paris Peace Conference* (1923 reprint ed., New York: Humanities Press, 1968); and Louis, "The United States and the African Peace Settlement of 1919: The Pilgrimage of George Louis Beer." As chief of the colonial division of the American Commission to Negotiate Peace in 1918, Beer quickly gained recognition as the most influential member of the Commission, with the exception of the plenipoteniaries. He sat on seven international committees, including the committees on Morocco, the German colonies, and the mandates commission. In addition, he represented the United States on the three committees appointed by the peace conference to settle the revision of international acts.

74. Du Bois Papers, Reel 8, Frame 226.

75. Diary of George Louis Beer, p. 33, DLC.

76. Counselor of American Embassy to Dr. W. E. B. Du Bois Paris, 8 March 1919, Du Bois Papers, Reel 8, Frame 286.

77. Paris Peace Conference "Log Book" of Edward M. House, Vol. III, p. 91, MS Group No. 466, Sterling Memorial Library Yale University.

78. The memorandum was found in the Du Bois Papers in Ghana, a copy of which was supplied by Professor Imanuel Geiss. The last of his three questions was already posed by Du Bois in 1915, when he wrote in anticipation of the future Pan-African movement: "The Pan-African movement when it comes will not, however, be merely a narrow racial propaganda. Already the more far-seeing Negroes sense the coming unities: a unity of the working classes everywhere, a unity of the colored races, a new unity of men. The

proposed economic solution of the Negro problem in Africa and America has turned the thoughts of Negroes toward a realization of the fact that the modern white laborer of Europe and America has the key to the serfdom of black folk, in his support of militarism and colonial expansion. He is beginning to say to these workingmen that, so long as black laborers are slaves, white laborers cannot be free. Already there are signs in South Africa and the United States of the beginning of understanding between the two classes." (*The Negro* [New York: Oxford University Press, 1970 (1915)], pp. 145–46).

79. "A Second Journey to Pan-Africa," *The New Republic* 29 (December 1921): 39.
80. "My Mission," *Crisis,* pp. 8–9.
81. Janowsky, *The Jews and Minority Rights, 1898–1919,* chaps. 7–9.

Shortcuts to the Mainstream:
Afro-American and Jewish Notables in the
1920s and 1930s

David Levering Lewis

"I know that a lot of people think that Jews and colored are alike because the same kinds of things happen to them," a Jewish merchant in Philadelphia's black ghetto explains in Lenora Berson's *The Negroes and the Jews* (1971). "They think that if Jews get ahead, so can the colored if they copy us. But let me tell you, and I'm not prejudiced, the colored might be a lot of things, but one thing they are not is Jews." That obvious conclusion is the conceptual bedrock of this essay which undertakes a tentative exploration of the assimilationist strategies of Afro-American and Jewish elites during the end of the first to the middle of the third decades of this century, a topic of personal interest dating from the writing of *Prisoners of Honor: The Dreyfus Affair* (1973), my second book, and greatly stimulated by the work on *When Harlem Was in Vogue* (1981), my current study of art and politics in Afro-America.

It seems evident, when their objectively similar historical moments and a certain degree of psychological affinity are contextually evaluated, that Afro-Americans and Jews possess quite different, if not antipodal, cultural pasts—intersecting, rather than parallel, *mentalities*. Forced and persistent analogies between these two ethnic groups, pertaining to slavery, Diaspora, subculture, and pariah status, are legacies of an era of slightly disingenuous underdog solidarity that once served a positive civil rights function for both parties, but tend now to clutter and distort impartial analysis. What Afro-Americans and Jews principally shared, of course, was not a similar heritage, but an identical adversary—a species of white gentile. Theirs was a politically determined kinship, a defensive alliance cemented more from the outside than from within.

To be sure, such an alliance could not have survived until the late 1960s had it been perceived wholly as an expediency. It was both necessary and natural for many of its members to believe fervently in the mystique of a special racial bond, an altruistic conspiracy of the dispossessed. Thus, in its editorial on the East St. Louis race riot of 1917, the *Jewish Daily Forward* compared it to the terrible Kishinev pogrom of 1903: "Kishinev and St. Louis—the same soil, the same people. It is a distance of four-and-a half thousand miles between these two cities, and yet they are so close and so similar." Another *Forward* editorial, in a similar vein and at about the same time, lamented: "Whenever there is an upheaval, all of Israel is oppressed, not just for the deeds of a few Jews, but even for imaginary crimes. And here, in our own free state, in our great and progressive democracy, this is the lot of the black race." Far more than politics united Negro and Jew, the *Forward*'s Abraham Cahan wrote, after being deeply stirred by *The Green Pastures:* "In this play . . . the souls of two nations are woven together . . . the soul of the Jews and the soul of the Negroes." Not prone to Cahan's rhetorical transports, and ever careful to acknowledge Anglo-Saxon superiority, Booker Washington was given to extolling the European Jewish community as the model for Afro-America— advice which the black Jews of Harlem later took literally.

For all this *apparent* rather than *real* soul-fellowship, dissimilarity and opportunism underlay the Afro-American-Jewish coalition. This is certainly not meant to derogate this once progressive coalition—or what remains of it—nor, a fortiori, to applaud the emergence of uncoordinated and even antagonistic Jewish and Afro-American policy agendas. The point is rather to describe and to explain some of the consequences of a misperceived ethnic propinquity. The argument of this analysis, simply stated, is that there was a time when a small number of privileged Afro-Americans and Jews believed that full acceptance—assimilation—into American society could be accelerated through collaborative strategies of overt and covert assistance, opportunistic symbiosis, and, on the part of the Afro-Americans, mimesis of the intellectual and organizational behavior of Jews. Both groups saw each other more as means to ends, rather than as syncretic and equal partners in a struggle for citizenship without disabilities. Both tended to misunderstand each other (necessarily, since full understanding would have been deleterious to collaboration). In the case of the Jews, collaboration achieved much of its purpose, and the misunderstandings were minimally problematical. The collaboration was, at least in the short term, minimally beneficial to the Afro-Americans, and the misunderstandings were crucial—giving rise to an unworkable paradigm of group success.

The foundations of the coalition of Afro-Americans and Jews were laid about ten years before "Negro Harlem" began to discover itself, in the aftermath of the Springfield, Illinois, riot of August 1908. Appalled by the quickening rhythm of racial violence in the urban North, the well-born Southern socialist William English Walling, assisted by other pedigreed New England socialists—Oswald Garrison Villard, Moorfield Storey, Mary White Ovington, Charles Edward Russell, inter alia—called into being the National Negro Committee and the Committee of Forty to build a program and create an organization for the attenuation of Afro-American subjugation. The initiative for and most of the first whites prominent in what became the National Association for the Advancement of Colored People were gentiles; but the passage at the NAACP's founding conference of the so-called "Russian Resolution" (condemning Czarist expulsion of Jews from Kiev) reflected the planning committee labors of Rabbi Stephen Wise, Columbia economics professor Edwin R. A. Seligman, and social worker Henry Moskowitz. The following year, it should be recalled, a similar white rescue operation, this one comprised overwhelmingly of moderate Protestants, led to the incorporation of the National Urban League; but, once again, Edwin Seligman's chairmanship, and the presence on the board of Felix Adler, Lillian Wald, Abraham Lefkowitz, and, shortly thereafter, Julius Rosenwald, principal Sears, Roebuck Company stockholder, forecast significant Jewish contributions to the League. By mid-decade, the NAACP had something of the aspect of an adjunct of B'Nai B'rith and the American Jewish Committee, with the brothers Joel and Arthur Spingarn serving as board chairman and chief legal counsel, respectively; Herbert Lehman on the executive committee; Lillian Wald and Walter Sachs on the board (though not simultaneously); and Jacob Schiff and Paul Warburg as financial angels. By 1920, Herbert Seligman was director of public relations, and Martha Greuning served as his assistant. The *Jewish Daily Forward* fittingly captioned an interview with Du Bois, "The Negro Race Looks To Jews for Sympathy and Understanding." Small wonder that a bewildered Marcus Garvey stormed out of NAACP headquarters in 1917, muttering that it was a white organization.

The motives of these Jewish Negrotarians were complex. There were Talmudic prescriptions of charity, reinforced, for many, by the status-enhancing opportunity to rebut gentile stereotypes about Jewish acquisitiveness that philanthropy among blacks afforded. There was abstract affinity for another race torn from its homeland and historically persecuted. ("Only a Jew can fathom" the depths of the Negro problem, says a character in Herzl's novel, *Altneuland.*) There was fascination with certain aspects of Afro-American life, some of it Freudian and voyeuristic. There was Jazz Age fame and profit in commercializing music, presenting plays, and publishing manuscripts based on Afro-American life (e.g., Calverton, Gershwin, Knopf). There were individual personality factors, ranging from the nefarious to the noble.

Affecting all of these, of course, was the steady erosion, beginning in the 1880s, of the professional and social gains of the small Sephardic and larger Ashkenazic American Jewish communities. Although Herbert Feingold reminds us that "Puritan love of things Hebrew did not necessarily carry over into love of the Hebrews who lived among them," practically all of the civil disabilities affecting the descendants of the first American Jews (1654) had been lifted by 1815. True, General Grant issued a blunt order expelling Jewish merchants from his command, and New Hampshire delayed granting the franchise until 1877. On the plus side, however, Harvard had awarded the Master of Arts to grammarian Judah Monis in 1720, its first to a Jew; Columbia College had appointed a rabbi as trustee in 1784; the Sephardic Franks had intermarried with the lordly Delanceys; the South Carolina Baruchs achieved impeccable social credentials, and Judah Benjamin the secretaryship of state of the Confederacy; and the most exclusive gentile clubs, churches, colleges, and resorts were open to the Jewish plutocracy—to Guggenheims, Kuhns, and Lehmans, Strauses, Gimbels, and Filenes. The accepted date, 1877, when the era of gentile-Jewish good feelings ended, marks the refusal by the Grand Union Hotel of Saratoga, New York, to admit Joseph Seligman to his customary rooms that summer. Summer resorts began to refuse Jewish patronage. In the early 1890s, Jewish merchants were physically harassed in the South, and "No Jews Allowed" signs spread across the nation. In 1893, the Union League closed its symbolic doors to Jewish membership. The public set to reading the invidious novels of Henry Adams (*Esther,* 1884) and Ignatius Donnelly (*Ceasar's Column,* 1891). Finally, in 1898, the financial leader Jacob Schiff objected publicly to the policies and the "tacit understanding" excluding Jews from the "trustee rooms of Columbia College, of the public museums, the public library and many similar institutions." Eight years later, Schiff, Rosenwald, Oscar Straus, and Louis Marshall helped establish the American Jewish Committee (AJC) and, in 1908, the New York Kehillah as instruments against anti-Semitism.

These are the familiar details of the beginnings of American anti-Semitism, recounted with amplitude of analysis and fact in Baltzell, Dinnerstein, Feingold, Gossett, Higham, Poliakov, and others. They provide the background for emerging Jewish interest in the problems of

Afro-Americans. They do not explain why that interest greatly intensified after 1910, taking on the urgency of a special mission; why Jews of influence and wealth rapidly moved from a racial altruism barely distinguishable from that of neo-abolitionist and parlor socialist WASPs to virtual management of Afro-American civil rights activity. The predisposing factors just enumerated lack the force of inevitability to produce such a commitment. Indeed, they suggest a more compelling rationale for avoidance of a special relationship with Afro-Americans. The case study of German-Americans discussed in Andrew Greeley's *Ethnicity in the United States* (1974) offers a suggestive, if extreme, example of ethnics who, confronted with a choice of affiliation or disengagement during World War I, elected to disappear, rather than to maintain their cultural separatism. If German-Americans renounced their identity in order to assert their patriotism, American Jews might well have concluded that bad matters could worsen if they were perceived as special friends of Afro-Americans, in the minds of many whites a menace as detestable, if less potent, as the Kaiser's legions. The literature, as I imperfectly know it, is silent about debate on this issue, but it is a safe presumption that Jewish leadership carefully weighed the pros and cons. Nor does it seem to be wildly speculative to suppose that a majority may have favored a policy of aloof philanthropy calibrated to complement that of liberal WASP donors. For the moment, Jews stood at a policy crossroads.

On 17 August 1915, Leo Frank was hauled from his cell in Marietta, Georgia, and lynched. Frank's grandfather had been a decorated Confederate officer. Frank, a Cornell graduate, was a leading Atlanta businessman, his match factory a cynosure of Henry Grady's New South philosophy. Accused of the murder-rape of a white female employee, he was the first white in the postbellum South to be convicted of a capital offense on the testimony of an Afro-American, one Jim Conley. When Conley, a Frank employee himself, recanted and confessed to the crime, then reaffirmed Frank's guilt while the case was being appealed, the Jewish-owned *New York Times* demanded that Georgia authorities clear Frank and try Conley. Afro-American outrage at what was seen as a ploy to redirect the fury of Tom Watson's Georgia rednecks led James Weldon Johnson to denounce the *Times* as racist in the *New York Age*. Steven Bloom's doctoral dissertation, "Interaction Between Blacks and Jews in New York City" (1973), states that the Frank case briefly threatened Afro-American and Jewish goodwill. Tom Watson's incendiary speeches and the Marietta mob's barbarism made it clear that the business man's guilt was established by his money and race, rather than by facts. "Frank belongs to the Jewish aristocracy," the fallen Georgia Populist leader ranted, "and it was determined by rich Jews that no aristocrat of their race should die for the death of a working girl." The impact of the Frank case (the simultaneous American counterpart of the "blood libel" cause celebre of Mendel Beiliss in Russia) was, as Lenora Berson and others have written, to "escalate Jewish involvement in civil rights."

Jews saw that they would be increasingly menaced by much of the violence and many of the institutional handicaps to which Afro-Americans had been long subjected. It is no exaggeration to say that the older Ashkenazim leadership was panic-stricken. Nurtured in the flexibility of Reform Judaism, possessing wealth and, many of them, great culture, families such as the Schiffs, Wises, Rosenwalds, Adlers, and Spingarns had placed their bets on assimilation. The long German migration of 1830 to 1880 was over, and descendants of Bavarian, Baden, and Wurttemberg Jews had striven to becocme less distinguishable from other white Americans, decade by decade. The title of Israel Zangwill's play, *The Melting Pot,* had become their credo, and Emma Lazarus had banked on the tired, huddled Jewish masses shedding kaftans, earlocks, and the rest of the *Shulchan aruch* in time for registration at City College. But the new migrants from the Russian Pale—1.4 million of them between 1900 and 1914—were not melting. Too many and too different, they played havoc with the assimilationist timetable.

When Moses Rischin wrote in *The Promised City* that "the thoroughly acclimated American Jew . . . has no religious, social or intellectual sympathies" for the new immigrants, he wisely added, "The uptown mansion never forgets the downtown tenement in its distress." The American branch of the Paris-based Baron de Hirsch Fund and the Jewish Colonization Society (JCA) had established the Industrial Removal Office in New York (1901) to implement the so-called Galveston Plan for dispersal and resettlement in the Southwest of the East European Jews—an enterprise endowed with five hundred thousand of Jacob Schiff's dollars. Shaken by police commissioner Theodore Bingham's 1908 charge that Jews caused most of New York City's crime, and greatly exercised by the *Immigration Report of 1911,* alleging national seduction by Jews of gentile girls, upper-crust Jewry established the Kehillah and other defense organizations, and mobilized the formidable scholarship of anthropologists Franz Boas and Alexander Goldenweiser. Nevertheless, restrictive immigration bills failed to become law by narrowing congressional margins or executive veto only, while the pseudoscientific eugenics of Galton and W. E. D. Stokes swept the land. Jewish Notables in 1915 were strenuously insisting on the fundamental sameness of human beings, minimizing observable differences as transitory, and, in the case of Jacob Schiff, pleading with immigrant parents not to speak Yiddish to their children.

Afro-American leadership in the North found itself at a similar crossroads after 1915. During the ascendancy of Booker Washington, it had commanded little of the loyalty of the masses of its own people nor the attention of white philanthropy—to say nothing of being heeded by elected officials. By 1917, however—two years after the Great Accommodator's death—perhaps as many as one million Afro-American peasants were resettling in the urban North and East. Bookerites had few answers to the socioeconomic questions raised by the Great Migration. After 1916, the bearers of the great names of the Gilded Age turned from Tuskegee to the urban, mostly Northern men and women who had never forsworn faith in full civil and social equality, and for whom the NAACP's Du Bois, Boston's Monroe Trotter and Archibald Grimke, Washington's Kelly Miller, and Chicago's Ida B. Wells were heroes. Many of these Talented Tenth Afro-Americans were stamped in what E. Franklin Frazier describes as the "genteel tradition of the small group of mulattoes who assimilated the morals and manners of the slaveholding aristocracy." But its nucleus was black Methodist and Puritan. It was descended from tiny colonial slave and free Negro populations concentrated in Boston, Brooklyn, Philadelphia, and Providence, Rhode Island, gradually reinforced by Underground Railroad fugitives and, after the Civil War, by Southern families with some or all of the endowments of pedigree, professional distinction, good morals, and racial admixture (but acceptable only if derived from an antebellum liaison). A few names—Forten, Nail, Murphy, Purvis, Syphax—represented moderate wealth from real estate, insurance, publishing, medicine, construction, but most had depended for generations on solid, middle-class incomes from service occupations historically monopolized by free Negroes: barbering, draying, catering, carpentry, tailoring, preaching.

As established Jewish leaders were separated from the post-1880s migrants by geographic provenance, religion, culture, and wealth, so, too, were Northern Afro-American leaders of a different mold from the folk of the Great Migration. They, too, had believed themselves (episodic riots notwithstanding) well along toward full citizenship by not asserting themselves as a political bloc, by good manners, education, and frugality, by quiet cultivation of influential WASPs, and by ostentatious patriotism. Public transportation had been accessible without discrimination; department stores had politely encouraged their patronage; most public schools had accepted their children; and there had even been a handful of elected municipal and state officials in Massachusettes and Illinois. Without exception, studies of Northern urban Afro-Americans report their nostalgia for the golden days before the Great Migration (Drake and Cayton, the two Johnsons, Mossell, Kosmer, Katzman). "There was no discrimination in Chicago during my childhood days," a a matron tells Drake and Cayton, typically, in

Black Metropolis, "but as Negroes began coming . . . in numbers it seems they brought discrimination with them." Like Uptown Jews who lived in terror of some Hester Street anarchist's mad act, Talented Tenth leaders complained, "We all suffer for what one fool will do." Churches and fraternal orders housed and fed the Southern migrant; the Urban League located jobs for him—all amid a chorus of grief about "ignorant and rough-mannered" newcomers, "inefficient, grop- ing seekers for something better." Uptown Jews asked their East Side cousins not to speak Yiddish; Urban League workers distributed soap along with lectures on boisterousness and shabby clothing. Nancy Weiss recounts the earnestness of Afro-American Urban League officials who spoke of "civilizing" and "Americanizing" the Southern migrant. "The Negro . . . needs help only in securing the opportunity to embrace American advantages," Dr. George Edmund Haynes, the League's Fisk and Columbia-trained executive director frequently said.

By the early 1920s, assimilationist Jews and integrationist Afro- Americans needed each other more than ever. The Palmer raids and Red Scare of 1919 had exacerbated anti-Semitism, while the riots and lynchings of the Red Summer of 1919 had arrested and, in many cases, reversed the wartime socioeconomic gains of Afro-Americans. As the melting pot turned into a skillet, dynamic new theories and ideologies of Afro-American and Jewish progress arose to challenge the melior- isms of the upper-class leaders. In his 1915 essay, "Democracy Versus the Melting Pot," and the 1924 book *Culture and Democracy in the United States,* the Harvard-educated philosopher Horace Kallen re- jected assimilationism and proposed, instead, that Jews retain and en- rich their "racial" uniqueness, the better to enrich and contribute to American society. Pluralists Isaac Berkman, Julius Drachsler, and Judah Magnes further energized the debate—ultimately at the cost of destroying the New York Kehillah. By the early teens, in addition to Kallen, intellectuals such as Du Bois (Pan-Africanism), Randolph Bourne ("trans-nationalism"), the Hapgood brothers (variety), and Robert Park (racial "temperaments") had begun to modify or abjure the once sacrosanct paradigm of "Anglo-conformity." Yet even as an intel- lectual exercise, cultural pluralism alarmed Jewish Notables because of its potential to raise the dual loyalty charge. Even more terrifying, such ideas could serve as Trojan horses for Zionism. They had not forgiven Louis Brandeis his 1915 Faneuil Hall address, "The Jewish Problem and How to Solve It." The former assimilationist legal scholar had unveiled the concept of "differentiative development," subse- quently explaining that he meant: "To be good Americans, we must be better Jews, and to be better Jews, we must become Zionists."

The Kallen and Brandeis heresies distressed Jewish Notables far more than similar separatist or nationalist ideas worried the Talented Tenth, but neither leadership class was equipped to deal with the new, dynamic, and mass-based ideologies of black and white Zionism. Not only did the *New York Times* deplore the Balfour Declaration, but even the *Forward,* porte-parole of Jewish socialism, assailed the separate homeland idea. The great majority of the Jews closely connected with the NAACP and Urban League—Louis Marshall, president of Temple Emanu-El and a founder of the American Jewish Committee; Jacob Billikopf, Marshall's distinguished lawyer son-in-law; Franz Boas, the Columbia anthropologist; the Altmans, Lehmans, Strauses, Spingarns, and Rosenwalds—were opponents of Zionism. Judah Magnes, the Kehillah leader and Marshall's brother-in-law, Juliusm Mack, the Chicago Zionist leader and Rosenwald intimate, and Felix Frankfurter were significant exceptions. Most Notables saw Zionism not as the solution to Jewish problems, but as a deadly manifestation of the problem itself—failure to assimilate. Zionism was a declaration of national disloyalty and a license for new immigrants to retain the strange culture of the *shtetl.* The correct approach—more urgent than ever—was to defuse American racism, but to do so with minimum visibility and vulnerability. When Julius Rosenwald told a friend that he was not "in the least anxious to see many Jews in politics or even on the bench," he spoke for most Notables, for whom high public profile *as Jews* was anathema. By establishing a presence at the center of the civil rights movement with intelligence, money, and influence, the Notables could fight against anti-Semitism by remote control. "By helping the colored people in this country," the *American Hebrew* suggested, "Mr. Rosenwald doubtless also serves Judaism."

For the Talented Tenth, heightened Jewish collaboration was extremely beneficial, for it, too, had been caught unprepared by the Zionism of Marcus Garvey's Universal Negro Improvement Association (UNIA). The Garvey movement's leadership was largely West Indian, as was the majority of its true believers, but its growing appeal among Afro-Americans extended coast to coast and deep into the South. The reasoned conviction that Garvey's Liberian beachhead would collapse under French and British pressures, the valid fears that emigrationism would detract from the struggle against racial discrimination, the genuine disgust caused by UNIA financial profligacy and dishonesty, the anger over Garvey's bid for Ku Klux Klan support, and the clash of personalities—all contributed to make relations between Garveyites and the Talented Tenth increasingly stormy. On the other hand, from Martin Delany to Booker Washington, Afro-American leaders had periodically espoused a variety of emigrationist and separatist philosophies. Du Bois, Garvey's nemesis, was himself regularly in attendance during this period at Pan-African congresses. It was less

Garvey's ideas that consternated the Talented Tenth than it was fear of having to share and, perhaps, even yield its leadership of the Afro-American masses. Garvey was not blustering when he charged that "the Negro who has had the benefit of an education of forty, thirty and twenty years ago is the greatest fraud and stumbling block to the real progress of the race." Nor was he guilty, as some thought, of applying an inappropriate West Indian color-status theorem to Afro-American leadership. If it was vicious to call attention publicly to the light complexions of the Talented Tenth (the perennial Afro-American taboo), it was also extremely effective against Du Bois, Jesse Moorland, Walter White, and their kind.

Professor Tony Martin's examination of Justice Department files uncovered the FBI's determination, as early as September 1919, to have Garvey prosecuted for mail fraud, but it is significant that the federal authorities moved against the president-general of Africa only after eight prominent Afro-American civic and business leaders (among them, the owner of the *Chicago Defender*) dispatched an open letter, in 1923, to the attorney-general of the United States demanding he take action "completely to disband and extirpate this vicious movement." With Garvey's imprisonment for mail fraud the following year, Black Zionism rapidly lost momentum. Its deflation presented the Talented Tenth leaders with an acute credibility crisis, however, for they now had to prove that Garvey's extreme pessimism about the future of the race in America was unjustified and that, by helping to scuttle the fervent mass movement, they had not consigned eleven million Afro-Americans to economic and social perdition. But the evidence and trends overwhelmingly supported the Garveyites. The practices, policies, and laws of the post-War years were meant to "put the nigger in his place," to keep him out of the officer corps, out of labor unions and skilled jobs, out of the North and quaking for his existence in the South, and out of politics everywhere. Louise Venable Kennedy's classic 1930 study, *The Negro Peasant Turns Cityward,* found that the proportion of Northern Afro-Americans in manufacturing had steadily declined during the 1920s, and that "numbers of them have gone back into . . . domestic and personal service, while many of the Negro women who had given up outside employment have been forced to return to work."

Talented Tenth anxieties about this dilemma permeated Alain Locke's famous introductory essays in the special 1924 issue of *Survey Graphic* devoted to the "New Negro." "The migrating peasants" were stirring, the Rhodes scholar stressed, "and the challenge of the new intellectuals among them is clear enough." "The only safeguard for mass relations in the future must be provided in the carefully maintained contacts of the enlightened minorities of both race groups." But time was running out, Locke warned. "There is an increasing group who affiliate with radical and liberal movements. . . . Harlem's quixotic radicalisms call for their ounce of democracy today lest tomorrow they be beyond cure." The race's leadership must be clearly seen to have influence among movers and shakers in the white world. Interracial enterprises as dazzlingly mounted and publicized as those of the UNIA were called for; promotion and celebration of symbolic racial break-throughs were indispensable. Given the near-total contemporary civil rights impasse, however, Talented Tenth opinions were limited to the obvious strategy of redoubled advocacy before the courts and in Con-gress, and to the novel game plan of harnessing art and literature for civil rights. For both approaches, support of Negrotarian Jews was invaluable. From a purely theoretical optic, it is true that Talented Tenth leaders could have opted for a more radical course, and thrown their support behind the Marxian socialists led by Asa Randolph and Chandler Owen of *Messenger* magazine, or behind Cyril Briggs of the African Blood Brotherhood. But not even Du Bois was yet prepared to take this ideological plunge. Furthermore, not only was it not in class character, it would have alienated their Jewish allies, who enthusiasti-cally commended litigation and literature as weapons of choice.

Court victories afforded Talented Tenth leadership maximum public-ity and, given the failure of enforcement on the state and local level, minimum practical inconvenience to white bigots. Afro-Americans won potential, distant benefits by such decisions; Jews hoped to derive more immediate advantages because of their color. Not all the NAACP's lawyers were Jewish before the 1933 shift to the brilliant Harvard-trained Charles Hamilton Houston and his Howard protégé Thurgood Marshall. Other Afro-Americans, James A. Cobb and Scipio Jones, served expertly in the background before the Association risked a black face at the bar. Moorfield Storey, an American Bar Association president and president of the NAACP, presented the winning 1923 U.S. Supreme Court argument that "mob spirit" had denied Arkansas sharecroppers a fair trial, a decision that drew Louis Marshall into NAACP work, as Marshall had unsuccessfully used the same argument before the Supreme Court in the Leo Frank appeal. Clarence Darrow won the famous Ossian Sweet case. But as August Meier notes, there were less than a thousand Afro-American lawyers in the entire country in 1920, few of them well trained. The vacuum was filled, usually pro bono, by Arthur Spingarn and his partner Charles Studin, by Louis Marshall and his son James, by Nathan Margold, the first salaried Association counsel, and by Felix Franfurter as valuable advisor. The NAACP's James Weldon Johnson, himself a lawyer, exploited every opportunity to draw parallels between Jewish and Afro-American dis-abilities and to urge Marshall and others to arouse the Jewish public.

"It seems to me," Johnson urged Marshall in the successful restrictive covenant case of *Corrigan* v. *Buckley* (1924), "that you might be willing to make a statement on the case calling its importance to the attention of the Jewish people."

Jewish support, legal and monetary, afforded the civil rights movement a string of legal victories—*Moore* v. *Dempsey* (1923), racial jury exclusion; *Corrigan* v. *Buckley* (1924), residential segregation; *Nixon* v. *Herndon* (1927), white primary exclusion—as well as important help in lobbying the unsuccessful Dyer and the Costigan-Wagner federal anti-lynching bills. Important support also went to Asa Randolph's Brotherhood of Sleeping Car Porters battle with the Pullman Company for recognition. There is little exaggeration in an American Jewish Congress lawyer's claim that "many of these laws were actually written in the offices of Jewish agencies by Jewish staff people, introduced by Jewish legislators and pressured into being by Jewish voters." It is conceivable that, without playing this major civil rights role, the overt signs of Afro-American anti-Semitism emerging in the mid-thirties in Harlem would have been less manageable. According to Hasia Diner, the Yiddish press began fleetingly to address the issue of black anti-Semitism at this time, mindful as it and readers of the Uptown *Hebrew Standard* were that, for most Northern ghetto dwellers, the Jewish corner store symbolized the harsh world of business capitalism. The Harlem riot of 1935 principally victimized Jewish merchants. The Talented Tenth continued, meanwhile, to speak warmly of the "special relationship" with Jews, James Weldon Johnson and Walter White routinely scrutinized obituary columns for Jewish legacies that the NAACP might tap, and drew up lists of prospective contributors, a disproportionate number of whom were Jewish. "The clue to Pierre Du Pont [is] that his wife is a Jewess," White wrote crudely, and mistakenly, of this potential donor (Du Pont's mother was Jewish). Faith in Jewish largesse was, generally, rewarded. During the Depression, William Rosenwald made a three-year grant to the NAACP, on condition it be matched by three others. Herbert Lehman, Mary Fels, and Felix Warburg matched—and Edsel Ford. The second largest Urban League funding source from 1924 to 1931 was the Altman Foundation.

Collaboration of the Talented Tenth and Negrotarian Jews in the Harlem Renaissance is complex. The Renaissance was the Talented Tenth's primary answer to Black Zionism, a synthetic substitute for a grass-roots ebullition. However regnant the influences of white dilettantes like Carl Van Vechten, or of professional primitivists like Mrs. Osgood Mason, there was a significant, Afro-American countervailing force at work in the Harlem Renaissance, frequently of sufficient potency to minimize and even manipulate those who were its ostensible sovereigns. The half-dozen or so Talented Tenth orchestrators of the

Renaissance—Charles Spurgeon Johnson, James Weldon Johnson, Walter White, Jessie Fauset, Alain Locke, Casper Holstein, Arthur Schomburg—conceived of it as serious racial politics, as art for politics' sake, or civil rights by copyright. This contention may be less obvious than it seems. It is neither crudely reductionist (viz., all art can be ultimately interpreted politically—Arnold Hauser) nor meaninglessly broad (viz., artistic enterprise tends to have social consequences—Victor Berger). Renaissance art and literature were artificially created through glamorous ceremony (NAACP- and Urban League-sponsored banquets and galas), prizes and fellowships (Guggenheim and Rosenwald grants, Spingarn medals and Holstein prizes), traveling art shows and well-advertised volumes of fiction and poetry (Boni and Liveright, Alfred Knopf), and national recruitment of talent by Jessie Fauset of the *Crisis* staff and Charles Johnson, editor of *Opportunity*. Charles Johnson's Urban League staff culled the Afro-American press for talent, kept files on promising artists or poets in remote towns, and arranged for temporary housing and employment (or stipends) for them, once they had accepted Johnson's risky invitation to relocate in Harlem from, say, Topeka, Kansas. Jessie Fauset discovered Jean Toomer and Langston Hughes. Walter White boasted that he had persuaded Paul Robeson to forsake the law for the concert stage.

Students of American culture from Van Wyck Brooks to S. P. Fullinwider have seen the Harlem Renaissance as another creative bubble in the melting pot, a savory ingredient in the concoction of New England, Knickerbocker, Hoosier, and Yiddish artistic efflorescence. "The Negro writers were caught up [in] the spirit of the artistic yearnings of the time," Fullinider argues. Of Langston Hughes and Jean Toomer alone was that the case. Nothing could have seemed to most Afro-Americans more extravagantly impractical as a means of improving racial standing than writing poetry or novels, or painting. Nor did the race's minute college population contain, as did the white, third-generation middle-class Yale and Princeton dropouts heading for writing seminars in Paris cafés. Upwardly mobile Afro-Americans were at least a generation away from the special cultural alienation—the insider-as-outsider syndrome—of the Lost Generation. With the decisive infusion of white philanthropy and publishing (much of it Jewish), the entrepreneurs of the Renaissance were able to mount a generation-skipping movement, diverting and recruiting to its ranks men and women who, in the natural course of events, would have become teachers, lawyers, dentists, doctors, and morticians. By the early thirties, the influence of Walter White in Alogonquin circles, of Locke in the Harmon Foundation, of James Weldon Johnson as a trustee of the Garland and Rosenwald funds, and of Charles Johnson as all-purpose

advisor had contributed to make the Renaissance a well-oiled arts ma-
chine, turning out a total of twenty-six novels, ten volumes of poetry,
five Broadway plays, innumerable essays and short stories, two or
three performed ballets and concerts, and a large output of canvas and
sculpture. Du Bois was as impressed as he was disapproving of such
manufactures, asking in a late 1926 *Crisis* editorial,

> How is it that an organization like this, a group of radicals trying to
> bring new things into the world, a fighting organization which has
> come out of the blood and dust of battle, struggling for the right of
> black men to be ordinary human beings—how is it that an organiza-
> tion of this kind can turn aside and talk about art? After all, what
> have we who are slaves and black to do with art?

Although it does not appear that Jewish Negrotarians were the first
to encourage the civil-rights-through-arts program, the paradigm of
Jewish success, as the Talented Tenth perceived it, stamped the program. The Afro-American upper crust described itself as an ancient,
special people, achieving superiority through suffering and intelligence. Jessie Fauset's novels insisted that her class was superior to
privileged whites by virtue of culture and attainments that had been
much harder to acquire because of racism. James Weldon Johnson
publicly claimed that Afro-Americans had made the sole authentic contribution to American life—music—and called on the race to emulate
the Jew in measuring up "brain to brain" with mainstream Americans.
The Jewish dictum, "the more learning, the more life," appealed because, for the Talented Tenth, more learning also meant more status.
Although Locke, Weldon Johnon, and Schomburg frequently wrote as
cultural nationalists and Pan-Africanists, the ultimate goal of their Renaissance was assimilation by way of a civil rights triad: (1) mobilization
of mass Afro-American support for artistic and literary achievement;
(2) racial breakthrough of a critical mass of talent sufficient to rebut
demeaning stereotypes; and (3) the public perception and private reality of access to and leverage upon the white world of power and influence in order, in a decade or more, to improve the lot of the masses
of Afro-Americans. Unlike their Jewish models, however, the Talented
Tenth minimized the kind of grimy success of Jewish migrants as a
basic condition for the perpetuation and diffusion of cultural achievement. Racial aristocrats, steeped in classical educations, they missed
the significance of the butcher and tailor shops, the liquor stores and
pawnshops. They overstressed psychological and social, at the ex-
pense of economic and political, solutions to race problems. "The
greatest handicap he experiences," said Walter White of the Afro-
American, "is that he is not permitted to forget that he is a Negro. . . .
The economic and social strictures do not play, in my opinion, so large

a part." In an extraordinary *American Mercury* article, the NAACP's Johnson hailed the trend of Afro-American professional men to marry light-skinned women. A few months later, Johnson informed *Harper's* readers that, after trying "religion, education, politics, industrial, ethical, economic, sociological" approaches, the Afro-American was, finally, on the right social track. "Through his artistic efforts the Negro is smashing" race barriers "faster than he has ever done through any other method."

Just a bit more talent, then, more culture, more professional distinction, and the race problem would be behind them—provided the masses behaved themselves. Jewish Notables and Talented Tenth leaders noticed and protested the Ivy League quotas and dormitory restrictions, and, as Ludwig Lewisohn discovered, the absolute ban on university professorships. Howard University professors Ralph Bunche and Abram Harris documented Afro-American political impotence, financial handicaps, and exclusion (with the notable exception of the ILGWU) from organized labor. Distressed, but still confident, both leadership groups held fast to the 1921 conclusions reached by Franz Boas, based on a vast study of race and culture:

> It would seem that man being what he is, the Negro problem will not disappear in America until the Negro blood has been so much diluted that it will no longer be recognized, just as anti-Semitism will not disappear until the last vestige of the Jews has disappeared.

Parallels in the Urban Experience

Herbert Gutman

A central fact in the Afro-American experience in the past century has been the continuous rural-urban migration, consisting of phases I (1890–1930) and II (1940–1965). Migration involves adaptation, the alterations of old cultures, changes by migrant populations, and, indeed, the creation of new styles of life. Urban migration and the subsequent creation of community, or new communities, is not, to be sure, a distinctly Afro-American experience. It is a universal experience that varies over time and from place to place, making comparisons possible that allow us to illuminate similarities and differences.

When looking at the twentieth century, unfortunately, there is no Afro-American version for the early twentieth-century migrants that compares to the "world of our fathers"; just as there is no "world of our mothers" for Jewish-American experience. In the vast area of Afro-American history, the least studied, or the most inadequately studied, area is the first rural-urban, South-North migration. It is one of the richest areas of study in American Jewish history, and makes the parallel comparison an uneven one. For example, take the work of someone like Carol Stack, who, in her study of Afro-Americans in the second urban migration, examines how Afro-Americans adapted to urban poverty, as well as used principles of reciprocity as a means of exchange in dealing with urban conditions. There is presently no way of linking, historically, this study to the early urban migration from rural areas.

I will draw some parallels in time and over time. Parallels will be drawn in several ways by other contributors and you can compare the experiences and behavior of Jews and Afro-Americans over time or in time. Following our coordinates to their intersecting points will enable you to also compare the perceptions and treatment of Jews and Afro-Americans in time, at moments in time, or, over time, and their relationship to the mainstream culture.

A comparison such as this poses very important questions for students of Afro-American history concerned with migrant and urban experiences between 1900 and the Great Depression, for the differences between the two groups that emerge from the comparison are striking. Let us examine the Afro-Americans first and then the Jews. My comparison looks at three measures. One of them is the occupational or class structure—the overall class structure of the community. A second is the demographic structure of the community, gender ratios and matters of that kind—age distributions. The third comparison, and I think in many ways the least important, are familial arrangements.

Let me summarize the finding on the Afro-American household in New York City in 1905. Early twentieth-century migration from the rural South to the urban North did not shatter the Afro-American family. This fact was disclosed in a study of the occupational and household status of about 14,000 Afro-American residents in the two major Manhattan Afro-American communities at the beginning of the first migration. Allow me to characterize that population prior to any comparisons. Perhaps as many as three-fourths of this population's adults had been born in the South, mostly in Virginia and the upper South. About two-thirds were between the ages of fifteen and thirtynine. Adult women significantly outnumbered adult men, a phenomenon that would continue over the next two decades, and about one in four women, age fifteen and over, was a lodger or lived alone.

The occupational status of Afro-Americans could not have been worse by early twentieth-century urban standards. In other words, about 5 percent of the black population were neither unskilled laborers, service workers, or skilled workers, which means that 94 or 95 percent of the population were laborers, wage earners of one or another kind. Nine percent were skilled workers. One in four Afro-American males living in New York City in this sample was either an actor or a musician. There were fewer Afro-Americans with skills working in the New York City building trades then working as actors or musicians. The scarcity of skilled workers meant that migrant blacks did not threaten the occupational status of native-born or immigrant skilled white workers. Instead, these men had been bypassed by the industrial advances identified with the development of capitalism in the nineteenth and early twentieth century. They either carried few skills with them or they were excluded from many urban unskilled or skilled occupations open to native and immigrant white New Yorkers.

Less than three hundred males of the thirteen thousand to fourteen thousand who listed themselves under an occupation could nominally deserve to be classified as middle class. Three or four of the so-called white-collar workers were postal employees, and federal custom-house employees; ten called themselves foreman or managers; but most of the professionals were clergymen. The San Juan Hill and Tenderloin districts had as residents three black lawyers and two black school teachers. The work of seventy-seven men engaged in enterprise also indicated the overall depressed status of the black community. Twenty-four ran restaurants or were caterers, one manufactured trunks; very few supervised petty retail enterprises. There are more examples but these are enough to make the point clear. Most black men, 86 percent, were employed as day laborers or held in-service jobs; and vast numbers of adult Afro-American women labored as service workers, washerwomen, and laundresses.

Largely a young-adult population, the economically depressed blacks in New York, did not live in disorganized households. Less than 10 percent lived alone or in boarding houses. Overall, about six of seven New York Afro-Americans lived in households that had at their core two or more persons related either by blood or marriage. Most families took in one or two lodgers, relatively few took in more than three. About one in six households contained kin other than members of the immediate family. There were many subfamilies, families living in families. These were most often members of extended kinship networks inside the household: members of the family of origin, mothers-in-laws, the head of household's adult siblings, and adult nephews and nieces. The evidence generated in relation to migration patterns, particularly the changing composition of the Afro-American household among New York City Afro-Americans in 1905, does not support the hypothesis that husbands and fathers were less frequent within a family than in the South in 1880 and 1900. Quite the opposite! In the North, they were more frequent than in the South of that time. Most of the households headed by women were headed by older women, widowed women; a small but significant percentage were headed by unmarried younger women. The typical New York City Afro-American household in 1905 had as its head a poor, male, unskilled laborer or service worker. Six in seven adult New York City Afro-American men were either laborers or service workers; and six in seven fathers were living with their wife and children, or just with their children.

A useful but problematic comparison between the households of New York City Afro-Americans in 1905 with the households of immigrant Jews living that same year in New York City is made possible by examining the composition of about thirty-seven hundred Lower East Side Jewish households in the same year. Meaningful comparisons require that two or more social groups being analyzed share a good deal in common so that similarities and differences between them can be explored. The age and gender distribution of the Afro-Americans as well as their occupational status differed very much from that of the

Jews. One can say that Afro-American inhabited the same island as Jews and other immigrant groups, but lived in a different world.

A striking difference between Afro-Americans and Jews resulted from the disparity in their age and gender structure. New York City Afro-Americans in 1905 differed radically from all the immigrant groups; Jews in this case being an example, and even from the Afro-American national population, which is migration specific. In 1905, the Afro-American population was predominantly adult in composition, and this differed from the Jews. Three-fourths of Afro-Americans were at least twenty years old; among the Jews the figure drops to 47 percent. This tells something about the migration. Children not yet fifteen years old were proportionately twice as numerous among Jews as among Afro-Americans. These differences can be explained but only by many more factors than the high infant mortality rate among New York blacks.

The *pattern* of migration by Afro-Americans, shaped by the opportunities open to them in Northern cities like New York, differed from the pattern of opportunities available to Jews. Family migration and the migration of married men without families, a form of delayed family migration, characterized the Jewish migration to New York. Few single adult women migrated alone among the Jews. On the other hand, single migrants, both men and women, were an important component of the Afro-American migration. This is seen simply by examining the household status of middle-aged Afro-American and Jewish women. Slightly more than one in five Afro-American women between the ages of twenty-five and forty-four were lodgers. About 3 percent lived alone and about the same percentage boarded with blood relatives. Jewish women knew exactly opposite circumstances. Among two thousand Jewish women, ages twenty-five to forty-four, one hundred twenty-nine (less than 7 percent) lived as lodgers. Twenty-eight lived as single women with relatives (less than 1 percent), and five lived alone.

Different patterns of migration also meant that the Afro-American adult gender ratio diverged dramatically from the Jewish adult gender ratio. In 1900 the New York City Afro-American adult gender ratio (for those twenty and over) was eighty-two men for every one hundred women. Immigrant Jews, in particular, had nearly an opposite gender ratio in the 1905 population study; it was one hundred twenty-eight men for every one hundred women.

In other Northeastern cities of their mutual and comparative residence, significant demographic differences paralleled equally important occupational differences between the New York City Afro-Americans, Jews, and Italians. In *The Early Bostonians,* Professor Thurstrom has shown that the "last of the immigrants theory" in no

way explained the economic and social disadvantages among native
and migrant Boston Afro-Americans between 1880 and 1940. That was
also the case among early twentieth-century New York City Afro-
Americans. It was more than the fact that large numbers of married and
older Afro-American women worked, in contrast to the white immigrant women. It was also that the Jewish male occupational structure
differed radically from the Afro-American male occupational structure.
Large numbers of Jewish men worked in New York City's clothing
industry. How many were skilled remains obscure. The fact that many
among them were described as tailors and not operators suggests the
retention of skills by some in a rapidly changing industry. If we assume
that half of the men listed in the clothing industry had factory skills,
most Jewish men studied, to be sure, were blue-collar workers—73
percent. Most black males were blue-collar workers—95 percent, but
there were very important differences between the Afro-American
workers and the Jewish workers.

Interestingly enough, these differences were similar to those that had
distinguished, Southern urban Afro-Americans from white Southern
urban workers in the late nineteenth century. Nearly three out of five
Jewish male workers had skills, but slightly less than one in ten Afro-
American workers had skills. Put another way, 30 percent of the Jewish
workers were unskilled laborers and service workers compared to 86
percent of the Afro-American men. The Jews experienced far greater
occupational and class diversities than the Afro-Americans and these
were not merely quantitative differences. Nearly 10 percent of all Jewish males, for example, were skilled building-trade workers as compared with less than 2 percent of all Afro-American males. There
existed a larger white-collar community; a larger professional and en-
terpreneurial community.

Too much is known from the nonquantitative material to idolize the
material condition of large number of 1905 Lower East Side Jews and
immigrant working-class families. The high percentage of teenagers
who labored in families of skilled immigrant workers and even in the
families of petty entrepreneurs damages that type of optimistic view.
Nevertheless, it was much more difficult to be Afro-American and
lower class than to be white, lower class, and foreign-born in New
York City in 1905. The measures suggest little family disorganization
among the Lower East Side Jews. Fewer than 6 percent in this predominantly working-class world lived in single-parent or irregular
households.

The Tenderloin and San Juan Hill Afro-Americans differed greatly in
their age and occupational structures, so much so, that to attempt
comparisons between their households and those of immigrant Jews is
both difficult and dangerous. At best, such a comparison illustrates

how demographic, social, and economic differences shape diverse patterns of lower-class adaptation to migration—early twentieth-century migration. Such a comparison indicates that immigrant Jews, as contrasted to migrant Afro-Americans, were drawn into the developing urban sector and thereby allowed to begin a precarious existence, but, nevertheless, one of great advantage compared to the migrant Afro-Americans. Their material and occupational circumstance's damage the assertion that migrant Afro-Americans arrived in the American city too late when contrasted with the experience of immigrant Jews prior to the First World War. In cities like New York, it becomes clear that the timing of Northern Afro-American migration is not the reason their entry was fraught with difficulty.

In conclusion, the implications of this brief comparison are as follows. In the Afro-American family, migration was not the overshadowing experience. The cited evidence is proof that the arguments put forth in books, like *Beyond the Melting Pot* and *The Moynihan Report,* is spurious. It further proves that patterns of adaptation between Jews and Afro-Americans differed because of distinctive cultural traditions and especially different structures encountered. The comparison, however, in *The Black Family* was inadequate and it posed a number of questions. Many questions were unasked and therefore unanswered in the book. A singular question has to do with the adaptation patterns of different migrant groups, the way in which different migrant groups form communities, especially in relation to Afro-Americans.

This brief comparison between Jews and Afro-Americans poses the following interesting questions that demand study. First, how did the dramatic differences in gender ratios, male and female, the so called excess of females, effect the developing role and status of women in the Afro-American community in New York City? The second question has to do with the opportunity structure; the differences in the class structure of the Afro-American and Jewish communities in 1905. The Jews were occupationally far more diverse than the New York City Afro-Americans. The Afro-American community was 94 percent working class, which was a remarkable figure at any time in American history.

This is the critical question that one has to address in studying such a population: How do groups of men and women that are occupationally homogeneous constitute themselves communities? How does the community stratify itself? How do leaders emerge in such communities? All the stratification models or prevailing stratification models for the United States ethnic groups, including WASPS and Jews, assume that economic and class differences usually form the basis of group stratification. Such differences were relatively insignificant among migrant Afro-Americans but a community developed. Therefore, how did it stratify itself? This is a central question in the Afro-American experience, the slave experience, and in the rural and urban Southern experience. How do relatively economically homogenous rural and urban communities stratify themselves?

A central question remains for students of the Afro-American experience, once we put aside the pathological and deficit culture models, about the Afro-American experience out of which communities stratify themselves: What principles give coherence to this aggregate of men, women, and children? What traditional structures are used to create a community that is distinctive? What are the important traditional institutions from the rural areas and what are the important innovative ones that emerge in the urban areas?

Jews and Blacks: What Happened to the Grand Alliance?

Nathan Glazer

It is well known that Jews and Afro-Americans were closely allied in the civil rights struggles of the 1950s and 1960s, and that then something happened in the 1970s. It is not my intention to justify the position that Jews and Jewish organizations took, in the 1970s, a position that has badly split and damaged the alliance. It is rather my intention to explain the split—to explain why Jews and Afro-Americans, on the whole, took different positions on the new civil rights issues of the 1970s. We should not absolutize these differences. Most Jews probably are still supporters of the new civil rights positions taken up by black organizations on such controversial issues as affirmative action; and some blacks, such as Thomas Sowell and Walter Williams—but very few—joined the substantial body of Jews who opposed affirmative action. Still, it is fair to say that there was a Jewish–Afro-American split, and it was particularly clear when it came to the Jewish defense organizations, the Anti-Defamation League, the American Jewish Congress, and the American Jewish Committee. Obviously I understand the Jewish position on these matters better than on Afro-American matters—I am no believer in pure distance and objectivity in understanding these matters. Nevertheless, I will also comment on the Afro-American position.

The basic alliance between Jews and Afro-Americans on civil rights matters was forged in the 1940s, and extended through the 1950s and 1960s. It was an alliance based in the desirability for both groups of getting laws passed that would ban discrimination on grounds of race and religion. Blacks and Jews were both subject to such discrimination. It was in New York City, and in other cities in which there were large communities of Jews, and of Afro-Americans, that this alliance was forged. New York was the most important center of Jewish Afro-Americans cooperation—in the forties it had half the country's Jews and the largest Afro-American community in the country. It was also the headquarters of both the Jewish defense organizations (as the Jewish civil rights organizations are called), and of the major Afro-American civil rights organization, the NAACP. It was also a liberal state, whose governors for many years were such men as Franklin D. Roosevelt, Herbert Lehman, Thomas Dewey, Averill Harriman, and Nelson Rockefeller—and all these men, whether Democrats or Republicans, were liberals on issues of race and civil rights. So I will make much reference to developments in New York State. But the fact is that what happened in New York State also happened in all the major Northern industrial states with substantial populations of Jews and blacks in their large cities. Whether it was Pennsylvania, or Illinois, or New Jersey, most such states saw a civil rights alliance between Jews and Afro-Americans in the 1940s, 1950s, and 1960s that had substantial success in passing civil rights legislation at the state level, long before there was any such legislation at the federal level.

There were three areas to which Afro-American and Jewish organizations in the 1940s fought for new laws to overcome this discrimination. Of greatest concern to both groups was discrimination in employment. But, of course, different kinds of discrimination in employment concerned them. For Jews, then involved in a major push into the professions, and with high proportions of their children entering colleges, it was discrimination in professional employment that was the greatest concern—for example, discrimination in big law firms. Or discrimination by hospitals in the affiliation of doctors. Or discrimination by major employers taking on managerial trainees. For Afro-Americans, the greatest concern was discrimination in skilled labor and in trade unions. Both groups were indeed concerned with the entire range of employment discrimination. But they concentrated on different parts of the spectrum.

Perhaps second to employment discrimination was concern over discrimination in education. Again, there were differences in emphasis. Jews were most worried about discrimination in medical schools; they also worried about discrimination in good four-year colleges. Blacks were more concerned about the quality of elementary and secondary education their children were getting. As a result, Afro-American efforts focused on matters that would improve this education. In the middle 1950s, following the Brown decision, and because of the prominence of Kenneth Clark, Afro-Americans concentrated on demonstrating that segregation was a problem in the New York schools too. But after a good deal of disappointment in getting programs to deal with segregation, much Afro-American political energy, in the later 1960s, shifted to community control. All along, the principal aim was to improve education at the elementary and secondary level—though of course entry into colleges and professional schools was also a matter of concern for Afro-Americans. But the numbers involved at these levels was small. When they became larger, in the late 1960s, there were already affirmative action programs in many colleges and universities. The aim then shifted from overt discrimination to standards for admission.

Finally, another area in which Jews and blacks joined was discrimination in housing. Both groups faced discrimination. But for Jews, already strongly represented in the middle class, the issue of discrimination in housing generally arose as they tried to move into upper-middle-class suburbs, or into exclusive apartment houses for the wealthy. For Afro-Americans, the issue of housing discrimination was far more serious: huge stretches of middle-class and working-class housing were closed to them.

These divergences in position and interest seemed to matter little throughout the 1940s and 1950s, as far as the Jewish–Afro-American alliance was concerned. In New York State, and in other states with substantial Jewish and Afro-American populations, a gamut of state legislation was in place long before the Congress bestirred itself to pass the key civil rights legislation of 1965 and 1968. In New York State, the pioneer in these matters, there were state laws against discrimination in employment, education, and housing.

One major area that was of great concern in the South and at the national level was not a matter of dispute in New York and other Northern and Western states: access to the ballot. Whatever the situation in the South, there was little argument in the 1940s and 1950s that Afro-Americans in the North were not discriminated against in registering and voting.

As we know, the alliance broke up, and one may well ask, what happened? Here we enter a zone of controversy. It is often said that what happened was that liberal whites, and Jews, were happy to support civil rights as long as it didn't affect them; when it did, their position changed. In other words, Jews were fair-weather liberals, or limousine liberals. As long as their children are not going out for jobs as plumbers and electricians, they were all for affirmative action for Afro-Americans. As long as Afro-Americans were interested in the elementary and secondary schools, Jews in the law and medical schools, Jews and Afro-Americans could work together. But if affirmative action meant that their children had less chance in law and medicine, the Jews said no. I think that is the predominant Afro-American interpretation of the Jewish role in such major affirmative action cases of the 1970s as *DeFunis* and *Bakke*. It may even be supported by the fact that the

Jewish organizations did not unanimously support Webber in his case—and the interpretation might be, they didn't because it was no loss to Jews if training positions in factories went to Afro-Americans.

There is some truth in this interpretation, but only some. Undoubtedly if the issue was desegregation of Southern schools, Northern Jews were all for it. But even though there were not that many Jews in the South to be affected, most of them were liberal on civil rights issues, and supported school desegregation. When school desegregation began to mean busing of white children into Afro-American neighborhoods, whites objected, and Jews among them. As long as the issue was no discrimination in entry to colleges and professional schools, Jews and Afro-Americans stood shoulder to shoulder. When it became affirmative action for Afro-Americans and fewer places for whites, Jews objected. And when we come to no discrimination in housing, Jews were often the targets of civil rights action. An urban people, a business-minded people, working their way up out of poverty, Jews invested in housing and in property: and if landlords generally were worried about losing control over whom they could rent to, Jewish landlords worried as much as all the rest. Jews were very well represented as landlords in Afro-American residential areas. One of the reasons there were so many Jewish landlords in Afro-American areas was that these were formerly Jewish areas into which Afro-Americans were moving. For there does seem to be a pattern of ethnic residential mobility in which Afro-Americans follow Jews more than other groups. One of the reasons this takes place is that Jews are not as militant as some other groups in opposing Afro-American entry. It may not appear that way now, after the experience of Israel, but Jews on the whole have avoided violence.

But let us get back to the breakup of the alliance. One interpretation, as I have suggested, is that Jews supported nondiscrimination in the abstract—as long as other people were involved; opposed it in the concrete—as long as they were personally involved. I think this interpretation ignores a key issue. While people do find it possible to simply act in defense of their interests, regardless of their principles, they do like, if possible, to keep their actions in harmony with their principles. And Jews found that their shift against the positions of the major Afro-American civil rights organizations not only did not do violence to their principles—it defended their principles.

Because while the alliance of Afro-Americans and Jews fought against discrimination, what could be ignored was a potential conflict in the principle under which one fought discrimination. For Jews, the principle was never in doubt: it was that each person should be judged abstractly, on the basis of exterior and impersonal measures. The judgment should not take account of religion. It is revealing that one of the first triumphs of the alliance in New York State was a prohibition against institutions of education asking for a picture from applicants. Why did Jews fight for such a prohibition? Because many Jews could conceal their religion or ethnic identity by changing their names. They could change their first name from Irving to John, and their second from Cohen to Irving. But if a picture was required, sharp-eyed admissions officers might detect a "Jewish nose" lurking behind an Anglo-Saxon application form. Afro-Americans were also against pictures— without pictures, it was not easy to tell whether an applicant was black or white, and we are talking of the forties and fifties, long before the days of affirmative action.

So common interest bound Jews together in attacking discrimination in employment, or education, or housing. But underlying the common interest was a divergence in the principles on the basis of which this discrimination was attacked. Jews had no objection to the use of abstract and impersonal tests. Indeed, they wanted them. Jews did not have a problem doing well in tests, whether tests to get into college, or medical school, or law school, or the civil service, or, if there are such paper-and-pencil tests, into managerial jobs. Jews perhaps may have done worse on manual tests—but that's not what they were after anyway. Jews also had no problems meeting the abstract qualifications for better housing—income, savings, credit ratings. So they were willing to, indeed eager to, go on the record.

Blacks were willing to, too. They were being discriminated against because of their color. If this became illegal, some who could not get into a college, or a good job, would.

The great transformation of the later 1960s was caused by the discovery that abstract and impersonal tests, while they were good for many Afro-Americans, were not good for Afro-Americans on the whole. The facts are well known. Whether they are tests for admission to selective colleges, to medical or law schools, or to the civil service, Afro-Americans on the average, did worse. Why they did worse is a complicated question, and it need not concern us here. Because the mere fact they did worse meant that the color-blind, abstract, and impersonal tests that the Jews wanted would not do the Afro-Americans—on the average—much good. The Afro-American–Jewish civil rights alliance of the 1940s, 1950s, and 1960s, broke up in the 1970s as a new principle emerged, with a great deal of support from government, to supplement the principle of nondiscrimination: the principle of affirmative action. This principle meant you would need the picture on the application form. You would require people to report their race and ethnic affiliation. Because only thus could one make special efforts for previously discriminated-against groups that, unhappily, did not on the average do well on tests.

It is no accident that the two great conflicts on which the alliance broke up were the cases of Marco DeFunis—applying to law school—and Allan Bakke—applying to medical school. Law and medicine are the two Nirvanas toward which Jews strive. Jews are greatly overrepresented in law and medicine, even more overrepresented on the faculties of law and medical schools, most overrepresented on the faculties of the most elite law and medical schools. A new principle of selection, one that took minority status into account and reduced, even moderately, Jewish chances to get into these highly selective institutions, was sure to arouse Jewish defense organizations—and Jews generally. And it did.

It is interesting, as I have suggested, that affirmative action in the skilled trades, which we have had since the late 1960s, did not really bother Jews much. It is true—and I believe it—that Jews were responding in defense of a principle. But there are many violations of principle in the world, and one chooses to fight on those that are close to one, and affect one's personal interests. This explains why, even though I believe most of us are committed to the defense of human rights, we really don't care much about the violation of rights in, say, Burundi. We are much more concerned with the violation of rights in Soviet Russia—our enemy—or El Salvador—a country in which we may have to fight. The fact that we take one rights violation more seriously than another, depending on the degree to which our interests are involved, does not mean we are indifferent to the principle. Similarly, the fact that Jews chose to fight on law school and medical school admissions did not mean that Jews did not take the principle of abstract merit seriously.

Now we must ask, is there any chance of reconstituting the alliance? One alternative is the common agreement of Jews and blacks on the principles of affirmative action, as they have evolved. This means the justice and rightness and desirability of meeting statistical standards in each area in which desirable goods are distributed (admissions to selective educational programs, employment in desirable jobs). The common principle would be equal representation. Leaving aside all the other arguments that may be made against this, this is not a principle Jews can ever accept. As 3 percent of the American population, they cannot accept a principle that says that Jews may not be 10 percent of doctors, lawyers, and college professors, because they are above their proportion. If the alliance means anything to Afro-American leaders, they must realize that Jewish acceptance of a principle with such implications is impossible. Many liberal Jews may go along, but it will simply not be acceptable to the Jewish defense organizations and most of the Jewish population.

Is there another basis for reconstituting the alliance? I believe there is. The other basis for reconstituting the alliance is the principle of the growing pie. If the worst problems of Afro-Americans could be mitigated—high unemployment, poor jobs, and everything these bring in their wake—it would be less important for Afro-American leaders to measure to a percentage point how many Afro-Americans are making it into law and medical schools.

I believe that one reason that the alliance broke up in the 1970s was that Afro-American progress economically—which had been pretty steady since World War II—stopped. There is a lot of evidence for this, and it is very distressing. Charles A. Murray has been analyzing the decline of poverty in postwar America, a matter of great interest to Afro-Americans, since they are overrepresented among the poor. In 1949, by a standard governmental statistical measure, 33 percent of the American population were poor—still FDR's famous one-third of a nation. The percentage dropped steadily, under Truman, Eisenhower, Kennedy, Johnson. In 1968 it was 13 percent and it has stuck therefor fourteen years, sometimes a little less, but never dropping below 13 percent for long. This means that since 1968 we haven't seen very much Afro-American progress, either. Mr. Murray asks how this is possible, when we have expanded programs for the poor enormously since the Johnson years. We spent twice as much on direct cash income transfers in 1980 than in 1970 (adjusted for inflation).

He gives two answers, one noncontroversial, the other rather controversial. The first answer is Afro-American progress is based on economic growth, and that the 1970s were a bad decade in terms of economic growth. Indeed, in three years of the 1970s, the GNP actually went down, in constant dollars. The second answer is that one of the reasons it was a bad decade is that we were spending too much government money on programs for the poor, and thereby depriving the economy of needed saving and investment, the taxpayer of needed incentive to work more and earn more, the entrepreneur of the needed incentive to invest more. Whether or not we accept the second answer—and perhaps in the next few months we will get a clearer answer as to whether this "supply side" answer makes sense—no one will argue with the first answer. If progress out of poverty has been so abysmal in the 1970s, I suspect no one will argue with a third conclusion: affirmative action doesn't do much good if the economy is stagnant, and jobs are scarce. And when the economy is buoyant and jobs are plentiful, we don't need affirmative action—as the experience of the prosperous 1950s and 1960s, in which Afro-Americans made substantial progress, attests.

I conclude that the reforging of the alliance on the basis of affirmative action, the new phase of civil rights action that has been embraced by many black leaders, just won't happen. It can be reforged on the basis of increasing the pie of economic growth. That, it strikes me, is the greatest need facing us if we want Jews and Afro-Americans to work together. Of course, just what measures they can agree upon to increase the pie, is itself a difficult question.

Blacks and Jews in the
Civil Rights Movement

Claybourne Carson, Jr.

I don't know whether any further discussions of Afro-American–Jewish relations would be productive. To merely describe the mutually supportive relations that have existed and continue to exist between some Afro-Americans and some Jews would probably not reduce the mutually hostile relations that have existed and continue to exist between other blacks and other Jews. Thus, despite the fact that no major civil rights group—and certainly not the NAACP—has ever taken an official position that was hostile toward Jews or toward Israel, considerable attention has been directed toward black individuals and non–civil rights groups that have taken such positions. One might suggest that Afro-Americans and Jews who wish to cooperate should do so, but, for reasons rooted in history, many of those who wish to cooperate are often unable to avoid focusing their attention on those who do not.

This is clearly evident, for example, in the ever-growing body of writings by Afro-Americans about black anti-Semitism. During the past forty years, a highly stylized ritual has developed that involves Afro American writers explaining to a largely Jewish readership why anti-Jewish sentiments exist in Afro-American communities. The avowed purpose of these writers is to reassure Jews, but the fact that reassurance is not lasting and that the process is repetitive suggests that other motives might be involved. James Baldwin's article, "Negroes Are Anti-Semitic Because They're Anti-White," published in 1967, added little of substance that had not already been stated in Lawrence Reddick's article, "Anti-Semitism among Negroes," published in 1942, or Kenneth Clark's "Candor in Negro-Jewish Relations," published in 1946.[1] One suggests that Baldwin, Reddick, and

Clark each realized that their Jewish friends would not be completely reassured by their rejection of anti-Semitism and their simultaneous inciteful explorations of the sources of anti-Jewish sentiments in the life experiences of millions of Afro-Americans.[2]

Can we move beyond ritualistic disavowals of anti-Semitism and equally ritualistic efforts to locate anti-Jewish attitudes within the logic of Afro-American history and Afro-American culture? Can a black person comment on the problem of Afro-American-Jewish conflict without becoming part of the problem? I am not sure about the answers to these questions, but I believe that the questions at least lead us beyond the confines of the existing literature on Afro-American-Jewish relations. The questions lead us away from efforts to express and explain intergroup attitudes toward an attempt to understand the historical settings that sometimes alters these attitudes and affects their social salience. I am not sure whether we can ever conclusively decide whether black anti-Semitism or Jewish racism are becoming more or less significant or whether Afro-American and Jewish concerns are diverging or converging. Perhaps, however, we can leave behind sterile intergroup arguments about such matters and look instead at the multitude of historical factors that affect the perception each group has of the other and that periodically produce conflicts between the two groups. I would argue that previous writings on Afro-American-Jewish relations have succeeded more in expressing the hopes and fears of the writers than in altering the attitudes each group holds toward the other.

My hope nonetheless is that historical perspective will enable us to view anew a few incidents during a recent period of Afro-American-Jewish conflict by placing the incidents in the web of individual lives and of history. I will argue that many of the Afro-American–Jewish conflicts of the period after 1966 were manifestations of internal conflicts and ambivalences within the Afro-American community, and that these conflicts among Afro-Americans had significant parallels among Jews.

Ambivalence and complexity certainly characterize the attitudes and actions of blacks associated with the Student Nonviolent Coordinating Committee (SNCC), a group that became enmeshed in the Afro-American-Jewish conflicts of the period after 1966. Most SNCC workers did not seek to become involved in these conflicts, but the history and character of the organization insured that it would play a singular role in them. Because SNCC was unique among civil rights organizations, its history of interactions with Jews was also unique. Unlike the NAACP and CORE, which had had significant Jewish involvement since their inceptions, SNCC only gradually attracted Jews in noticeable numbers. Moreover, Jews who associated themselves with SNCC did so on terms established by the black student militants who dominated the organization. SNCC's relations with Jews, and with other whites, cannot be compared to the high-level alliance that existed among leaders of other civil rights and Jewish organizations, because SNCC offered no quid pro quo in return for Jewish support. As political scientist Michael Walzer noted during the early stages of the black student sit-ins, black students did not "ask, or even hint, that whites should join their picket lines. It will be better for them, and for us, I was told, if *they* came unasked."[3] Jewish SNCC supporters gave their support without asking for SNCC support of Jewish causes; indeed, Jews did not call attention to their religious background. From SNCC's perspective, they entered the Movement simply as whites, although some would leave as Jews.

Founded by Southern black students who had led the lunch counter sit-ins of 1960, SNCC developed into a cadre of full-time activists and organizers, most of whom were Southern blacks. Whites who joined SNCC's staff were primarily Southern whites, and even the handful of Northern whites were, during the early 1960s, more often Christians than Jews. Publicist Dotty Miller, a graduate of Queens College, and adviser Howard Zinn, then a professor at Spelman College, were, in the early 1960s, among a small number of Jews directly involved in SNCC's work. Even after an influx of Jewish volunteers during the Mississippi Summer Project of 1964, Jews working full time with SNCC were considerably outnumbered by white Protestants and even more by blacks, Northern and Southern.

SNCC's reliance on ad hoc fund-raising efforts outside the South led to the development of extensive ties between SNCC and Northern Jews. This indirect involvement contained seeds of future conflict, however, since it led SNCC leaders to ignore the increasingly evident divergences between the prevailing Jewish conception of the civil rights movement as an effort to gain new legal protections against discrimination and the increasingly accepted view among blacks that it was an effort to gain direct government intervention on behalf of blacks to overcome past racial inequities. Although it is impossible to determine precisely what proportion of SNCC's financial support came from Jews, there are many indications that it was considerable. During SNCC's early years, crucial support came from radical lawyer Victor Rabinowitz. Subsequently, Rabinowitz and other Jewish lawyers associated with the National Lawyers Guild made it possible for SNCC to avoid becoming dependent upon the more restrictive legal assistance provided by Jack Greenberg's NAACP Legal Defense Fund.

From 1963 through 1966, SNCC's New York office, headed by Elizabeth Sutherland, concentrated its efforts on attracting Jewish support and succeeded in raising far more contributions than any other SNCC office. At least one-fourth and sometimes more than half of the

monthly contributions SNCC received during this period came from
the New York area.[4] Prominent Jewish supporters such as Theodore
Bikel also aided SNCC by participating in fund-raising concerts or
cocktail parties. A symbiotic relationship developed between SNCC,
which needed financial support yet refused to compromise its militancy
in return for that support, and a radical minority of Northern Jews,
who were attracted by SNCC's uncompromising militancy and by its
singular willingness to have help from sources that would have been
viewed with suspicion by more moderate civil rights groups.

SNCC's decision to concentrate its fund-raising efforts in the Jewish
community and the positive response of that community, even as
SNCC became more radical, was an outgrowth of a shared Afro-
American–Jewish radical culture. This culture was the product of a
long history of cultural and historical interactions, concentrated particularly in the Communist party during the years after World War I and
especially evident in New York City. Although SNCC's early leaders,
often training for the Christian ministry, initially directed their appeals
toward the Northern Christian student movement, SNCC's radicaliza-
tion and the redirection of its fund-raising efforts each resulted from
the entry into the group of blacks who were products of this radical
culture centered in New York.

Thus the often-noted parallels between the Biblical stories of Jewish
oppression and the travails of Afro-Americans were less significant in
accounting for SNCC-Jewish ties than were the common experiences
of a small minority of Afro-Americans and Jews: those whose attitudes
were shaped by awareness of secular radicalism and political dissent,
from labor organizing in the 1930s to more isolated protest activity
during the 1940s and 1950s. To refer to the outgrowths of these common experiences as a culture may stretch the term somewhat, but I
would argue that a number of blacks and Jews became similarly
alienated from prevailing white cultural values to the point that they
became more like each other than like the most culturally distinctive
members of their own group.

One does not have to accept Harold Cruse's conclusions about the
damaging consequences of Afro-American–Jewish interactions within
the Communist party to recognize the validity of his view that Afro-
American–Jewish radicalism never encompassed Jewish culture, for
that was known to be the preserve of Jews alone.[5] Because Cruse was
so determined to condemn black radical intellectuals for separating
themselves from black nationalist culture, he was reluctant to admit
the understandable appeal, particularly during the period from Garvey's fall to Malcolm's emergence, of a dynamic, activist-oriented,
intellectually vibrant, Afro-American–Jewish radicalism over a

moribund, accommodationist, intellectually stagnant black nationalism.

Jewish radicals rejected the staid, thoroughly WASPish, approaches
of the Socialist party and actively sought black support even after the
Communist party lost its effectiveness as a vehicle for radical activism.
Especially in New York, an Afro-American–Jewish radical community
survived occasional internal conflicts during the 1930s, 1940s, and
1950s to become a seedbed for civil rights activism during the 1960s. It
was in this Afro-American-Jewish radical community that blacks
gained awareness of protest and propaganda techniques and a faith that
these techniques, despite the fact that they were used by small numbers of radicals, might someday change American society. No comparable faith existed among black nationalists of the period after Garvey.

Although he was by the 1950s a staunch anti-Communist, Bayard
Rustin was a crucial link between this Afro-American–Jewish radical
culture and the most radical of the civil rights groups of the 1960s:
SNCC. Because his political life bridged the years from the radicalism
of the 1930s to the rebirth of black militancy in the 1950s, Rustin was a
central fixture in the Afro-American-Jewish civil rights coalition that
developed in New York after World War II. He also influenced several
of the activists who would later steer SNCC toward a radical course. In
the early 1960s, when Rustin was organizing New York support for
Martin Luther King, Jr., he noticed the dedication of a young black
teacher at Horace Mann School, Bob Moses, who patiently worked
stuffing envelopes and doing other mundane chores.

It was Rustin who sent Moses to Atlanta to work with Martin Luther
King's Southern Christian Leadership Conference. After Moses spent
the summer of 1960 working alongside student activists in the SCLC
office in Atlanta, he returned the following summer to begin SNCC's
Mississippi Summer Project. Rustin also influenced several of the
Howard University students who would later play crucial roles in
SNCC's transformation through his meetings with members of the
Nonviolent Action Group at Howard University. Influential NAG
members included Tom Kahn, a Jewish socialist who had worked
closely with Rustin in New York, and Stokely Carmichael, who was
himself a product of the New York Afro-American–Jewish culture of
radicalism.

That Carmichael could be both a product of this culture and also a
central figure in the Afro-American–Jewish conflicts after 1966 may
require some explanation but also should not be surprising. The Afro-
American-Jewish radical culture is an urban culture, but in urban centers it coexists with a resilient black separatist culture (and also, for
that matter, with an irrepressible Jewish separatist culture). Although

Carmichael moved toward a black nationalist philosophy, his ideological development was initially more strongly influenced by Jewish radicalism. In this respect, he followed a pattern similar to that of West Coast black nationalist Ron Karenga, who also developed his initial political awareness as a result of extensive contacts with Jewish socialists in Los Angeles.[6] Like Moses, Carmichael's political development was influenced by the Jews he met after winning admittance into one of New York's selective secondary schools—in Carmichael's case, Bronx High School of Science.

He envied the greater intellectual awareness of his white classmates. "All the other kids I went to school with, their fathers were professors, doctors; they were the smartest kids in the world," he later told Howard Zinn.[7] One of his best friends was Gene Dennis, the son of a New York Communist party leader and a resident of Harlem—unlike Carmichael, whose family lived in an otherwise all-white neighborhood in the Bronx. Carmichael associated with various socialist and communist youth groups while in high school. His first demonstration was on behalf of Israel. He later recalled: "Someone at the U.N. had said something anti-Semitic; I can't exactly remember who, but [the Young Peoples Socialist League] drew up a big picket-line at the U.N."[8]

Ironically, it was through Carmichael's contacts with Jews, especially Dennis, that he became acquainted with Benjamin Davis and other black radicals who were themselves products of the Afro-American–Jewish political culture that developed inside the Community party. By the end of Carmichael's high school years, his world view had clearly been shaped by his contacts with Jews. His ambition was to go to Brandeis University and become a teacher. Only the attraction of being near the sit-in protests led Carmichael to give in to his parents wishes that he attend a black school. After arriving at Howard in the fall of 1960, Carmichael, like other Northern blacks, was attracted to those aspects of SNCC that corresponded to the values of the urban radical culture.

More than other civil rights groups, SNCC increasingly rejected bourgeois culture; it demanded a moralistic commitment to sacrifice one's welfare on behalf of oppressed people; it stressed the value of rigorous discourse as a component of political action. It distrusted the prevailing white-Anglo-Saxon-Protestant liberalism that made civility and respectability preconditions for effective political action, and, most importantly, it saw the black struggle as a necessary component of fundamental social change.

Carmichael's election as SNCC's chairman in May 1966 marked the culmination of the displacement of Southern black activists, such as former chairman John Lewis, by Northern blacks who saw Lewis as too moderate and as lacking the kind of political sophistication they saw in themselves. Many of SNCC's new leaders were directly or indirectly influenced by the Northern tradition of Afro-American–Jewish radicalism, although by 1966 they also reflected the influence of Northern black nationalism.

The newly elected head of SNCC's International Affairs office, James Forman, had become involved in civil rights activities while living in Chicago, but, as SNCC's executive secretary, he had guided the development of the group's Northern fund-raising network. His move to New York during 1966 was part of a general drift of SNCC personnel from the rural South to the urban North and part of a gradual shift of SNCC's emphasis from civil rights goals to broader economic and political objectives. Although this shift would ultimately result in conflict between SNCC and Jewish leftists, SNCC failed to recognize quickly the implications of the conflict between its objectives and its financial base. It remained permeated by the complex mixture of socialistic and nationalistic ideas advocated by Carmichael, Moses, Forman, Courtland Cox, Ivanhoe Donaldson, and many other Northern black activists.

Although these black activists were moving toward black nationalist ideas, which they hoped would allow them to express the sentiments of the urban black masses, they had initially stressed the need for socialistic economic reforms. By 1966, Carmichael and Cox had broken with Rustin and Kahn, but they were still part of a group of blacks, including Forman but no longer Bob Moses, who believed that interracial alliances were possible, if not probable, and still served as SNCC's primary links with Northern Jewish supporters.

After Carmichael's election as chairman and his subsequent highly publicized use of the "Black Power" slogan on the Mississippi march of June 1966, Carmichael was portrayed as a proponent of black nationalism, but he is more accurately seen as a man who stood uneasily between an urban black nationalist tradition with which he had had little personal contact and the radical culture that continued to shape his rhetoric. In his "Black Power" speeches he often pointed to parallels in Afro-American and Jewish experiences, sometimes misreading the historical evidence but always seeking to place blacks in the historical continuum of militant ethnic politics. He often mentioned Jews as a group that Afro-Americans should emulate while seeking to build a basis for social power.

Carmichael reflected earlier currents of Afro-American-Jewish radicalism in his verbal attacks on the hypocrisy of conventional liberalism and middle-class values. At the same time, he departed from that tradition by bringing to the fore issues of racial and ethnic identity that had always been a problematical, though still significant, part of the Afro-American-Jewish radical tradition. Significantly, Carmichael did not refer to the Jewish model in his discussion of the need for black cultural autonomy, perhaps recognizing that to do so would be to suggest that black separatism might become as conservative as were some forms of American Jewish Zionism.

Carmichael's expressed goals at the time did not extend much beyond the pluralism best articulated by Jewish liberals. Having abandoned Jewish socialism, Carmichael's views unwittingly converged with those of sociologist Nathan Glazer, who in 1964 had revealed the divisions among Jews regarding civil rights reforms by pointing to the conflicting interests of Afro-Americans and Jews, because, he argued, Afro-Americans sought equality of economic results while Jews sought equality of opportunity. Carmichael also foreshadowed the black consciousness theme by suggesting that blacks should not continue to break down the legitimate barriers imposed by surrounding ethnic groups while failing to preserve what was valuable to their own group.[9]

Despite his public reputation, within SNCC Carmichael was a firm advocate of maintaining contacts with those whites who were sufficiently alienated from the white majority to support SNCC on terms set by blacks. He remained on close terms with individual white activists and supported the use of SNCC funds to help white organizers found the Southern Students Organizing Committee and resisted efforts to expel whites from SNCC.

Carmichael's efforts to translate the new black militancy into terms SNCC's former white supporters could understand took the form of articles in the *New York Review of Books* and the *New Republic,* certainly not forums designed to reach the black urban masses. It also took the form of numerous appearances at predominantly white colleges and on radio and television shows, including extended interviews on "Face the Nation" and on the David Susskind show.

Many Jews, like other former SNCC supporters, were not willing to accept the new militancy, but Carmichael's background helps account for the successes he had in making black power a topic worthy of serious discussion within the Jewish Left. For some Jews, continued support for SNCC brought them into conflict with more conservative Jews who were only too willing to use SNCC as an example of the terrible consequences of Jewish radicalism. Despite their growing vulnerability to attack from other Jews, many Jewish SNCC supporters remained optimistic that SNCC would continue to be worthy of support.

Jewish Currents was among the Jewish journals to defend SNCC, arguing in 1966 that it was "particularly important for Jews, who are so alert to the dangers of racism as it affects them, to avoid misjudging an idealistic, heroic movement like SNCC, which is dedicated consciously to abolishing racism."[10] Journalist I. F. Stone saw the cry for black power as "psychological therapy" rather than "practical politics," but nonetheless he applauded SNCC's opposition to the Vietnam War and expressed hope that black militancy would prod the nation into eliminating ghetto poverty.[11]

Although some Jews cut off their support to SNCC during 1966, most did so because they, like many former non-Jewish supporters, disagreed with SNCC's antiwar stance and with Carmichael's inflammatory rhetoric. I located only one letter in SNCC's files that suggested that Jewish supporters saw anti-Semitic overtones in the black power rhetoric. SNCC responded to this note from a New York attorney in a polite letter claiming that nothing in its policies or programs suggested anti-Semitism, adding that the organization was "very aware of the support it has received, both 'physical' and financial, from American Jews and appreciates it."[12] In contrast to this one negative letter were those like the one from a sixty-six-year-old Los Angeles Jew who wrote Carmichael to object to what he considered to be the effort by Susskind to inject the issue of anti-Semitism into Carmichael's discussion of black power.[13]

SNCC files also contain a revealing letter from the executive secretary of a Chicago temple, who gently chided Carmichael after the SNCC chairman had quoted Hillel and incorrectly referred to him as a German. Carmichael's apologetic reply insisted that he had quickly recognized his own mistake and that it did not betray a general lack of understanding of Jewish history.[14] It is likely that continued Jewish support of SNCC, even after it began promoting black power, was the result of the extensive history of personal contacts between SNCC workers and Jewish supporters. Thus, the support SNCC received from Rabbi Irving Ganz in California was at least partially the result of the fact that Ganz's son, Marshall, had worked with SNCC in Mississippi. Rabbi Harold Saperstein of Temple Emanu-El of Lynbrook, New York, who had worked for a brief time with Carmichael in Lowndes County, was one of those who did not agree with the black power theme but still understood SNCC workers' frustrations and continued to support the organization.[15]

Carmichael, Forman, and other blacks who remained close to the white Left during 1966 faced enormous pressures from SNCC's black separatists, however, and these pressures resulted in bitter internal conflicts that would have profound impact on SNCC's relations with an outside world that included Jews. At a staff meeting held in upstate New York during December 1966, SNCC's veteran leaders came under strong attack from separatists in SNCC's recently established Atlanta Project. Several of the Atlanta separatists were themselves from Northern backgrounds, but their ideological orientation was more strongly influenced by the black nationalist tradition than were the veterans. In place of an economic emphasis, they argued for great recognition of the importance of racial identity; rather than to Marx, they looked to Franz Fanon or Malcolm X for ideological guidance. Rejecting the previously dominant view that struggle itself was SNCC's reason for being, they insisted that ideological conversion was a necessary precondition for future struggles.

In their effort to purify SNCC of all white influences, the Atlanta separatists used as weapons the charge that SNCC's leaders had not cut themselves off from white people. Interestingly, just as SNCC's ties with the white New Left were based on common positions on foreign policy issues, the tenuous threads that held together SNCC's factions were more often support for Third World alliances than common positions about strategies for achieving black power. Although SNCC's officers hoped that the few remaining whites on the staff would not become an issue dividing black staff members, the Atlanta separatists were willing to disrupt the New York staff meeting until they had achieved their goal. Carmichael argued at the start of the meeting that SNCC needed white financial support and a "buffer zone" of white liberals to forestall repression, but the separatists repeatedly insisted "whites had to go."

After days of seemingly endless discussion, a vote was finally taken. Nineteen staff members voted for expulsion, eighteen against, and twenty-four, including most officers and all whites, abstained. Despite the expulsion, however, SNCC remained divided as the separatists continued to deny the racial loyalty of SNCC's leaders and sought to undermine their authority. During the winter of 1967, after repeated acts of insubordination, Carmichael fired or suspended all members of the Atlanta project. This firing was upheld at the March Central Committee meeting, but when the entire staff met in June a member of the Atlanta staff came to lambast those who had betrayed the cause of "blackness." His outburst established an atmosphere of hostility that permeated the rest of the meeting. It was in this tense atmosphere that the issue of SNCC's position in the Arab-Israeli conflict was raised.

Staff members elected H. Rap Brown as chairman, believing that he could remove SNCC from public controversy. They also voted to declare that SNCC would henceforth be a "Human Rights Organization" that would "encourage and support the liberation struggles against colonization, racism, and economic exploitation" around the world. In addition, they proclaimed a position of "positive non-alignment" in world affairs, indicating their willingness to meet with Third World governments and liberation groups and authorizing an application for Non-Government Organization status on the United Nations Economic and Security Council. To coordinate these activities, SNCC established an International Affairs Commission headed by Jim Forman. These actions to establish international ties were taken despite the almost total collapse of SNCC projects in Afro-American communities; indeed the redirection of SNCC's interests into those of the Third World served as a cohesive theme for a divided group, still torn between its roots in an interracial culture of dissent and its search for the illusive ideas that would unify Afro-Americans.

Reacting to the separatist demand that SNCC break its umbilical cord to white supporters, most of the seventy-six remaining staff members agreed that SNCC support for the Third World should extend to the Palestinians. They did not agree, however, about whether the group should allow the Palestinian issue to further separate SNCC from its declining body of white financial supporters.

Shortly before leaving on a trip to Africa, Forman cautioned Stanley Wise, who had replaced him as SNCC's Executive Secretary, about the dangers of taking an anti-Israel stand. Forman noted that such a stand would result in "a certain isolation from the press." Forman warned against adopting "a reactionary position that even the Syrians and the Egyptians do not articulate: namely a hatred for the people of Israel." He suggested that SNCC must begin to build bases of financial support in Afro-American communities to replace Jewish support if SNCC were to take a position against Israel. Forman also expressed sympathy for leaders of CORE, who had refused to take a stand on the issue for fear of dividing their organization. He stressed the need for staff members to educate themselves regarding the dispute and asked that SNCC be placed on the mailing lists of all the Arab nations. He argued that a public stand should not be taken until the staff became more knowledgeable and a special meeting was held to discuss the issue.[16]

Forman's cautionary admonitions were stated even more strongly in the first published statement by a staff member on the Arab-Israeli conflict. Veteran SNCC worker Fred Meely wrote an article for a SNCC newsletter called *Aframerican News for You,* in which he suggested that black leaders should not take a stand on the crisis, for they were "already under enough pressure" as a result of the black power controversy. "We black people neither need [nor] deserve the wrath of Arab or Jew, for we are even denied access to this debate that may well affect the future of all mankind."[17]

Soon after Forman wrote to Wise, SNCC's Central Committee meeting in the midst of Israel's six-day victory over Arab forces in June 1967, requested that SNCC's search and communications staff investigate the background of the conflict. Ethel Minor, editor of SNCC's newsletter, volunteered for this task. She recalled that the committee wanted an "objective critique of the facts." Minor was not impartial on the issue, however, for she had been close friends with Palestinian students during her college years and was acquainted with the urban black nationalist tradition through her involvement with the Nation of Islam. Minor never wrote a position paper, nor did SNCC ever conduct an extended discussion of the Middle Eastern dispute.

Nonetheless, SNCC suddenly found itself at the center of a bitter conflict with former allies when Minor published a piece that she claimed would provide staff members with information not available in the "white press." In the *SNCC Newsletter,* she listed thirty-two "documented facts" regarding "the Palestine Problem," including assertions that the Arab-Israeli war was an effort to regain Palestinian land and that during the 1948 war, "Zionists conquered the Arab homes and land through terror, force, and massacres." By itelf, the *Newsletter* article would have provoked controversy, but accompanying photographs and drawings by SNCC artist Kofi Bailey heightened its emotional impact through clearly anti-Semitic drawings. The caption on one of the photographs, which portrayed Zionists shooting Arab victims who were lined up against a wall, noted "This is the Gaza Strip, Palestine, not Dachau, Germany."[18]

Although Minor later claimed that those who prepared the article intended it for internal education rather than as a policy stand, other SNCC workers, particularly in the New York fund-raising office, realized immediately that the article would bring swift condemnations from Jewish leaders. Johnny Wilson, most recently installed as head of the office and unaware that the article would be published, called a press conference to announce that the article did not present SNCC's official position. Wilson's disclaimer went unnoticed in the subsequent press reports, however, because Minor and other workers at SNCC headquarters quickly called their own press conference to reiterate the anti-Israel position. Program Director Ralph Featherstone explained to reporters in Atlanta that the article did not indicate that SNCC was anti-Semitic, but he inflamed the emotions of Jews by criticizing Jewish store owners in Afro-American ghettoes. Forman, still out of the country when the newsletter was published, privately expressed his dismay that his counsel of caution had been ignored, but publicly backed the stand again Israel. He decided that SNCC should support the Arabs on the Palestinian question "regardless of how ragged the formulation of our position" and concluded that "no formulations of our position would have satisfied the Zionists and many Jews."[19]

Whether Forman was correct is disputable, but the strength of the negative response to the Minor article suggests that it symbolized more than it said. Actual incidents of publicly expressed black anti-Semitism were few in number, and none involved persons who still identified themselves as civil rights leaders. Most such incidents would not have gained much notice if they had not been brought to public attention by

Jews who saw them as indications of a trend, despite the fact that no civil rights group ever took an official anti-Israeli or anti-Jewish stand.

For blacks in SNCC, the anti-Israel stand was a test of their willingness to demonstrate SNCC's break from its civil rights past and a reconfirmation that ties with whites were inconsistent with their desire to express racial aspirations and frustrations without restraint. Veteran staff member Cleveland Sellers later acknowledged that afterward many donations "from white sources just stopped coming in," but he added: "Rather than breaking our will, this made us more convinced than ever that we were correct when we accused the majority of America's whites of being racists."[20]

Forman might have succeeded for a time in convincing SNCC's Jewish supporters to ignore or downplay the existence of private anti-Israel sentiments in SNCC, except that Jews who had long been hostile to SNCC quickly directed national attention to the Minor article. The executive director of the American Jewish Congress labeled the article "shocking and vicious anti-Semitism." Similar criticisms came from the heads of other Jewish groups and from black leaders Whitney Young, A Philip Randolph, and Bayard Rustin. Theodore Bikel and author Harry Golden added to the furor by announcing publicly that they were resigning from SNCC, an organization to which they did not belong. Bikel mentioned the sacrifice of Mickey Schwerner and Andrew Goodman, who had been lynched in Mississippi during the summer of 1964, saying that SNCC had no right to "spit on their tomb."[21] More restrained was the response of Rabbi Saperstein, who privately informed SNCC leaders that he could not continue to support a group that "so readily allowed itself to become a mouthpiece for malicious Arab propaganda."[22]

Although the highly publicized controversy over the *Newsletter* article was described in the press as a split in the civil rights movement, it was actually a more complex event. For some time, SNCC's goals had extended beyond civil rights, a fact confirmed by its self-definition as a human rights organization seeking ties with the Third World. Many SNCC workers had once shared a wide range of values with SNCC's Jewish supporters, but they had gradually and self-consciously separated themselves from that culture, because its values were not shared by the black masses whose support they sought. In retrospect, it is easy to see that the Pan-Africanism toward which SNCC workers were moving would not automatically guarantee widespread Afro-American support, but that was not evident in the heady political climate of 1967. SNCC workers were surprised at how rapidly and completely they had destroyed the bridges to their ideological past, but historical continuity was evident in their firmly held belief that it was their destiny, even as a small minority, to bring into being a better world.

Having destroyed their bridges, SNCC workers tried to build new ones in the less-known cultural territory of the Third World. Reacting to the criticisms of the earlier article, a *SNCC Newsletter* article in the fall of 1967 stated that SNCC had

> placed itself squarely on the side of oppressed peoples and liberation movements. . . . Perhaps we have taken the liberal Jewish community or certain segments of it as far as it can go. If so, this is tragic, not for us but for the liberal Jewish community. For the world is in a revolutionary ferment. . . . Our message to conscious people everywhere is "Don't get caught on the wrong side of the revolution."[23]

Even after SNCC workers had burned their bridges, however, they continued to insist that they were not anti-Semitic. Their defense of themselves rested on the semantic issue of whether attacks against Israel or against the role of Jewish businessmen in black communities necessarily constituted anti-Semitism. On occasion SNCC workers used the facile argument that Arabs were also Semitic peoples. Such arguments did little to bridge the gulf between SNCC and Jews, and SNCC workers were undoubtedly far more interested in establishing new ties to angry urban blacks than in reestablishing old ties with angered Jews. Whether SNCC could have found a way of expressing its opposition to Israeli policies without making itself vulnerable to the charge of anti-Semitism is an interesting question, but there is little evidence that SNCC workers expended much effort searching for such a way or that Jews expended much effort aiding in the search. For many Jews, there was no proper way for blacks to condemn Israel.

During the summer of 1967, Forman and SNCC's new chairman, H. Rap Brown, led a successful black effort at the National Convention for New Politics to gain adoption of an anti-Israeli policy stand. The fact that the resolution contained a statement that the condemnation of Zionist expansion did "not imply anti-Semitism" was not nearly as significant for Jews as the fact that it was introduced by the Black Caucus at the convention. An issue that, at the beginning of the summer of 1967, had unexpectedly cost SNCC needed financial support became by the end of the summer the central issue by which SNCC militants demonstrated their own militancy and tested the loyalty of their erstwhile white allies in the New Left.

Thus it happened that a few dozen black activists became the first, and for some time the only, major black organization to take a stand against Israel in the Middle-East dispute. SNCC itself rapidly disintegrated after the summer. Deprived of former sources of financial support and weakened by internal conflicts and external repression, it lost black support and access to power even as it made black power its central focus. The small SNCC staff had lost the ability to serve as a catalyst for massive mobilizations of black people, but they retained the ability to serve as a catalyst for a major disruption of the Afro-American–Jewish reform alliance of the post–World War II period. As ideological consistency gained priority over the goal of political effectiveness, they eagerly sought opportunities to display their independence from the constraints of alliances.

Many SNCC workers refused even to accept the constraints of working within their own organization and left it rather than compromise their militancy. Carmichael rejected SNCC's efforts to control his actions while touring the Third World in 1967, and after his return moved gradually away from SNCC until making a final break in July 1968. Forman was forced to resign a year later. There was a considerable degree of irony in Earl Raab's suggestion in the late 1960s that the black movement was "developing an anti-Semitic ideology,"[24] for it was only while the Afro-American–Jewish civil rights alliance lived that it was possible to speak of a black movement coherent and unified enough to possess a single ideology.

The hostility that developed as a result of SNCC's anti-Israel stand survived longer than did SNCC, however, because the hostility had many sources in the web of Afro-American–Jewish interactions. Once Jewish supporters of the civil rights movement had discovered evidence of what they deemed black anti-Semitism in SNCC, a group spawned by the Afro-American–Jewish civil rights coalition, it became much easier to find evidences of anti-Semitism in the more alien black world outside of SNCC, where its expression was less likely to be inhibited than in SNCC.

The publicity focused on SNCC during the summer of 1967 was redirected toward other isolated anti-Jewish statements, and the publicity itself probably stimulated the anti-Semitism that it sought to denounce. There is little evidence that anti-Jewish sentiments among blacks increased substantially during the late 1960s, but it is apparent that anti-Israeli or anti-Jewish statements symbolized a new willingness among that minority of Afro-Americans who had been part of the interracial civil rights movement to break with their past.

Former SNCC worker Julius Lester provides a final illustration of the complex motives that shaped black responses to issues of concern to Jews during the late 1960s. Lester was by no means a typical SNCC worker, if such a construct can ever exist, but his multifaceted experiences in the movement reflect many aspects of the dynamics of Afro-American–Jewish relations during the late 1960s. That he found himself a central figure in Afro-American–Jewish conflicts was both an accident of history and a consequence of historical trends that made such accidents inevitable. Lester was not exposed to the New York culture of radicalism until the early 1960s, when as a young folksinger and writer he came to New York with his new wife, a white socialist studying at the New School.

Despite growing up in the South and attending Fisk University, Lester had resisted joining the Southern civil rights movement until 1964 when he discovered that he and SNCC were each moving toward a new sense of racial identity. Unlike the Northern-born blacks who joined SNCC, Lester did not adopt Marxian ideas, and perhaps for this reason he did not feel compelled to supplant Marx with the "black" ideology of Fanon or Nkrumah or Malcolm X. In the spring of 1966, he left his wife to join the SNCC staff on a full-time basis as head of the photography department. Although he kept his feelings to himself during that spring, he was privately critical of the tendency of Moses and other SNCC activists to stress Afro American ties with Africa rather than identify with the unique racial consciousness that already existed among Afro-Americans who had not been exposed to such large doses of white culture as had SNCC's college-educated black nationalists. He later attributed this tendency to the Northern backgrounds of much of SNCC's leadership. Referring to his own upbringing, he was instructive:

> Those of us from the South had lived outside the perimeter of white culture; northern blacks were infected with it. Their black militancy was so strident that I regarded them as recent converts to the race, and their rage at whites, misdirected self-hatred.[25]

Lester did not express his reservations at the time, however, and instead became one of the chief propagandists for the black power theme. Among the large number of his writings were "The Angry Children of Malcolm X," a classic essay of the 1960s and the popular tract, *Look Out, Whitey! Black Power's Gon' Get Your Mama*. Both these uncompromising statements of black militancy demonstrated the extent to which he became caught up in the angry mood of the time. They also demonstrated how completely he suppressed any feelings of doubt. Much later he would comment, "I was so determined to be a revolutionary that I refused to look at anything within me which might contradict who I wanted to be."[26]

After leaving SNCC in 1967, Lester returned to New York, where he observed the eruption of Afro-American–Jewish conflicts during the dispute over the firing of nine white teachers from the black-controlled Ocean-Hill–Brownsville school district. The teachers' union president, Albert Shanker, accused the local school board of anti-Semitism, a charge that led to bitter exchanges between striking Jewish teachers and black parents and students.

Lester invited a black teacher, Les Campbell, to appear on his weekly radio show, and when Campbell showed Lester an anti-Semitic poem that had been written by a black student, Lester encouraged the teacher to read it on the air to indicate how the strike was affecting the attitudes of black youths. For two weeks after the broadcast, Lester heard no protests—probably a result of the limited nature of his audience—but early in 1969 the United Federation of Teachers announced that they were asking that the license of Lester's station be revoked because of the airing of the poem. As had been the case for SNCC in 1967, the controversy around the program intensified as Lester found that his refusal to condemn the poem encouraged some blacks to view the controversy as an opportunity to demostrate to other blacks how completely they ignored Jewish and white sensibilities.

Soon afterward, a black high school student appeared on the show and offhandedly remarked, "Hitler didn't make enough lampshades out of them." Lester wrote that he "found the remark obscene and personally offensive, but [said he] lacked the maturity to know how to dissociate myself from it while upholding the student's First Amendment right to make it."[27] The student's remark prompted demonstrations at the station by the Jewish Defense League and further poisoned an already volatile atmosphere. When Lester replied to his critics on the air, his comments echoed those of Baldwin, Reddick, and Clark, for they superficially appealed for Jewish understanding while simultaneously providing a rationale for anti-Jewish sentiments among Afro-Americans. He announced that the "old relationship" that had existed between Afro-Americans and Jews had "been destroyed and the stage [was] set now for a real relationship where our feelings, *our* views of America and how to operate has to be given serious consideration."[28]

Despite Lester's announcement of a new relationship, the continuities of history were displayed in interesting subtle ways. The board of the Pacific Foundation, which operated Lester's stations, stood firmly behind him throughout the controversy and no one remained more firm than board member Bob Goodman, a Jew and the father of Andrew Goodman, who had been lynched in Mississippi in 1964.

Even as the Lester controversy continued, Nathan Glazer provided an indication of the extent to which Afro-American-Jewish conflict reflected intra-Jewish as well as intrablack conflicts. As in his earlier article mentioned above, Glazer continued to oppose black militancy (although his definition of it had changed since 1964) and Jews who supported such militancy. In *Commentary,* he combined an attack on Afro-American leaders, who he said were guilty of "justifying and legitimizing" black anti-Semitism, with an even stronger attack against Jewish radicals, who "abetted and assisted and advised" black intellectuals.[29]

Glazer may have exaggerated the degree of consensus among black militants about issues of concern to Jews, but his twofold attack on black militants and white radicals clearly demonstrated the close connection between the issue of Afro-American–Jewish conflict and the broader political currents that brought the issue public attention during the late 1960s.

The lack of communication between black militants and Jewish critics of black militancy during this period is revealed in the contrasting conclusions drawn by Glazer and Lester. For Glazer, black militancy was infected with anti-Semitism and could be supported only by Jews who had a nihilistic view of American society and its political system. "All they can do is give the blacks guns, and allow themselves to become the first victims,"[30] he wrote. Lester followed a different route to arrive at a similar state of cynicism. While Glazer was defining his conditions for continued Jewish support of black civil rights efforts, Lester and other blacks were insisting that conditional white support was no longer acceptable. "Black anti-Semitism is not the problem," he answered his critics.

Jews have never suffered at the hands of black people. Individuals, yes. But en masse, no. The issue is not black anti-Semitism. This issue is what it has always been: racism. . . . If this fact cannot be faced, then there is little else to be said. It is this which black people understand. I guess it just comes down to questions of who's going to be on what side. If there are Jews and other white people out there who understand, never was there a more opportune time for them to let their voices be heard. All I hear is silence, and if that's all there's going to be, then so be it.[31]

Notes

1. James Baldwin, "Negroes are Anti-Semitic Because They're Anti-White," *New York Times Magazine*, 9 April 1967, pp. 26, 27ff.; L. D. Reddick, "Anti-Semitism among Negroes," *Negro Quarterly* 1 (Summer 1942): 112–22; Kenneth Clark, "Candor in the Negro-Jewish Relations," *Commentary*, February 1946, pp. 8–14. See also bibliography in *Negro-Jewish Relations in the United States,* Papers and Proceedings of a conference convened by the Conference on Jewish Social Studies, New York City, (New York: Citadel Press, 1966), pp. 67–71.

2. Earl Rabb probably spoke for many Jews when he suggested that Afro-American writers were in danger of crossing the fine line between explanation and rationalization. He charged that

Negroes trying to reassure Jewish audience repeatedly and unwitting make the very point they are trying to refute. "This is not anti-Semitism," [black writers] say. "The hostility is toward the whites. When [blacks] say "Jew," they mean "white." But that is an exact and acute description of political anti-Semitism: "The enemy" becomes the Jew, "the man" becomes the Jew, the villain is not so much the actual Jewish merchant on the corner as the corporate Jew who stands symbolically for generic evil.

See Earl Rabb, "The Black Revolution & the Jewish Question," *Commentary*, January 1969, p. 29.

3. Quoted in Clayborne Carson, *In Struggle: SNCC and the Black Awakening of the 1960s* (Cambridge: Harvard University Press, 1981), p. 17.

4. Available financial statistics are incomplete, but the following table is representative:

May 1965:	New York provided $50,000 of the $82,292 SNCC received.
June 1965:	$12,000 of $37,997
July 1965:	$8,000 of $29,300
April 1966:	$12,000 of $30,753.45
May 1966:	$20,000 of $29,910,37

See SNCC Papers, Subgroup B, New York Office, Series III (Microfilm edition by Microfilming Corporation of America); and Civil Rights Movement in the United States Collection, Box 8, University of California, Los Angeles.

5. Cf. Harold Cruse, *The Crisis of the Negro Intellectual: From Its Origins to the Present* (New York: William Morrow, 1967).

6. Karenga's political development is revealed in my extended interview with him, conducted on 4 October 1977.

7. Interview conducted in Mississippi during the summer of 1963.

8. Ibid.

9. See Nathan Glazer, "Negroes & Jews: The New Challenge to Pluralism," *Commentary,* December 1964, pp. 29–34.

10. "Is SNCC Racist or Radical" (editorial), *Jewish Currents,* July–August 1966.

11. I. F. Stone, "Why They Cry Black Power," *I. F. Stone's Weekly,* 19 September 1966.

12. Myron Cohen to Stokely Carmichael, 9 November 1966; unsigned letter to Cohen, 11 November 1966. SNCC Papers, Series I, Chairman's Files, New York.

13. Fred Buch to Stokely Carmichael, 9 November 1966, SNCC Papers, Series I, Chairman's Files.

14. Mrs. Joseph Walzer to Stokely Carmichael, 17 January 1967, SNCC Papers, Series I, Chairman's Files.

15. See Rabbi Harold I. Saperstein to H. Rap Brown, 5 January 196[8], SNCC Papers I. Chairman's Files.

16. See letters in James Forman, *The Making of Black Revolutionaries* (New York: Macmillan, 1972), pp. 492–96.

17. Fred Meely, "The Chicken or the Egg of the Middle East," *Aframerican News for You,* July 1967.

18. "Third World Round Up; The Palestine Problem: Test Your Knowledge," *SNCC Newsletter,* June–July 1967, pp. 4–5.

19. Forman, *Black Revolutionaries,* p. 496; Jean Wiley interview with author, 11 May 1978, in Washington, D.C. See also "S. N. C. C. Charges Israel Atrocities," *New York Times,* 15 August 1967; "Zionism Assailed in Newsletter of SNCC," *Los Angeles Times,* 15 August 1967; "SNCC and the Jews," *Newsweek,* 29 August 1967.

20. Cleveland Sellers, with Robert Terrell, *The River of No Return: The Autobiography of a Black Militant and the Life and Death of SNCC* (New York: William Morrow, 1973), p. 203.

21. "Bikel Scores Attack on Jews by S.N.C.C. and Quits the Group," *New York Times* 17 July 1967; "Golden Criticizes S.N.C.C. and Quits," *New York Times,* 22 August 1967.

22. Saperstein to Brown, 5 January 196[8].

23. "The Mid-East and the Liberal Reaction," *SNCC Newsletter* September–October 1967, p. 5.

24. Raab, "Black Revolution," p. 29.

25. Julius Lester, *All Is Well* (New York: William Morrow 1976), p. 130.

26. Lester, *All Is Well,* p. 131.

27. Lester, *All Is Well,* p. 153.

28. See text in Lester, *All Is Well,* p. 158.

29. Nathan Glazer, "Blacks, Jews & the Intellectuals," *Commentary,* April 1969, pp. 33–39.

30. Ibid., p. 39.

31. Lester, "A Response," in *Black Anti-Semitism and Jewish Racism* (New York: Richard W. Baron, 1969), p. 237.

Africa and the Middle East:
What Blacks and Jews Owe to Each Other

Richard L. Sklar

> A man should fight for what he believes in—and the
> fact that he fights is his reward. I owe him nothing.
>
> —Ossie Davis[1]

The United States of America is a multinational society. Many ethnic nationality groups retain their cultural identities as hyphenated Americans. Most of them cherish sentimental ties to an "old country" and to kith and kin abroad. Black Americans are deeply attached to the progress of Africa and the cause of black liberation. With the passing of European colonial rule in Africa, this passionate commitment has been focused upon the white supremacist state of South Africa, where 4.5 million whites dominate more than 23 million blacks. Similarly, Jewish Americans are passionately committed to the security and well-being of the Jewish state of Israel, where 3 million Jews constitute 85 percent of the population. Neither of these foreign commitments is exceptional for a cultural nationality in the United States.

Nations and "peoples" define their essential interests to include survival and freedom. The survival, freedom, and well-being of national groups abroad are primary interests for their ethnic brethren in the United States. Given this conception of primary interest, the Afro-American community does not have a strong primary interest of its own in the Middle East; nor does the Jewish community in America have a strong primary interest of its own in Africa. However, Afro-Americans and Jews do have significant secondary interests in the Middle East and Africa respectively, and these have given rise to unforeseen conflicts between them.

Conflicts of Interest

Over the years, black political organizations in the United States have upheld the principle of self-determination for oppressed and subject peoples. This principle has been crucial to the cause of freedom for black people in many lands. On occasion, it has been invoked by African peoples against independent African states. In two such cases, namely the unsuccessful Biafran secession from Nigeria (1967–70) and the Southern Sudanese rebellion of 1967–72, many Afro-Americans favored the separationist cause. Naturally, the well-publicized plight of a displaced and downtrodden people in the Middle East, namely the Palestinians, evokes a sentiment of solidarity among all peoples who experience comparable grievances. So it is not surprising that many blacks respect and endorse the Palestinain struggle for national self-determination.

In the late summer and fall of 1979, Afro-American and Jewish community leaders were antagonists in a bruising political dispute about the question of Palestinian representation. Andrew Young, then United States Ambassador to the United Nations, incurred the wrath of pro-Israeli groups because he wished to include the Palestine Liberation Organization in negotiations for peace in the Middle East. These critics were not mollified by his personal and publicly avowed belief in Israel's right to exist within secure borders. He resigned as Ambassador, for the convenience of the president if not at his request, after it had been disclosed (allegedly by Israeli sources and with intent to undermine his position) that he had held an unauthorized meeting with an official representative of the PLO. Reacting sharply, a major black organization, the Southern Christian Leadership Conference, "resolved to support the courageous stand taken by Ambassador Young."[2] At meetings with representatives of the PLO and the government of Israel, the Reverand Joseph E. Lowery, president of the SCLC and the Honorable Reverand Walter E. Fauntroy, chairman of the board of directors of the SCLC and congressional delegate for the District of Columbia, urged both sides to renounce violence and "respect the mutual right of each to state sovereignty and territorial integrity."[3] Shortly thereafter, some two hundred thirty "leaders and representatives of civil rights and other major black organizations" met in New York to formulate a common position. As Jake C. Miller has reported, they

defended the right of the SCLC to speak out on foreign policy issues, and deplored the double standards which had been used in judging Ambassador Young, whom they considered to have been performing his duty in preparation for assuming the presidency of the Security

Council. The leadership group felt that it was Young's prerogative, in the above role, to meet with all parties involved in the pending United Nations debate on the Middle East.[4]

At this juncture Yasser Arafat, chairman of the PLO, invited the leaders of the SCLC and their prominent colleague, the Reverand Jesse Jackson, founder of People United to Save Humanity (PUSH), to discuss their proposals with him in Lebanon.[5] Two separate groups, one headed by Lowery and Fauntroy, the other by Jackson, went to the Middle East in September 1979. The former group, characterized by Fauntroy as "a mission of reconciliation,"[6] visited Lebanon only; Jackson's group went to Israel as well as to Lebanon and other Arab countries. At all times, both the SCLC delegates and Jackson affirmed their support for both Israel's right to exist and the PLO's effort to secure national rights for the Palestinians. Upon his return to the United States, Jackson created something of a stir by stating, frankly and repeatedly, that he expected to receive Arab financial assistance for PUSH in return for his support of the Palestinian cause. Black support for the PLO, he declared, was not for the asking but strictly for sale. Overnight, the anger of his critics turned to scorn while the awe of those who had taken his professions of principle at face value gave way to more cynical estimates of his political acumen.

Meanwhile, various influential Afro-Americans and Jews, including Young, Benjamin L. Hooks, executive director of the NAACP, Henry Siegman, executive director of the American Jewish Congress, and Vernon E. Jordan, president of the National Urban League, tried to repair the damage that had been done to Afro-American-Jewish relations.[7] In Los Angeles, a coalition of Afro-American and Jewish community leaders convened under the informal auspices of Mayor Tom Bradley to deliberate on various divisive issues. Mayor Bradley, an architect of this so-called coalition in the early 1960s, was reported to feel that "an ongoing dialogue between representatives of the two communities would help maintain the historically strong bond between them."[8] In addition to declarations on affirmative action, education, and economic development, the public "statement of conscience" on "Black and Jewish Issues" included a section on the state of Israel. In keeping with a commitment to "dialogue with candor," the statement reported a fundamental disagreement between "most Jews" and "many Blacks" on the legitimacy of the PLO.

While most Jews disagree, many blacks believe that dialogue between the PLO and the Israeli Government should take place. They view this as an avenue by which the PLO could be convinced to abrogate and renounce violence and terrorism. Such cessation would be a necessary first step toward recognition of Israel's sovereignty and right to exist by the PLO and concommitantly that Israel recognize that the Palestinian Arabs, as a part of an overall peace, are entitled to exercise the right of self-determination. Blacks believe firmly that each of these steps is necessary for a just settlement of this Middle East question.[9]

Occasionally, Afro-American political groups have condemned Zionism and the Jewish state as evils in themselves. This aberrant attitude was adopted by the Student Non-Violent Coordinating Committee, an Afro-American nationalist organization, in 1967, and by the National Black Political Convention at Gary, Indiana, in 1972. The latter adopted a resolution in favor of action to "dismantle" Israel and deny her both economic and military aid. The vote on that resolution, ten years ago, marks the zenith of broadly based Afro-American hostility to a fundamental Jewish interest. It was quickly repudiated by the Congressional Black Caucus, the NAACP, and many leaders of Afro-American opinion. As finally published in the *National Black Political Agenda,* the resolution merely "condemned" Israel for her "expansionist policy" and occupation of Arab territory.

In addition to wide-ranging support for the cause of Palestinian nationhood, many blacks are particularly critical of Israel's growing cooperation with South Africa regardless of the justifications that have been advanced on Israel's behalf. During and immediately after the Yom Kippur War of 1973, twenty-one African states broke diplomatic relations with Israel. They did so in affirmation of their solidarity with Arab members of the Organization of African Unity and with the expectation of financial aid from the Organization of Arab Petroleum Exporting Countries to ease the burden of a sudden fourfold increase in the price of oil.[10] This proved to be a false hope; meanwhile Israel and South Africa exchanged ambassadors for the first time in their histories as independent states. In 1975, Israel agreed to sell military equipment to South Africa; economic and military relations between the two countries were expanded significantly after Prime Minister B. J. Vorster of South Africa visited Israel in April 1976. Although Israel has been singled out by antiapartheid groups for disproportionate criticism, the turnabout in her policy toward South Africa since the Yom Kippur War is undeniable. It is also antithetical to the interest of Afro-Americans in African liberation.

Hence, devoted friends of Israel in the Afro-American community have joined the chorus of critical voices. For example, in August 1976, Bayard Rustin, director of Black Americans to Support Israel Committee, wrote Rabbi Arthur Hertzberg, then president of the American Jewish Congress, "to express a deep sense of concern and disturbance

about the recent visit to Israel by Prime Minister Vorster of South
Africa and the plans to expand commercial and other relations between
the two countries." He continued:

> Not only I but every friend of Israel in the Black community was
> chagrined by this news. Our support of Israel has been based not
> merely on pragmatic considerations nor even on what we may con-
> ceive to be the best national interests of our country but rather on
> moral concerns, on our historic and deep sense of solidarity with the
> Jewish people and our appreciation of the State of Israel as a pro-
> gressive and democratic society.[11]

Rabbi Hertzberg's reply began with these words of personal tor-
ment:

> I daresay there was not a thinking, sensitive Jew in the world whose
> heart did not sink at the news of the visit of South Africa's Prime
> Minister Vorster to Israel, a society dedicated to the salvage of hu-
> man life and the pursuit of human values.

He then reported, on the basis of a recent visit to Israel, the universal feeling of aversion for apartheid by political and intellectual leaders
there. But, in Israel's defense, he cited her "virtual isolation in the
world" since 1973, "when most of Black Africa broke diplomatic relations and commercial ties with Israel." Moreover, he noted, many
states, including a substantial number of Black African states, have
been expanding their economic and commercial ties with South Africa.

> Stronger states than Israel continue to have dealings with countries
> with whom they disagree profoundly. The repressive ideology and
> cruel behavior of many of these nations are little less hideous than
> South Africa's. Let us not ask of Israel what we do not ask of the
> countries of Black Africa and the rest of the world. There can be no
> double standard in judging the behavior of nations; there cannot be
> one rule for the great and powerful and another for the small and
> weak.[12]

Rustin's criticism of Israel was strictly moral. Hertzberg's defense
shifted the ground from morality to *realpolitik* (national interest nar-
rowly conceived from an Israeli point of view). However justifiable this
line of defense may (or may not) be from a Jewish and Israeli standpoint (it would surely be questioned by Jews who believe that Israel
should set a high moral standard of political conduct), it is essentially
irrelevant and unpersuasive from an Afro-American and African standpoint. Jews cannot expect Afro-Americans to tolerate support for
white supremacy in Africa for the sake of Israel's security and well-
being. Jews should acknowledge the cogency and validity of this criticism of Israel by Afro-Americans. Its validity does not diminish when

it is voiced by Afro-Americans who are less sympathetic to Israel than Bayard Rustin.

I turn to conflicts that arise from Jewish interests in Africa. In the United States, many Jewish individuals have been involved in cultural, economic, and educational relations with Africa and Africans. The academic careers of numerous American Jewish scholars, like me, have been reared upon their contributions to African Studies. Disproportionate (I use this word in a statistical sense only, without moral connotation) Jewish prominence in African Studies is a temporary condition; it is attributable, I think, to these two causes: first, the prominence of Jewish scholars in American social science after the Second World War. Many of them sensed that the time had come to create human and social sciences on a truly universal basis. They responded with alacrity to the methodological and scientific challenges that bold thinkers encountered on the frontiers of social research in the newly developing countries. Second, African Studies attracted idealistic American scholars, who viewed their research as a contribution to racial liberation. Since racial domination is based upon ignorance and prejudice, racial liberation, they believed, would surely be promoted by science and knowledge.

Jewish scholars in the postwar world of African Studies took pride in Israel's contribution to African development. The Israeli labor movement and its political representatives had long supported the movement for colonial freedom in Africa. In turn, Africans were inclined to regard Israel as a shining example of national achievement by a liberated people in a poor country. They were anxious to benefit from Israeli technical assistance in many fields; Israel responded to that desire with enthusiasm by establishing successful projects in many African countries and by subsidizing programs for African students and trainees in Israel.

Israel's influence in Africa declined during the mid-1960s as a result of pro-Palestinian pressures in Northern and Southern Africa. In Southern Africa, the principal African liberation movements are socialist revolutionary movements with pronounced Marxist-Leninist tendencies; nearly all of them have been and remain aligned with the Soviet Union or (until recently) China in world politics. A great patron ensures the supply of arms, the provision of military training, and the steady flow of financial assistance. The leaders and representatives of these movements are widely respected throughout Africa; their views are influential and do reinforce the tendency of numerous African governments to side with the Palestinian Arab cause against Israel. In other words, they work for a cause that is not their own both as a matter of practical necessity and in defence to liberationist solidarity.

Moreover, the most influential liberationist doctrines today link Israel with South Africa as "outposts" of monopoly capitalism. These doctrines teach that the struggle against racial oppression cannot be separated from the struggle against capitalist imperialism. Hence they minimize the deep antagonism between Afrikaner nationalism and pragmatic capitalism within South Africa; and they underestimate the disposition of major capitalist powers to press for racial justice and social reform in South Africa as an alternative to social revolution. Those who contend that capitalism, imperialism, and racism constitute a unified enemy, which must be combated all at once, severely restrict their own political vision and strategic options. Simplistic or not, their beliefs do find Israel guilty by association, since she, like South Africa, has close political ties with the United States.

Among the black liberationist organizations in Southern Africa, including the parties that have gained power in Angola, Mozambique, and Zimbabwe, the African National Congress of South Africa is particularly hostile to Israel. That organization is firmly allied with the South African Communist party, which is well known for its emphatic pro-Soviet orientation. In the words of a recent study by authors with impeccable revolutionary and socialist credentials:

> Of course, the precise nature of the link between these two bodies [the African National Congress and the South African Communist party] is not known outside fairly narrow circles, but it is close. Nor, in exile, has the SACP been one of the more "open" and independent of Communist parties; any revolutionary socialist who is not greatly enamored of Soviet definitions of reality must experience a certain unease in reading the SACP's *African Communist,* for example, or indeed in reading some of the ANC's own publications.[13]

During the latter 1960s and early 1970s, ANC publications, notably the official Party organ, *Sechaba,* charged that the racial policies of Israel and South Africa are essentially similar. That propaganda line achieved an infamous success in November 1975, when twenty-eight African states voted for the UN General Assembly's condemnation of Zionism "as a form of racism." Only five African countries (Central African Republic, Ivory Coast, Liberia, Malawi, and Swaziland) voted against the resolution while twelve abstained. By this time, many Jews had concluded that black nationalists in Africa and America were inveterately hostile to Jewish nationalism and its cherished manifestation in Israel.

No serious discussion of Afro-American-Jewish relations in the sphere of American foreign policy can overlook Afro-American and Jewish views of the Soviet Union's role in the movement for black liberation in Southern Africa. In the absence of survey research data, my observations are bound to be impressionistic. Doubtless, in the current era, most Jews regard the Soviet Union as the main threat to Jewish culture and Israeli survival. By contrast, Afro-Americans know that the Soviet Union supports the African National Congress of South Africa and other revolutionary liberationist groups materially and without equivocation. Black American responses to Soviet support of the armed struggle for African liberation are distributed over a wide spectrum of opinion. At one extreme, Afro-Americans associated with the conservative American-African Affairs Association, founded by William Rusher and Max Yergan, oppose socialist revolution in Southern Africa at any cost; at the other extreme, black Leninists affirm the identity of African and Soviet goals. The vast majority of blacks adopt intermediate positions that include these attitudes: that black liberationist movements are motivated by nationalism, not communism; that such movements would never be subservient to a non-African communist patron; that the struggle against white racial domination takes priority over all other ideological considerations. These beliefs underlie the statement on this subject in the 1976 "African-American Manifesto on Southern Africa."

A people's quest for freedom is a driving, unyielding force. Freedom and self-determination are objectives that have always been obtrained by whatever means necessary. To suggest that nationalists are motivated by communism, or that those who achieve independence through the assistance of socialist countries will perforce become communist sattelite states, is to ignore African political history. African nationalists have not and will not give up colonial domination for communist domination. The issue is not the choice between democracy and communism, but rather the authority and power to decide for oneself a preferred system of government. . . . It is false to portray the incumbent South African and Rhodesian governments as bulwarks against communism, for it is their very existence that forces Africans to struggle to end their oppression, and in face of racist intransigence, to seek allies from responsive governments without regard to ideological persuasion.[14]

As this statement indicates, blacks everywhere will support effective black liberation movements regardless of their personal ideological preferences, much as Jews everywhere once supported socialist Zionism regardless of their personal ideological preferences. Unfortunately, Jewish understanding of and respect for this black attitude will not dissolve the objective conflict between Afro-Americans and those Jews who stand up to the enemies of Israel. Such Jews may seek to support black liberation groups that neither condemn Israel nor endorse the Soviet line in world politics. And such groups do exist in South Africa; but their prospects for success are minimized by conditions beyond Jewish or Israeli control, chiefly the South African government's refusal to end white domination. If South African whites would join with blacks to establish a free society based upon principles of racial equality, Jews who demand fair play for Israel would not be estranged from black nationalists in South Africa. But the policies of the South African government drive the forces of African nationalism into the violent channels of armed struggle and increasing reliance upon Soviet support. This reality should be faced by Afro-Americans and Jews in the United States; it has poisoned the well of Afro-American–Jewish relationships.

One incidental and minor consequence of the real divergence of interest between Afro-Americans and Jews in the field of foreign policy is the unmistakable decline of Jewish involvement in African Studies. For several years, I have had the impression that few Jews enroll in my African Studies courses, especially graduate courses where professional interests are evinced. Doubtless other explanations, such as the constriction of the academic job market, are equally pertinent. However, the era of the Left-cosmopolitan Jewish intellectual is over and relatively few Jews mourn its passing. Yet the dilution of Jewish names in African Studies will not result in academic symmetry between the Afro-American and Jewish communities because it will not be balanced by a proportionate Afro-American presence in Jewish studies. Africa is a continent; Africans comprise a major section of humanity; African studies will be pursued by scholars in all parts of the world. Israel is a speck of land; Jews are a small people, a tribe that knows unending strife and imposes itself on world history in every generation.

The Assertion of Interests

Let us recapitulate and systematize the interests of Afro-Americans in the Middle East and Jews in Africa. Although neither group has a strong primary interest of its own in the "other" region, a few such interests in the survival and freedom of blacks in the Middle East and Jews in Africa can be identified. Blacks are alert to reports of official discrimination against the small community of black Hebrews and other blacks in Israel. In addition, Afro-American members of Muslim congregations in the United States may be expected to identify with their coreligionists in conflicts between Muslims and other religious communities in the Middle East.

On the Jewish side, the persecution of Falashas, or black Jews of Ethiopia, since the seizure of power by revolutionaries has occasioned bitter exchanges between an American Association for Ethiopian Jews and the advocates of "quiet diplomacy" in both Israel and the United States. The Falashas, of whom there are an estimated twenty-eight thousand in Ethiopia and fourteen hundred in Israel, have been recognized as Jews under the Israeli "Law of Return" since 1975. In an entirely different context, some Jews view the Jewish presence in South Africa with disquiet. Concerned American Jews have urged the South African Jews, who number some one hundred twenty thousand, to emigrate. However, many progressive Jews in South Africa believe it is their duty to stay put and work for racial equality in the country of their birth.

The secondary interests of each group in the "other" region are by far more consequential to their relations with one another. Afro-Americans deplore Israeli ties with South Africa and support the principle of self-determination for Palestinians, while Jews decry African condemnations of Zionism and the alignment of African liberation groups with Soviet foreign policies. In addition to these "principled" secondary interests, the members of each group also have material and financial interests in the "other" region that should not be overlooked. A few Afro-American leaders, notably the Reverend Jesse Jackson, anticipate financial assistance from Arab donors in return for their political support of the Palestinian cause. Similarly, on the Jewish side, the financial interests of certain businessmen coincide with their opposition to communist influence in Africa.

The severity of conflict between Afro-Americans and Jewish Americans in the field of foreign policy depends upon the matter in which their respective foreign interests are asserted. Two alternative models for the assertion of interest may be perceived in the instances of Afro-American initiative by Rustin, Bradley, Jackson, and Lowery-Fauntroy (SCLC) to which I have referred. Thus, in 1976, Bayard Rustin sought to enlist Jewish support for his disapproval of Israel's growing relationship with South Africa. In addition to his role as director of the Black Americans to Support Israel Committee, Rustin was (and is) executive director of the A. Philip Randolph Institute, a center for social thought. His letter to Rabbi Arthur Hertzberg, president of the American Jewish Congress affirmed "our historic and deep sense of solidarity with the Jewish people" and referred to the alliance between Afro-American and Jewish organizations in the struggle for civil rights in America. The power of this appeal should not be underestimated. Whatever their differences, Jewish and Afro-American intellectuals are apt to remind one another for some time to come that they alone, among all the peoples of the world, were stigmatized in the racial theory of the Nazis as "culture-destroying" races. There is a firm moral foundation for the Afro-American–Jewish alliance, or Rustin model of interest assertion. But it has thus far failed to mobilize organized Jewry for a combined black-Jewish effort to halt Israel's rapprochement with South Africa.

For example, we have seen that in 1979, Los Angeles Mayor Tom Bradley and his associates activated an old Afro-American-Jewish "coalition" to ponder a range of problems in the relationship between these two communities. The resulting "Joint Statement" of November 29, 1979, conspicuously omitted any mention of Israel's relationship with South Africa. I have learned that this issue was dropped because the participants could not formulate a mutually acceptable statement of their *disagreements,* as they had been able to do for the vexing question of PLO participation in the Middle East peace process. The Los Angeles dialogue was an event of national significance in Afro-American-Jewish relations because the participants included persons of national stature and both sides conferred regularly with their counterparts in other cities and at the national level. In view of Mayor Bradley's strong affirmation of the historic bond between Afro-Americans and Jews, and his personal commitment to a Afro-American-Jewish dialogue, I shall henceforth refer to a Rustin/Bradley model of interest assertion.

An alternative to the Rustin/Bradley model emerged with the Jackson and Lowery missions to the Middle East. This initiative was roundly condemned in Jewish circles as an assault upon Jewish interests, although some Jews would surely agree with Jackson and Lowery that black interlocutors who oppose terrorism and defend Israel's right to exist should be appreciated by Jews.

In fact, the Jackson/Lowery model of interest assertion in the Middle East had been anticipated by a Jewish organization for its own purposes in Africa. In 1978, the American Jewish Committee inaugurated a program of seminars, conferences, and informal meetings for "Jewish and African intellectuals and diplomats" intended to improve "Jewish-African and Israeli-African relations."[15] In the letter that I received, there was no mention of Afro-American intellectuals and diplomats or Afro-American organizations.

The most dramatic example of Jewish organizational diplomacy in Africa must be the meeting of 4 December 1981 in New York, convened by Maxwell E. Greenberg, National Chairman of the Anti-Defamation League of B'nai B'rith, between President Mobutu Sese Seko of Zaire and the representatives of four major American Jewish organizations, namely, the American Jewish Committee, the American Jewish Congress, the American-Israeli Public Affairs Committee, and the Anti-Defamation League.[16] Mobutu had previously expressed his intent to resume diplomatic relations with Israel in concert with the leaders of a few other African governments. This venture in private diplomacy would hardly endear the Jewish organizations to Afro-Americans who are informed about African affairs. It is just as unpopular in Afro-American circles as were the Jackson/Lowery missions in

Jewish circles. Mobutu's regime is an autocratic dictatorship. In office, Mobutu has accumulated an immense personal fortune. His overthrow would be greeted with joy by most black scholars, who must wonder what he wanted and received in return for his gesture toward Israel. They may also wonder what benefits may accrue to businessmen who are associated with the Jewish organizations. As in the case of the Jackson/Lowery mission, Greenberg's diplomacy may be misrepresented and underappreciated by those who regret its occurrence. But intergroup resentment is an invariable by-product of the Jackson/ Lowery/Greenberg model of interest assertion.

Just as the Jackson/Lowery model has its Jewish counterpart, so too is the Rustin/Bradley alliance model attractive to Jews. The best example of a de facto Afro-American-Jewish alliance in foreign policy may be found in the Congress of the United States. The foremost Jewish proponent of this alliance is probably Representative Stephen J. Solarz (D-N.Y.), who represents the largest Jewish electorate for the House of Representatives in the United States. A member of the House Foreign Affairs Committee since his election to Congress in 1974, Solarz is reputed to be the most effective proponent of Israeli interests in the House. He is also a member of the Subcommittee on Africa, having served as its chairman during the ninety-sixth (1979–80) Congress. He has earned the respect and trust of his Afro-American colleagues for his knowledge of African affairs and his dedication to African interests. In 1979, he persuaded the entire Foreign Affairs Committee to support a bill that allowed President Carter to refrain from lifting sanctions against Rhodesia before the conclusion of a negotiated settlement of the war in that country. This approach prevailed in the face of powerful opposition in both the House and the Senate. It was a major contribution to the emergence of Zimbabwe as an independent country with a popular and universally recognized government.

In 1978, Solarz proposed legislation to prohibit both new investments, including bank loans, in South Africa by American citizens and unfair labor practices by American companies in that country. His current bill on this subject would prohibit bank loans by American financial and lending institutions to the South African Government and its parasitical agencies; it would also prohibit the importation of South African gold coins for sale in the United States, and require Americans who control enterprises in South Africa to comply with an enforceable code of fair employment practices. This bill is co-sponsored by seven members of the Congressional Black Caucus, although the Caucus, itself, prefers legislative action that would also prohibit new investments and require the withdrawal of existing investments. Solarz agrees with the moral rationale for that approach, but he contends that it is not politically feasible at the present time. He defends his own proposal on the ground that it is more realistic and would, if enacted, have a considerable impact on South Africa.[17]

Jewish support for black interests abroad in the House of Representatives is reciprocated by the congressional Black Caucus. For example, in October 1981, eighteen of the nineteen Afro-American members of Congress voted against the sale of AWACS surveillance aircraft to Saudi Arabia; the sole exception did not vote. As Solarz has observed, "By and large, the Blacks strongly support Israel, and the Jews strongly support the Black position on Africa."[18] In American politics, vote trading is known as *logrolling*. In foreign policy, Afro-American and Jewish members of Congress are mutually engaged in ethnic logrolling. Good relations emanate from the Rustin/Bradley/Solarz alliance/logrolling model of interest assertion. Conceivably, the congressional allies will be able to accomplish more than their organizational counterparts in coping with the bitter conflicts of secondary interest between Afro-Americans and Jews abroad. Yet the mood for Afro-American–Jewish legislative logrolling is likely to be dissipated by the persistence of intercommunity wrangling.

Beyond Logrolling

In the United States, Afro-Americans and Jews have often joined forces to combat racial and religious discrimination. The Rustin/Bradley/Solarz alliance/logrolling model of interest assertion presupposes the existence of a special relationship between Afro-Americans and Jews. For many members of both groups, the alliance, rooted in common struggle, has sentimental as well as practical value. However, a growing number of Afro-Americans and Jews question the value of this partnership and criticize its restrictive effects. For example, Robert S. Browne, director of the Black Economic Research Council and a critic of Afro-American congressional support for military aid to Israel, has wondered whether "black leadership is so intimidated by its ties to the Jewish community that it cannot articulate positions which might collide with Jewish aspirations."[19] Afro-Americans who take this stand, like Jews who cry "halt" to affirmative-action programs, are damned for their ingratitude and betrayal of the common cause.

The Jackson/Lowery/Greenberg self-interest model has unloaded a lot of sentimental baggage in order to maximize freedom of action. This model does not dispense with the practice of ethnic logrolling. (Henceforth, I shall use this term expansively to signify, not merely legislative vote trading, but all types of reciprocal support by political groups.) On the contrary, it frees each group to choose among numerous potential logrolling partners. Hence Jackson's switch from Jews to Arabs may be matched by a Jewish switch from Afro-Americans to white Southern Baptists, and so forth. This strategy will appeal to many ethnic politicians. It frees them to follow the course of ethnic and religious self-interest. From this standpoint, cultural nationalities have no strictly moral obligations to one another. The strength and weakness of this strategy, its allure and moral inadequacy, are limned in Rabbi Hillel's famous saying two thousand years ago:

> If I am not for myself, who is for me?
> And if I am for myself alone, what then am I?

The Jackson/Lowery/Greenberg model has gained favor because Afro-Americans and Jews have obviously tired of their special relationship. It has become a burden that ethnic politicians and their community organizations are no longer willing to bear. In the field of foreign affairs, many blacks are inclined to criticize Israeli policies while many Jews are distressed by African expressions of support for the isolation and destruction of Israel. Neither blacks nor Jews should expect members of the other group to forbear from criticism of one another's foreign friends.

Individual Afro-Americans and Jews are highly critical of African policies on the one hand and Israeli policies on the other. However, the sternest critics of their ethnic brethren abroad are likely to defend the primary interests of their communities in Africa and the Middle East. With few exceptions, Afro-Americans firmly support the liberation movement in South Africa and the right of all African states to choose their own forms of political and economic organization. Similarly, Jews, with few exceptions, seek to ensure the survival, enhance the security, and promote the well-being of Israel. These primary interests can be pursued effectively without resort to ethnic alliances or logrolling. They coincide with the measure of understanding, respect, and support that each cultural nationality owes to all cultural nationalities without exception. Blacks and Jews as individuals can and should support one another on these vital matters of ethnic and religious group obligation without logrolling or the expectation of reciprocal special favors or ethnic preference.

In a multicultural and multinational society, such as the United States of America, each group should respect the commitments of all groups to defend the vital interests—survival, freedom, and well-being—of their cultural kin-groups abroad. Afro-Americans and Jews can and should expect no more, or less, from one another than they expect from any other group. Afro-Americans cannot expect Jews to support organizations, like the African National Congress of South Africa, which anathematize Zionism as a racist "enemy . . . of mankind."[20] They can, on moral grounds, expect Jews and Americans of all ethnic and religious backgrounds to oppose American actions and policies that tend to perpetuate white supremacy in South Africa. The Jewish opponent of American bank loans to South Africa should not be expected to support African nationalist organizations that defame Israel. Some Jews do support such organizations for various reasons of their own; but their commitment to racial liberation and brotherhood is no greater than that of Jews who insist upon equal treatment for Jewish nationalism.

Jews and Jewish organizations adopt positions on many facets of American foreign policy toward the Middle East. These positions do not necessitate special relations with the Afro-Amerian community. Jews can ask Afro-American and everyone else to support fair play for Israel. Blacks fulfill their obligation to their Jewish compatriots when they show an equal measure of respect for the national rights and freedom of Arabs and Jews in the Middle East. They cannot be expected to side with Israel; nor could Jews honestly promise to give any more support for African interests than they should give in any case on humanistic grounds and in keeping with their own avowed principles.

Must we, then, conclude that the historic relationship between Afro-Americans and Jews in America has (or should have) little or no contemporary significance in foreign affairs? Not in my opinion. In the various conflicts between their respective interests abroad, Afro-Americans and Jews have discovered the outer limits of ethnic logrolling. This painful discovery may prove to be an important contribution to the theory and practice of American democracy.

The limit to logrolling between Afro-Americans and Jews in foreign policy is signaled by this unmistakable fact: neither group has been able to prevail upon the community organizations of the other group to criticize the policies of their foreign brethren. On the two occasions noted here, Afro-Americans with impeccable credentials of friendship for Israel, namely Rustin in New York and the Bradley group in Los Angeles, failed to persuade Jewish counterparts to either criticize or undertaken to change the policy of Israel toward South Africa. There are, to be sure, many individual Jews who, while they admire Israel, are nonetheless willing to raise their voices against specific Israeli policies. However, community organizations are led by ethnic politicians who usually represent an exaggerated version of the common sense of their respective groups. In these organizations, the principled views of independent intellectuals have little weight.

For good and ill, multinational America, with 5 percent of the world's population, has an immense impact upon the world at large. The contribution of every American nationality group to world history is measured by its influence on America's role in world affairs. Groups form coalitions and practice logrolling to extend their influence. In foreign affairs, however, ethnic alliances are subject to unbearable and disruptive strains. The only secure basis for interethnic collaboration in foreign affairs is the universal standard of equal respect for all nationality groups. In the pursuit of universal ends, intergroup solidarity is irrelevant; special relationships are inoperative; everything depends upon individual understanding, conviction, and commitment. America's vocation in the world is founded upon an individualistic creed. Afro-Americans and Jews have made that remarkable discovery.

Notes

I wish to thank Gary Remer and C. R. D. Halisi for their contributions to my thinking about this subject.

1. *Freedomways,* 7, no. 1 (Winter 1967): 78.
2. "Statement of the Southern Christian Leadership Conference following its Middle East Peace Initiative, Dr. Joseph E. Lowery, President, Honorable Walter E. Fauntroy, Chairman, Board of Directors, September 21, 1979," Appendix E of "Report of Honorable Walter E. Fauntroy . . . on the SCLC Fact-Finding Mission to Lebanon, September 17–21, 1979," reprinted from the *Congressional Record* (House of Representatives), 11 October 1979, and quoted in *Journal of Palestine Studies* 10, no. 2 (Winter 1981): 165.
3. Ronald W. Walters, "The Black Initiatives in the Middle East," *Journal of Palestine Studies* 10, no. 2 (Winter 1981): 3. Professor Walters has summarized the SCLC proposals and subsequent events.
4. Jake C. Miller, "Black Viewpoints on the Mid-East Conflict," *Journal of Palestine Studies* 10, no. 2 (Winter 1981): 43.
5. Walters, *Black Initiatives,* p. 4.
6. "Report of Honorable Walter E. Fauntroy . . . on the SCLC Fact-Finding Mission to Lebanon," p. 158.
7. Miller, *Black Viewpoints,* pp. 47–49; Henry Siegman, "The PLO Is Not the Real Black-Jewish Problem," *Congress Monthly* 46, no. 6 (September/October 1979): 3–4.
8. Press Release by the Mayor's Office, Los Angeles, 29 November 1979.
9. "Joint Statement on Black and Jewish Issues," Los Angeles, 29 November 1979.
10. Ethan A. Nadelmann, "Israel and Black Africa: a Rapprochement?", *The Journal of Modern African Studies* 19, no. 2 (June 1981): 207–11.
11. Bayard Rustin to Rabbi Arthur Hertzberg, 27 August 1976. (facsimile copy of letter).
12. Arthur Hertzberg to Bayard Rustin, 1 September 1976 (facsimile copy of letter).
13. John S. Saul and Stephen Gelb, *The Crisis in South Africa: Class Defense, Class Revolution* (New York: Monthly Review Press, 1981), p. 137; also Sheridan Johns, "Obstacles to Guerrilla Warfare—a South African Case Study," *The Journal of Modern African Studies* 11, no. 2 (June 1973): 299–300.
14. *Journal of Southern African Affairs* 1 (October 1976): 183–84.
15. Ronald Glassman to Richard L. Sklar, 8 March 1978.
16. *The Jerusalem Post,* International Edition, 13–19, December 1981.
17. *Congressional Record* (House of Representatives), 6 April 1981.
18. Quoted in Wolf Blitzer, "Blacks and Jews in Congress," *Hadassah Magazine* (April 1981).
19. Quoted in Bayard Rustin, "American Negroes and Israel," *The Crisis* 81, no. 4 (April 1974): 115.
20. Statement of the African National Congress of South Africa, July 1976, in Richard P. Stevens and Abdelwahab M. Elmessiri, *Israel and South Africa* (New York: New World Press, 1976), pp. 162–64.

The Fallacies of Pragmatism: Israeli Foreign Policy Toward South Africa

Naomi Chazan

The Paradox of Israel's South African Connection

Few other topics in Israeli foreign policy have been subjected to such intense scrutiny and heated debate as its burgeoning relations with the Republic of South Africa. During the past decade, Israel and South Africa have developed an intricate web of interactions on a variety of levels. The evolution of this relationship has proceeded at a rapid pace and in the most demonstrative of manners. In effect, Israel has appeared to relinquish the cause of liberation in Southern Africa at precisely the same time as an international consensus has coalesced on the obsolence of white domination in that area.

Rhetoric on this topic, not surprisingly, abounds. Israel's detractors have pointed an accusing finger at an alliance that to them furnishes ultimate proof of the illegitimacy and nefarious predilections of the Jewish state. Israel's friends are constantly embarrassed by a move that runs against their most ingrained principles. In response, Israel's defenders appeal to the logic of national interest, detail the extent of duplicity of its attackers, and decry the double standards of morality in international politics. The emotional tone and the vitriolic nature of these exchanges have tended to obscure the substance of the subject matter and to deflect attention from the main issues involved.

From an Israeli perspective, the South African link has engulfed policymakers in a twofold paradox. First, an enormous gulf exists between Israel's declared position against apartheid and the continuation of ties with South Africa. Israel's consistent antiapartheid stance is by no means mere posturing. Judaism condemns the immorality of racism. Jewish history is littered with instances of anti-Semitism and racial persecution. The state of Israel was established in the aftermath of the most horrifying genocide. As Israel's delegate to the United Nations Committee of Human Rights declared: "Israel's opposition to the concept and practices of apartheid has been repeatedly voiced in the United Nations. I wish to reaffirm this position. Its roots are found in Jewish history and in the Jewish faith."[1] It has become increasingly difficult for Israelis to reconcile their antipathy to any overt manifestation of racism with their collaboration with South Africa.

The second aspect of the Israeli dilemma centers on the contradiction between the persual of the South African connection and the damage that this has wrought. Unquestionably, the spotlight focused on this topic has harmed Israel in a multiplicity of ways. In international forums Israel has experienced condemnation and increased isolation because of its contacts with South Africa. This process commenced with the juxtaposition of Zionism and racism by the United Nations in November 1975.[2] Since then Israel has been berated repeatedly in UN organs for its choice of allies.[3] The extent of the isolation of Israel in international gatherings was driven home most dramatically in the General Assembly's recent decision to impose sanctions on the country. Although Israel's gradual ostracization from the world community can hardly be attributed solely to its South African ties, these have furnished an all too convenient pretense for the expression of anti-Israeli sentiment.

Israel's bilateral relations have also been adversely affected by this connection. African states have frequently utilized this link not only to excuse their reluctance to reestablish diplomatic relations with Israel, but, more pertinently, to publicly expound on the difficulties inherent in their joint efforts to attain concerted action against the South African regime.[4] The Soviet bloc and the Arab world, predictably, have pounced on this alliance as further evidence of Israeli imperialism.[5] Even Israel's traditional partners in Western Europe have voiced dismay and discomfort over Israel's close ties with the white regime.[6] In the United States criticism has come both from official circles, and from leaders of the American Jewish community.[7] The South African relationship has further marred the atmosphere of Afro-American-Jewish interactions, and caused severe stress in the ties between these two communities.[8]

The ramifications of the South African enterprise have therefore exposed Israel to public wrath. This association has tarnished the Iraeli image abroad, and despite attempts to minimize the backlash, it has strengthened the hands of those who have tried to establish the existence of a Tel-Aviv-Pretoria-Taipei axis.[9] Attribution of membership in an international club of pariah states is hardly comforting. Israeli policymakers are now confronting the need to balance the benefits accruing from the South African link against the palpable harm to Israel's global standing and credibility that it has unleashed.[10]

Given the very real hesitations stemming from the dual currents of Israel's South African paradox, the predominant question that arises revolves around the reasons for the persistence of this connection. If indeed, this link is so problematic, and even detrimental, why does it continue and expand? What underlies the progression of this relationship? The purpose of this analysis is to tackle the key components of this puzzle in an attempt to come to grips with the concrete issues surrounding the conduct of Israel's present foreign policy toward South Africa.

Specifically, this exploration will deal with three interrelated facets of the problem. First, it will briefly outline the dynamic of the Israeli political association with South Africa. Second, it will examine in depth some of the proferred reasons for this alliance, and suggest several alternative explanations. Third, it will evaluate the immediate and long-term repercussions of this association in order to assess the possibilities for change.

The main contention of this investigation is that Israel has become embroiled in an unequal relationship with ambiguous returns. The scope of exchanges, though diverse, is meager. The benefit Israel derives from these interchanges is unclear; in any event it is in no way commensurate to that reaped by the other partner in the equation. Thus, this analysis will attempt to demonstrate—popular myths notwithstanding—that this policy from an Israeli viewpoint makes very little sense indeed.

If, as this essay posits, Israel's South African connection has been maintained by a bewildering admixture of emotion, lack of knowledge, external machination, and inertia, then it might be possible to illuminate the ambivalence that surrounds its underpinnings and consequences. On this basis, it would not be too farfetched to suggest that the time might be ripe for a thorough revision of Israel's policies in Southern Africa.

The Political Backdrop

The evolution of Israel's relations with South Africa may be divided into four distinct phases.[11] The first stage commenced with the establishment of the state of Israel in 1948, and extended until 1961. During this period, which coincided with the consolidation of Afrikaner power in South Africa, Israel supported correct, albeit not overly cordial, contacts with South Africa. An Israeli legation was set up in Pretoria, and though South Africa was content to allow Britain to represent its interests in Israel, the foundations for diplomatic communication were laid down. Some exchanges of visitors did take place: Moshe Sharett, then foreign minister,[12] went to South Africa in 1951 at the behest of the Jewish community. South African Premier D. F. Malan came to Israel in 1953, the first head of state to make an official visit to the country. But beyond these formalities and the cementing of Israeli contacts with the South African Jewish community, these years were uneventful.

The second stage in Israeli–South African contacts covered the years between 1961 and 1967. In 1961 Israel joined an antiapartheid censure initiative in the United Nations. In 1962, this vote was repeated, and by 1963 Israel had withdrawn its diplomatic delegate to South Africa, unilaterally reducing its representation to a consular level. In keeping with its efforts to woo the new states of Black Africa, Israeli officials avoided any unnecessary association with the South African regime. These moves suggested that when Israel had a choice between Black Africa and South Africa, it opted unequivocally for the former.[13] The new direction in Israel's policy culminated in 1966, when Israel voted to relieve South Africa of its mandate over Namibia. During this phase, Israel's ties with South Africa cooled perceptibly. By 1967 real contacts had dwindled to a mere trickle.

Following the Six-Day War, a certain thawing was evident, at least from the South African side. South Africans praised Israel's military victory, and the South African government began to make overtures toward Israel. Between 1967 and 1973, a period of transition, efforts were made to reestablish trade and commercial contacts, and the South Africans set up a consulate in Tel-Aviv. Israel, for its part, responded only partially to these gestures. While the vigor with which it had pursued antiapartheid measures waned, Israel continued to back efforts to effect a change in Southern Africa. In 1971 the government offered a financial contribution to the Organization of African Unity's African Liberation Committee. Although this donation was rejected by the OAU, it led to an almost total break in Israel-South African relations.[14] Israel also resisted requests to upgrade its representation in South Africa. Gradually during these years, however, Israel's links with South Africa improved. And, as ties with Black African states became more precarious, this connection assumed a new prominence.

The events of 1973 constituted a turning point in Israeli-South African interactions. Three interrelated occurrences led to a drastic reversal of previous trends. First, the Yom Kippur War (which South Africa followed with more than casual interest[15]) severely shattered the equanimity that had characterized Israeli policies after 1967. Second, the Arab oil embargo altered the relations between Israel and the West, creating a breach in what had heretofore been the backbone of Israel's international support system. And third, by the end of 1973 all but four

African states had severed diplomatic relations with Israel.[16] This confluence of upheavals, by rendering Israel exposed in the international arena, laid the groundwork for the launching of the fourth, and ongoing phase in Israeli–South African relations.

In early 1974, the Israeli government decided to reinstate its diplomatic representation in South Africa. Mr. Yitzhak Unna, then consul general, was appointed Israel's ambassador to Pretoria. In that year, senior Israeli officials (including Moshe Dayan and Haim Herzog) visited South Africa and held talks with South African leaders. The then minister of information, Dr. Connie Mulder, came to Israel. Trade relations between the two countries took on a new impetus. By 1975 the Israeli-South African link had begun to solidify. Following the anti-Zionist resolution in November, South Africa appointed its first ambassador to Israel, Dr. Charles Fincham. In April 1976, Prime Minister Rabin treated Prime Minister B. J. Vorster to an official state visit, indicating that Israel was now willing to reciprocate the South African initiatives of previous years.[17] At the end of this demonstrative tour, Israel and South Africa concluded a comprehensive pact that covered a range of commercial, trade, cooperative, fiscal, and, in all probability, military spheres. A joint ministerial committee, slated to meet at least once a year, was created to oversee the implementation of the pact.[18] The Vorster visit in effect drew Israel and South Africa into a complex network of mutual collaboration.

In 1976 Israel absented itself from antiapartheid votes at the UN.[19] And although cooperative ventures developed apace, Israel made attempts to downplay the South African connection and forbade ministerial visits to South Africa. Thus, when the Likud coalition under the leadership of Menahem Begin came to power, South African government circles expressed satisfaction with the selection of the new premier (who had visited South Africa and was the chairman of the Israel–South Africa Friendship Society).[20]

The Likud government has not exhibited the same unease with the South African association that characterized key figures in the Labor party leadership.[21] The South African minister for foreign affairs, R. F. Botha, visited Israel shortly after the political changeover and reaffirmed South Africa's support for Israel. The flow of official and unofficial exchanges since then has grown, and by early 1982 interaction on all levels reached an all-time high.[22]

The pattern of the progression of South African political relations with Israel over the past thirty-four years has vacillated significantly. Since 1967, however, with minor gyrations, what had been a casual encounter blossomed into a full-grown relationship. The intensity and rapidity with which this connection has been nourished requires more systematic explanation.

The Balance Sheet of Israeli Interests in South Africa

The reasons forwarded for the proliferation of Israel's South African connection in recent years rest on considerations of pragmatic self-interest. Although no public acknowledgment has been forthcoming, the underlying assumption of participants and observers alike has been that compromises on moral issues have been made in the name of more tangible concerns. It is therefore necessary to examine with some care precisely what interests are actually being furthered by this alliance, at what price, and to what end.

The Jewish Interest

The first Israeli national interest ostensibly served by the South African connection relates to the well-being of South Africa's Jewish population. Since the inception of the state a major leitmotiv of Israeli foreign policy has been its concern for world Jewry. Israeli leaders have viewed the South African Jewish community as a unique instance of the application of this guide rule.

The South African Jewish community, which numbers 117,099 in the 1970 census (3 percent of the white population) is extremely homogeneous and highly structured. The bulk of Jews are of Lithuanian extraction. Since the main influx in the late nineteenth century, South African Jews have been constantly caught between their Jewishness and their whiteness. A minority within a rigidly structured ruling minority, the economically secure Jewish community's response to their dilemma has been to organize around two guiding institutions: the South African Jewish Board of Deputies and the South African Zionist Federation.

Although this is hardly the place to detail the history of South Africa's Jews, three themes of this experience are pertinent.[23] The first strain in Jewish life in South Africa has been anti-Semitism. Even before the establishment of the Republic in 1910, Jews were systematically excluded from the mainstream of white society in the country. In the 1930s and 1940s, the Ossewabrandurag and the greyshirts used scare tactics against Jews. Segments of the Afrikaner leadership, avowedly racist and anti-Semitic, supported the limitation of Jewish immigration to South Africa in 1937, and spent the better part of the war in internment camps because of their Nazi sympathies. The National Party lifted its anti-Jewish ban only in 1954. The recurrence of anti-Semitic outbreaks persist to this day.[24] A second, and interrelated current of the South African Jewish fabric concerns its position vis-à-vis the dominant sociopolitical ethos of apartheid. Until recently, South Africa's Jewish leadership has systematically abstained from

provoking the ruling oligarchy. Individual Jews, however, have not
only served at the forefront of the antiapartheid struggle, but have been
vocal in their attacks on the quiescence and acquiescence of their
Jewish cohorts.[25] "If it is thus correct to say that many white liberals
and radicals were Jews, it is equally correct that not many Jews were
liberals and radicals."[26] In this context, Zionism, the third component
of the South African Jewish triangle, has served as both a prop and an
escape from the realities of Jewish existence in the country. Contacts
with the Zionist movement and Israel have constituted a prominent
dimension of Jewish life. The Zionist movement in South Africa repli-
cated party divisions within Israel, and links (on a personal, communal, normative, and financial basis) have been consistently close
throughout the years. This association has exposed South African Jews
to charges of dual loyalty at the same time as it furnished an important
outlet from the dilemma of being a Jew in contemporary South Africa.

The direct links between Israel and the Jews of South Africa have
followed several concurrent paths. First, and perhaps foremost, South
African Jews have contributed to Israel more per capita than any other
Jewish community in the world. This transfer of funds has been
facilitated by the government's agreement to permit the transit of Jewish funds to Israel despite strict restrictions on the exportation of
capital. While individual donations from South Africa are high, the
absolute quantity of monies received from South Africa falls far below
that of the much larger Jewish communities of the United States, Britain, France, and Canada, and its impact on Israel should not be exaggerated.[27] Nevertheless, the fund-raising activities of the Israel United
Appeal are an integral element of the annual calendar of South African
Jewry. These have provided for a steady flow of Israeli dignitaries to
South Africa, and of South African Jewish missions to Israel.[28]

South African Jews also maintain contact with Israel through ties
with immigrants from South Africa. Such prominent politicians and
diplomats as Abba Eban, Michael Comay, Shmuel Katz, and the late
Louis Pincus are of South African extraction. South African students
in Israel have frequently settled in the country, and the Zionist federation continues to encourage Aliyah (immigration) to Israel. Once again,
however, the magnitude of this personal link need not be overdrawn.
Since the establishment of Israel, twelve thousand South African Jews
have settled in the state, far less than the South African Jewish diaspora in London or Toronto. Moreover, the number of Israelis currently
residing in South Africa, estimated at twenty thousand, outnumbers
the total of Jews who have migrated to Israel.[29]

Alongside these ties, religious interchanges have flourished. Especially in thd 1970s the Jewish community in South Africa has looked
toward Israel's religious establishment for spiritual sustenance and

practical support. Israel supplies many Jewish educators and rabbis, and Israel's religious leaders have made frequent trips to the country. More recently, the political dimension of links has expanded, since the Likud government in Israel developed particularly close relations with the revisionist Herut faction that has dominated the South African Zionist Federation since the early 1970s.[30] Approval of these multifaceted links was granted by Prime Minister Botha, who stated that the special relationship with the Jewish state "has no bearing on the loyalty which I know our Jewish citizens hold for South Africa."[31]

That the links between South Africa's Jews and Israel are exceedingly close cannot be denied; what can be questioned is the degree to which Israel's affinity with and concern for South African Jews is forwarded by its growing relationship with the Republic of South Africa. The answer is far from clear-cut. In the first instance, Israel's collaboration with South Africa has hardly ameliorated some of the internal dilemmas of South African Jewry. Examples of continuous anti-Semitism have not abated.[32] The highest officials of the South African government continue to berate Jews for their dual identities.[33] And internal squabbles on the nature of the Jewish path have not been resolved in the wake of this tie. Second, and more puzzling, has been the tangible reduction in Zionist fervor in South Africa since the mid-1970s. The number of immigrants has dwindled, interest in Israel has lessened, and Zionist activities attract fewer supporters.[34] Third, and most problematically, Israel's links with South Africa have gained momentum at exactly the same time as South Africa's Jewish community has announced its commitment to the abolition of apartheid.[35] This renewal of the social justice role of South Africa's organized Jewry stands in blatant dissonance with Israel's collaboration with South Africa.

Even if, as some observers maintain, the South-African–Israeli link nevertheless provides Jews in that country with a short-term security blanket,[36] the long-term effects on the well-being of South African Jews are debatable. Were Israeli policymakers as truly interested in the future of South African Jews as they maintain, they would display a much greater sensitivity to the tides of change in South Africa and to the need to better define the Jewish place within this transformation. No such forward looking awareness is presently apparent. In this context, the claim that Israel's concern for South Africa's Jews justifies the improvement of relations with South Africa can hardly be supported either empirically or logically.

The feebleness of the Jewish argument is further corroborated by the fact that Israeli foreign policy has not been subservient to the sensitivities of the Jewish diaspora when other considerations have intruded.[37] Israel has not supported the Soviet Union because of its large and subjugated Jewish community. Recent moves vis-à-vis the United States have surely given little succor to American Jews. More to the point, Israel in the past took strongly antiapartheid positions in the name not only of morality and Israeli interests, but also of oppressed Jewish communities elsewhere.[38]

The suggestion that Israel's present policy in Southern Africa is an outgrowth of its Jewish concerns is not borne out under close investigation. Furthermore, this proposition has little explanatory value in understanding the reasons for Israel's recent rapprochement with South Africa.

The Economic Interest

A second interest-bound set of arguments for Israel's present South African policy highlights economic matters. The implicit assumption behind this category of reasons is that official contact can be shown to promote the Israeli economy. Verification of this justification rests partly on an assessment of the profitability of Israel's material exchanges with South Africa.

Israeli–South African economic links have mushroomed during the past decade. The substance of cooperation in trade and investment has been ironed out in a series of agreements reached between the two countries since the 1976 Rabin-Vorster pact. The nature and direction of economic contacts is supervised by the minister and senior officials of the economic and finance ministries of the respective countries, who have exchanged visits frequently since 1975.[39] Two organizations, the Tel-Aviv based Israel–South Africa Chamber of Commerce and the Johannesburg based South Africa–Israel Chamber of Economic Relations have coordinated the implementation of economic exchanges.

Trade is the first component of the new Israeli–South African economic alliance. South Africa exports to Israel include a variety of raw materials and semi-finished products, ranging from steel, timber, tobacco, hides, wool, sugar, to frozen meat, canned food stuffs such as beer, apple juice, peanut butter, and even, ironically, fresh citrus fruit and prefabricated wooden houses.[40] Three items account for the bulk of the trade. Steel alone comprises 50 percent of South Africa's exports to Israel.[41] Raw diamonds, crucial to Israel's cutting industry, while purchases through the Central Selling Organization in London, originate mostly from South Africa.[42] Lately, coal has assumed a most significant place on South Africa's export roster to Israel. The coal deal, negotiated in 1979, provides for the supply of $23 million of coal per annum for Israel's Hadera plant, thus making South Africa Israel's main source of coal.[43]

Israel, in turn, exports mostly finished products to South Africa.

These include agricultural machinery, textiles, and electrical goods. Of special note are South African purchases of sophisticated Israeli electronic equipment and diamond-cutting machinery.[44] In effect, then, trade between Israel and South Africa conforms to the well-known pattern of an exchange of raw material for manpower and technology.[45]

The volume of trade between Israel and South Africa has expanded tenfold in the past decade. From a level of $20.9 million in 1970, the figure jumped to $199.3 million in 1979.[46] South African exports grew from $10.2 million in 1970 to $151.1 million in 1979 (a factor of 15), whereas Israeli exports to South Africa expanded fivefold, from $10.7 million to $48.2 million in 1979. Thus, the rapid pace of growth is perhaps the key characteristic of Israel's commercial contacts with South Africa.

The second, and lesser-known, facet of Israeli–South African economic exchanges consists of mutual investments and joint ventures. South African financing has been instrumental in establishing joint companies in Israel, the most prominent of which is Iskoor, a South-African Iron and Steel Corporation (ISCOR) and Koor Industries venture for the distribution of steel in Israel.[47] South African investors have poured money into a variety of Israeli schemes, ranging from a new hydroelectric system that will divert water from the Mediterranean to the Dead Sea, regional development projects in the Negev, a plan for linking Eilat and Tel-Aviv by rail, the construction of the coal loading quay in Hadera, to investments in the Tel-Aviv marineland and dolphinareum and a brush factory on a kibbutz.[48] Subsidiaries of South African companies have sprung up in Israel, most notably Tagun Rubber, a Calan subsidiary, Transvaal Mattress, and Hendler and Hendler.[49] Other opportunities are being investigated systematically by South African business interests.[50]

In contrast, Israeli investment in South Africa is miniscule (indeed, it accounts for barely .01 percent of total Israeli investment per annum).[51] Tadiran, Israel's large electronic firm, has established several plants in South Africa in cooperation with the local Calan conglomerate. Other Israeli companies, mostly in construction and agricultural technology, have established South African subsidiaries.[52] But these efforts have been negligible, as witnessed by the real effort made in the past year to encourage greater Israeli investment in South Africa.[53]

The economic cooperation between Israel and South Africa on this level has been facilitated by the extension of a substantial credit line to Israel for imports from South African and by the special permission granted to augment the total of South African investments in the country.[54] The intense interest exhibited by South Africa in Israeli ventures derives in no small measure from the desire to utilize Israel as a stepping-stone for reaching European markets. Local processing of semifinished goods enables South African businessmen to relabel their products and bypass the severe controls on imports from South Africa imposed by the European Economic Community. Israel has thus come to provide, whether consciously or not, a vital bridgehead for South African exports in Europe and the United States.[55]

The diversification of economic contacts and collaboration has been the hallmark of the Israeli-South African economic changes of recent years. But whether this feverish activity is also economically worthwhile to Israel merits further examination. In fact, in purely economic terms this alliance is problematic from an Israeli standpoint on a number of counts. In the first instance, the scope of contacts with South Africa is really quite restricted. The South African market contributes only 1 percent of the export trade, and imports from South Africa account for barely 2 percent of totals. For South Africa the figures are even more infinitesimal, with the trade volume with Israel reaching not even 1 percent of per annum commerce.[56] For Israel, trade relations with black Africa still retain, in 1982, a more significant proportion of official statistics than do contacts with South Africa.[57] In comparison, the South African exchange with African states, with the Arab world, and with the West renders Israel's relative role close to meaningless.[58] It is exceedingly doubtful that the scope of Israel's ties with South Africa in the economic sphere justifies the undue attention that these links have drawn.

A second objection to this economic collaboration stems from the unequal benefits that Israel derives from this relationship. Israel has a growing negative trade balance with South Africa. Israeli goods have been subjected to stiff South African import levies.[59] Many South African imports compete with locally produced goods. The returns that Israel receives economically are hence highly equivocal. It might not be too rash to posit that during the past decade the Israeli economic position vis-à-vis South Africa has lapsed into one of rank inequality and incipient dependency.

Even short-term gains and statistical manipulations cannot, however, explicate the viability of economic entanglements of a demonstrative nature. Specifically, Israel's readiness to form economic links with the Transkei, Bophothatswana, the Ciskei, and the Bantu Investment Corporation possesses next to no economic virtue.[60] And the constant commentary on economic interactions cannot be shown to serve any real economic purpose.

In short, then, Israel's economic returns from the South African connection are much more problem-ridden than they appear on the surface. When coupled with possible economic harm brought about through the circumscription of contacts with potential partners, it becomes difficult to understand the rationale behind Israel's purported economic interest in South Africa. In any event, economic concerns per se by no means provide a viable reason for the continuation of Israeli interaction with South Africa.

The Cultural Interest

This conclusion holds even more firmly for the third set of interests supposedly upholding Israel's South African connection: those related to cultural, academic, and sports links. The presumption in this connection is that close formal ties are necessary to support ongoing links in an array of mutual endeavours. Once again, in order to evaluate the merits of this claim it is necessary to take a closer look at the exchanges involved.

The first is that of tourism. In the past decade, tourism between Israel and South Africa has grown moderately. In 1979 approximately ten thousand Israelis visited South Africa (of a total outward Israeli movement of some five hundred thousand).[61] The rise in visits from Israel prompted the South African Tourist Corporation to open a branch in Tel-Aviv. This office is actively engaged in promoting tourism in South Africa.[62] And the South African Travel Agents Association has held a conference in Israel. South African tourism to Israel has also been on the increase, with approximately twenty-five thousand tourists, many of them black, visiting Israel in 1980.[63] Despite the steady stream of visitors in both directions, their movement accounts for only small percentages of the tourist trade of the two countries. Moreover, the rise in tourism triggered a conflict between South African Airways and El Al about the frequency of travel and landing rights on the Tel-Aviv–Johannesburg route. Israel has had to make concessions to the South African carrier that have reduced profits on this line.[64]

There have also been sporadic cultural exchanges between Israel and South Africa. In 1973 and 1974 fashion models toured South Africa, as did the Israeli Philharmonic Orchestra. Some Israeli singers have performed in South Africa, including the Jerusalem Song and Dance Ensemble, and the prestigious Bat Dor and Batsheva dance troupes, who visited South Africa in 1976 and 1981 respectively.[65] A few Israeli artists have exhibited in South Africa. In the opposite direction some South African productions have stopped in Israel, among them the Johannesburg Youth Ballet and several plays.[66] These exchanges, however, have been mostly symbolic and may hardly be deemed of quantitative import. In fact, many Israelis have protested the tightening of cultural contacts with South Africa, and a diplomatic incident ensued after Israel's ambassador's refusal to attend the open-

ing of a white-only production of the musical "Golda."[67] In the same
vein, the striking of twin city agreements between Haifa and Capetown
and Simonstown and Akko have not gone uncriticized.[68]

Sports links have also often been more problematic than worthwhile.
Some South African rugby teams (a non-sport in Israel) have played in
the country. And South African and Israeli gymnasts have exchanged
visits. Similarly, two Israeli swimmers have competed in South Africa,
as has Israel's foremost tennis pro, Shlomo Glickstein.[69] But by and
large Israeli sports associations have shunned contact with South Africa, and rescinded a 1979 directive prohibiting all sports contact with
South Africa except under extreme political pressure.[70]

Some cooperation does exist between Israel and South Africa on the
academic level. In 1976 Israel's National Council for Research and
Development signed an agreement with South Africa's Council for
Scientific and Industrial Research. Other contracts have been com-
pleted in the medical and agricultural fields. Since then South African
scientific and medical personnel have participated in conferences and
colloquia in Israel, most recently a cardiology conference attended by
Dr. Christian Barnard.[71] Israeli academic visits to South Africa have
been of several sorts. Some Israeli scholars have toured South Africa
on a private basis at the invitation of the South African government.[72]
Others have come as guests of the South African Jewish community.[73]
And still others have carried on fund-raising missions for Israeli univer-
sities.[74] The delicacy of these academic contacts has prompted Israeli
academic circles to understand them as much as possible. The Hebrew
University has even forbidden members of its faculty to visit South
Africa in other than a private capacity unless on missions of purely
Jewish concern.

The extent of Israeli–South African links in cultural and educational
fields is simply very insignificant. Interest in these exchanges in Israel
is minimal, and they elicit no clear benefit: these contacts are, if anything a by-product of, rather than a reason for, Israel's South African
alliance. To suggest that these links lie at the root of this association is
to confuse cause with effect.

The Political Interest

The Jewish economic, and cultural interests supposedly underlying
Israel's continuing cooperation with South Africa have been shown to
be of little explanatory consequence. A fourth set of interests at the
core of this arrangement, of a political bent, appears on the surface to
be more compelling.

The contention that the Israeli–South African link is a manifestation
of vital Israeli political interests rests on two, rather contradictory,

arguments. The first school of thought claims that the Israeli involvement with South Africa is a spin-off of Israel's reliance on the West in general, and the United States in particular. To buttress their analysis, proponents of this view point to two key pieces of evidence. First, a fair amount of speculation has developed around publications that suggest that then secretary of state, Henry Kissinger, encouraged a stepped-up Israeli connection with South Africa as a way of bypassing the congressional decision to avoid an involvement in the Angolan War.[75] Second, Kissinger, Prime Minister Vorster, and the late labor foreign minister of Israel, Yigal Allon, were reported to have met in Bavaria in June 1976, in order to clarify modes of U.S.–Israeli–South African cooperation.[76] The motive behind the purported U.S. inducements to Israel on the South African question may be bound in the American desire "to use Israel as a clandestine conduit to South Africa."[77] Some observers have interpreted this evidence as an indication of a U.S. effort to form a U.S.-centered strategic triangle to counteract the African-Arab-European triangle that was emerging at this time.[78]

The theories that have evolved around this proposition and the meager data mustered to support it have been more concerned with proving American complicity with South Africa than in comprehending the reasons underlying Israeli actions.[79] Some hesitations as to the veracity of this explanation from an Israeli angle do come to mind. In the first place, while it is probably correct that Israel has in the past been overly associated with American and Western interests in the Third World and Africa, it is equally true that Israel's position as the weak link in this Western chain has been politically costly. The backlash that Israel experienced in Africa on this count in the early part of the 1970s has served as a warning signal for the resumption of a similar third-party role.[80] Second, the United States has repeatedly expressed its concern over the Israeli-South African venture. In the summer of 1976 the United States requested a clarification from Israel on reports that Israel was transferring American know-how to South Africa.[81] If the United States had conspired with Israel, it would not need to demand such an elucidation. In the same vein, in early 1977, the U.S. requested that Israel cease its arms deals with South Africa.[82] And during the Carter presidency the administration repeatedly berated Israeli-South African ties. These expressions of unease from Washington raise some grave doubts as to the validity of the complicity theory. Israel is unquestionably greatly dependent on the United States, and perhaps signs of this link have also spilled over to the South African arena. But Israeli politicians and pundits have never brought in the U.S. connection as an explanation for Israel's South African policy; and if they should do so in the future they would be hard put to present a convincing case for such a justification.

The alternative political interest theorem proffered for the Israel-South Africa alliance stems from an opposite set of propositions. It suggests that because Israel and South Africa are both beleagered states with few international options it is only natural that they should form a combined political axis.[83] Expounders of this thesis underline the fact that South Africa in the past made repeated gestures to Israel (as well as to Iran prior to the revolution and to Taiwan) to join an alternative South Atlantic Treaty Organization under its aegis.[84] In 1975, the argument runs, Israel, beseiged on all fronts, finally capitulated to these entreaties. In 1975 the Ford administration announced a reevaluation of its Middle East policy and cut off aid to Israel for a period of seven months. During this hiatus, Israel cemented its South African alliance as a way of breaking out of its total dependency on the United States.[85] Since then, it is advanced, Soviet intrusions in the Horn of Africa and the Indian Ocean have perpetuated this collaboration.[86]

The logic of this political explanation is almost as faulty as its opposite. Again, from an Israeli viewpoint, even if there is a similarity between Israel's precarious political position and that of South Africa—and Israel and South African leaders alike have hastened to emphasize this convergence—it is not at all clear how Israel's political future depends on closer ties with South Africa. No details have been furnished to explicate what Israel hopes to gain from such a political connection, and it may be unlikely that any such evidence exists. Even if such thoughts did play a role in the mid-1970s turnabout, they no longer hold water. The international political approbrium experienced by Israel on this count more than balances out the political returns to be glenaed from the continuation of such an association. It appears therefore, that the similarity of political circumstances provides a very weak political motive for Israel's South Africa policy.

The confusion adhering to the opposing political arguments raised to explain the Israeli–South African alliance highlights their fragility. The contradictions inherent in the two main approaches to this topic tend to cancel each other out. Those in search of reasons for this connection must turn elsewhere.

The Military-Strategic Interest

The final, and in view of the indeterminancy of the foregoing interests, perhaps the most interest-provoking, group of concerns behind Israel's South African ties lie in the military-strategic category. Israeli policymakers are understandably reluctant to discourse on military motives, or to expound possible Israeli strategic interests underlying their South African connection. A very strong impression, however, has been transmitted by both foreign observers and Israelis to the effect that the South African link is, however distasteful, a necessity vital to Israeli security. Israeli–South African military cooperation, it is posited, is an outgrowth of geopolitical concerns, of strategic interests, and of a joint aversion to Soviet expansion in the Middle East and Africa.[87] Its history goes back to 1967, when South Africa reportedly supplied Israel with crucial spare parts for French-made arms after France imposed an embargo on Israel prior to the outbreak of the Six-Day War. Since then the two so-called garrison states have developed a small, though heterogeneous, set of military interchanges. The following analysis seeks to summarize the (largely speculative) evidence on cooperation in these areas in an attempt to uncover the degree to which they might justify Israel's ongoing connection with South Africa.

The first documented area of Israeli–South African military exchange has been in the sphere of arms transfers. The list of Israeli sales of military hardware to South Africa concentrates on a limited number of items. Israel has supplied South Africa with six Reshef-class warships equipped with Gabriel surface-to-surface missiles. Two of the gunboats were supplied in early 1976 and the remainder of the shipment went through after Vorster's visit to Israel that year.[88] Israel has trained South African naval personnel in the use of this equipment.[89] South Africa has also purchased an unspecified number of Ramata patrol boats. Further transfers have taken place in military electronics, with Israelis providing assistance to the South African Air Force in aircraft computers, and in the production of electronic military fences.[90] In 1977 Israel undertook to modernize 150 Centurion tanks in return for rare steel needed to construct Israel's homemade Chariot tanks.[91] Contrary to popular presumptions, Israel has not been an important small arms supplier to South Africa, although Uzi submachine guns are being manufactured in South Africa under Belgian licence.[92] Moreover, Israel has not responded to South African requests for the sale of Israeli-made Kfir fighter bombers.[93]

This is the known extent of Israeli arms transfers to South Africa. The scope of these exchanges in no way parallels that of South Africa's major arms suppliers from the West.[94] It is not clear that the sum total of these deals even rivals some Eastern European and Arab sales to South Africa.[95]

To some observers even these small exchanges are damning. The more relevant question in the present context is whether this connection justifies the continuation of Israel's links with South Africa. In the first instance, the extent of these deals is simply not that great. Second, it is not at all clear that arms transfers have continued after the Security Council decision of November 1977 to impose an arms embargo on South Africa. While Israel at first balked at this dictate, to the glee of the South African press, the late Foreign Minister Moshe Dayan announced Israel's compliance with this order. Israeli representatives have repeated this decision to abide by Security Council Resolution 498 (1977) and have stated unequivocally that Israel "will not provide South Africa with arms or related materials of all types, including the sale or transfer of weapons and ammunition, military vehicles or equipment.[96] Although some rumors have circulated that Israel continues to defy this embargo, it has been impossible to offer concrete evidence to back these speculations.[97] A final caveat on the significance of this facet of Israeli-South African ties is provided by the South African arms industry itself. South Africa is today a net arms exporter, and is virtually self-sufficient in military hardware. It appears therefore that Israeli–South African arms transfers, however regrettable, do not help to explain the continuation of Israeli ties with that country.[98]

A second aspect of military links with South Africa is in the area of counterinsurgency techniques and joint training ventures. Several reports have been published to the effect that senior Israeli military personnel frequent South Africa to lecture on military procedures.[99] Other sources have insisted that Israel has trained South African teams in counterinsurgency warfare and quick-strike tactics.[100] And SWAPO spokesmen have claimed that Israeli advisers have been seen providing support to South African army raids against Namibian freedom fighters in Angola.[101] These reports have neither been verified nor proved to be false. If they are correct, Israel's motives for such an involvement are puzzling. At least overtly, there seems to be no good reason why Israel should give these services to South Africa, especially since there is no visible return for such an involvement. The claim that this is a repayment for South African moral support or for the fact that 1500 Jews of South African descent participated in the Yom Kippur War, is patently absurd.[102] On that basis Israel should be training the armies of Iraq or Syria—Israeli soldiers from those countries comprise a much higher proportion of the Israeli defense forces than Jews of South African origin. The reasons for these alleged actions remain a mystery. In any event, they must be seen more as a confirmation of IsraeliSouth African collaboration rather than a reason for this interaction.

The third, and unquestionably the most delicate and problematic, field of Israeli-South African military cooperation is the nuclear one. The conventional wisdom among strategic analysts is that Israel and South Africa are collaborating in the nuclear sphere. This collusion is perceived as one facet of South Africa's stepped-up nuclear development program that gained momentum as a result of German, French, British, Belgian, U.S., and Italian assistance during the past decade. The main known components in the South African atomic program revolve around the Valindaba uranium enrichment plant sited near the Palindaba atomic research facility. In the mid-1970s, South Africa gained access to the German nozzle process technique for the enrichment of natural uranium.[103] The uranium used to feed this program is supplied by South Africa's substantial uranium reserves (second only to those of the United States). The world's largest uranium mine at Rossing in Namibia produces 5,000 tons of uranium oxide per annum.[104] More recently, the first two French-built tight waterpower reactors became operational at Koeberg.[105]

Talk of some Israeli involvement in the extensive South African nuclear program began immediately after the signing of the 1976 scientific cooperation agreement. It has been claimed that South Africa receives help in its nuclear research from Israeli scientists and that Israeli personnel have been seen at the Valindaba plant.[106] Lately, reports have been published to the effect that South Africa hired Israeli consultants to advise on safety aspects of the commercial reactors.[107] When a Soviet satellite spotted a nuclear test site in the Kalahari desert, it was widely presumed that this was the location for a possible South African-Israeli test.[108] Recent evidence from a banned book on Israel's nuclear technology refutes this charge, claiming that Israel refused a Kalahari test site for Israeli experiments.[109]

The most widespread discussion of Israeli–South African atomic cooperation has centered on reports of joint testing of nuclear weapons. Although some mention has been made of a test in September of 1978,[110] most speculation focuses on a possible explosion on 22 September 1979. The probability of a low-yield nuclear blast on that date comes from a variety of sources, including the Los Alamos observatory, the U.S. observatory at Arecibo in Puerto Rico, and the U.S. navy research laboratory.[111] The U.S. position on this matter is that, "We do not have corroborating evidence that a nuclear blast took place; but neither do we have evidence corroborating any other explanation."[112] Talk of Israeli collusion in this test commenced in the spring of 1980, following a report by CBS correspondent Dan Raviv, broadcast from Athens to bypass the Israeli military censor.[113] Circumstantial evidence to support the Israeli connection—including a visit to South Africa by Israeli Defense Minister Ezer Weizmann and nuclear scientist Amos Horev—has been published in several reports.[114] If these publications of a South African explosion in 1979 are correct, the purported Israeli connection to this explosion does not rest on a solid empirical foundation.[115] Thus, it would seem that despite widespread rumors, no hard facts have been (or are likely to be) produced to verify either the existence of Israeli involvement in South Africa's nuclear surge or the extent of such collusion. Circumstantial evidence, including the fact that both countries are nonsignatories of the nuclear nonproliferation treaty and share some common strategic concerns does not suffice. It is just very hard to know exactly what links exist in this sphere.

Should more information become available at some future date, it would probably still be unclear what benefit Israel hopes to derive from such a nuclear connection. It is widely known that Israel has been independently developing its own atomic energy program for some years, and that Israel possesses the scientific know-how and in all probability the facilities to manufacture nuclear weapons.[116] Under the circumstances, what Israel has to gain from nuclear collaboration with South Africa is not self-evident. Two sets of hypotheses have been offered, the first of which centers on the possibility that South Africa is supplying Israel with enriched uranium.[117] But Israel, in all probability, has its own enriched uranium stockpiles and the scientific capacity to separate U-235 from natural uranium through the gas centrifuge and/or Laser isotope separation (LIS) methods.[118] Moreover, Israel can extract uranium from its ample phosphate reserves.[119] So the need to find an additional source of uranium is far from obvious. A second suggested reason for the South African nuclear connection relies on the possible Israeli need for testing space. But it is documented that Israel did not accept South African offers of testing sites in the past, and if some tests have occurred, one cannot be sure whether this reason is still operative.

The entire topic of nuclear research is covered with a cloak of secrecy in Israel. Far be it from a total novice to intrude on this most sacred of cows. But the questions raised above do cast a pall on the eagerness of Israeli defenders *and* detractors alike to find a convincing argument in this sphere for Israel's ongoing contacts with South Africa. Moreover, whatever the merit of opposing arguments in this regard, it is worthwhile repeating that even if some kernel of truth exists in this domain, it is not evident that the minor gains that Israel can possibly reap from this collaboration outweigh the damage that intimation of an Israeli–South African nuclear conspiracy has wrought.[120]

Ultimately, then, although Israel and South Africa have engaged in joint activities in the military and strategic spheres, as the preceding analysis has attempted to show, however unpraiseworthy this mode of interaction is, from an Israeli perspective there are severe reservations on what indeed Israel receives in return for these contacts. Israel in all probability has little long-term interest in serving South African military ambitions.

The Interest Weighed

The argument for the continuation of the Israeli association with South Africa, despite the serious complications that this has entailed, is predicated on the supposedly compelling nature of the interests involved. The foregoing exploration has sought to highlight the weaknesses inherent in such an approach.

The diversification of Israeli ties with South Africa have been subjected to exhaustive scrutiny in the academic and popular media.[121] The attention that this connection has drawn is out of all proportion to the magnitude of the contacts in question. On a comparative basis, the scale of Israeli involvement pales in comparison with those of other states. As Andrew Young so aptly stated: "It is unfair to link Israel to South Africa. If there is a link you must compare Britain, Germany, Japan and the United States. Israel becomes too easy a scapegoat for other problems we have."[122] Pointing to the hypocrisy of the holier-than-thou attitude adopted by Israel's critics (while it does go a long way toward putting this link in its proper perspective) in no way absolves Israel from responsibility for this connection. Even taking into account the recent ramification of Israeli-South African ties, the insubstantial scope of these links hardly justifies Israel's insistence on their significance. These simply do not occupy a quantitatively or qualitatively meaningful segment of Israeli trade, politics, or military activities.[123]

Arguments about the extent of Israeli–South African collusion aside, this investigation has gone to great pains to show that collaboration is not coterminous with benefit. In the separate spheres of Jewish, economic, cultural, political, and military interchanges, Israel's gains from its South African alliance are ambiguous at best. Even on a cumulative basis the results do not bear out the realpolitik considerations that one is lead to believe guide the policy. Israel has become entangled in an unequal partnership of a highly inconclusive nature.

Whatever the very short-term arguments that may be garnered to uphold this policy—and they are very sparse indeed—these exhibit a long-term policy weakness of the highest order. By linking Israel (if only by association) to South Africa, policymakers have not even taken the trouble to hedge Israel's longer-range political bets in the region. This smacks of a short-sightedness and lack of concern for Israel's future interests that raises serious questions regarding the political maturity of policymaking procedures.[124] Moreover, even the most persuasive arguments cannot justify the apparent intensity with which Israel has followed its South Africa course. The demonstrative nature of these links possesses no redeeming value in Israeli terms.[125]

Therefore, the contention that Israeli interests are promoted by its present policy in South Africa just does not stand up to close analysis. This argument can hence serve neither as a justification nor as a cause for ongoing contacts. It surely cannot act as a convincing counterweight to the moral queries evoked by this policy. In short, from a rational viewpoint, this attachment simply does not make very much sense.

Toward an Explanation for Israel's South Africa Policy

The absence of necessary or sufficient reasons for Israel's link with South Africa does not, however, explain how this policy evolved or why it continues. This analysis would not be even partly complete without an examination of some of the more salient factors that may account for its formulation and perpetuation. Three interlocking hypotheses come to mind.

The first rests on the deep sense of hurt and betrayal that Israelis have expressed in the wake of Israel's systematic abandonment by many of its former allies. The tightening of Israel's ties with South Africa scarcely a decade ago came in the aftermath of Africa's massive rupture of diplomatic relations with Israel. Israel had expended a great deal of energy, time, and devotion to the nurturing of common ties with African states during the period of decolonization and early independence. Not only had Israel designed a substantial and highly regarded program of technical assistance and cooperation in Africa,[126] it also had made efforts to adjust political stances to suit the sensitivities of African leaders.[127] The rise of anti-Israeli sentiment in Africa during 1971, 1972, and early 1973 was perceived as a deep breach of confidence. Israelis were particularly unnerved by the constant references in African gatherings to Zionism as an unmodified form of colonialism.[128] Feelings were further stirred when President Mobutu of Zaire, in his declaration on the severance of ties with Israel, compared Israel to a friend who could not replace a brother (the Arab states).[129] Emotions finally peaked during the October and November 1973 breaks.

The reasons for the actions of African states in 1973 are extremely complex, and in all probability these moves were taken despite a strong sense of affinity with Israel and appreciation for Israeli endeavors in the continent.[130] The periodic mention of Israel's ties with South Africa in some of the official proclamations on the cutting of ties were incidental to other, more weighty, concerns.[131] In any event, the Israeli press and the Israeli public reacted strongly and emotionally to what was treated as a sign of total perfidy. With few exceptions, the Israeli journalists inveighed against the infidelity of African states.[132] In a public survey, a cross section of citizens expressed dismay at the African political maneuver, and many decried the lack of reciprocity displayed by this action.[133]

In this charged atmosphere, it is hardly surprising that few voices of dissent were raised to protest the upgrading of diplomatic relations with South Africa in early 1974. The move was seen not only by the public but also by Israeli officials as a fitting quid pro quo to the African initiative.[134] Murmurs to the effect that only tragedies reveal who one's true friends are were rampant.[135] The 1973 African boycott and the nature of the Israeli response effectively neutralized Israel as an anti-apartheid force.[136]

In the same vein, some of the subsequent improvements in Israeli ties with South Africa since 1973 can be linked to an Israeli diplomatic setback involving Third World countries. Thus, the 1976 Vorster visit may be interpreted as part and parcel of the fallout of the 1975 correlation of Zionism and racism. The step-up in relations with South Africa in 1977 and 1978 coincided with the Afro-Arab summit convened in Cairo in the summer of 1977.[137] The African reluctance to review diplomatic relations after the Egyptian-Israeli peace treaty, despite an upsurge in nonformal contacts, has been seen as bearing out Israeli reactions.[138] By 1982, however, Israel's South African connection is as much a deterrent to the resumption of diplomatic relations as it was previously an excuse for the rupture of these links.[139]

The emotional vagaries evinced by Israel's relations with Africa, and by extension with South Africa, are bewildering. Reactions have ranged from self-righteousness to hysteria, from raw emotionalism to paranoia.[140] These changing feelings reflect, for better or for worse, some of the important undercurrents that fueled the reinstitution of close links with South Africa during the past decade. In the context of the events of 1973, these forces, however impracticable, do furnish an understandable explanation for the initial change of heart. What they do not explain is why, after emotions subsided, the South African connection has grown.

A second hypothesis, which harps on the similarity, empathy, and even conspiracy between Israel and South Africa, has been introduced to fill this explanatory gap. The gist of this argument is that Israel and South Africa share many common features (both countries are on the fringes of the world community, both feel beleaguered, both may be portrayed as minorities struggling for survival, both view themselves as the chosen people, both have to confront terror, both fear communism, both have deep religious roots), and that therefore their alliance is an overt manifestation of ongoing empathy.[141]

Proponents of this form of explanation came from two widely divergent camps. On the one hand, the South Africans themselves highlight this interpretation. South African officials have gone out of their way in recent years to drive home the similarities between Israel's situation and their own.[142] The convergence between the Jewish experience and the Afrikaner one (however bizarre the comparison) is constantly underlined.[143] White leaders in South Africa see Israel as a model for emulation, as the following statement by General H. Van den Bergh, the head of the South African Bureau of State Security, exemplifies: "I went to Israel recently, and enjoyed every moment there. I told the Prime Minister when I got back that as long as Israel exists we have a hope."[144] This sentiment was echoed last year by the state president, Marais Viljoen, who cited Israel as an example that "inspires us to stand firm and to work for peace, prosperity and safety for all South Africans."[145] In a recent public opinion poll, Israel even emerged as South Africa's favorite country.[146] From the expression of empathy it was only a short hop to the presumption of collaboration. South Africans have not only defended this cooperation on the grounds of a common battle against the Palestine Liberation Organization and the African National Congress, but have gone so far as to exalt the virtues of a pariah state status.[147]

The South African government has not, however, relegated its quest for the establishment of cooperation through an insistence on commonality to the academic plane. The South African embassy in Tel-Aviv has spent a small fortune on glossy publications detailing the virtues of South Africa and its propinquity to Israel. Articles originating from the South African embassy have appeared in the press. The South African legation has subsidized a veritable stream of visits by Israeli journalists to South Africa.[148] And no opportunity is missed to hammer home the common destiny of South Africa and world Jewry. Some of the single-mindedness with which this policy has been implemented came to light during the Muldergate scandal that rocked the Afrikaner hierarchy. Eschel Rhoodie, the former South African Information Department chief and the supervisor of the [dis]information slush money publicly acknowledged that some of the funds he managed were used to buy influence in "Jewish circles" in the United States, South Africa, and Israel.[149]

The South African campaign to establish a congruence between Israel and the white oligarchy has been rivaled only by the most strident anti-Israel elements. In the minds of Israel's critics on the Left and in the Arab world, the only viable explanation, since no other reasons hold, for Israeli-South African cooperation lies in the alliance of two racist states.[150] To the comparison of racism has been added on the notion of conquest and exploitative settler societies.[151] And, of course, the unholy alliance of imperialism.[152] "Israel-South Africa ties are becoming organic. . . . This relationship has a special quality unlike any other relationship South Africa has because of the worldwide awesome power and influence of Zionism especially in the United States."[153]

The government of South Africa and the radical detractors of Israel make strange bedfellows. Although the operative conclusions they draw from these comparisons are radically different, they both rest their case on the intimation of an Israel-South African conspiracy based on an acknowledged mutuality of interests. The problem with this hypothesis is that it has fallen mostly on deaf ears in Israel. Conspiracies need collaborators. Most Israelis reject out of hand (the validity of these comparisons aside) the suggestion that democratic Israel's struggle for security against external threats is in any way akin to a racist minority's quest for self-perpetuation.[154]

Vorster's visit gave rise to a public outcry against linking Israel's future to that of South Africa. Public pleas were made to shun an alliance with what was euphemistically dubbed a second Massada state. "With our hands we pour oil on the anti-Israel fire. He who opens his arms [to South Africa] becomes a partner to crime; a collaborator with a hated and cruel regime."[155] And in the same disassociating tone: "The white regime has no future; for us it is possible that things will turn out otherwise. It may come to pass that there might be agreement and understanding here; for these we must toil. And this difference must be stressed in every possible way."[156] Examples of such public periodic soul-searching are a regular feature of Israeli political discourse. With next to no exceptions, even supporters of cooperation with South Africa deny the similarity between the two countries and decry racism in South Africa. The uniformity of this attitude is perhaps best exemplified by the first Israel ambassador to South Africa's categorical statement that "the contention that Israel and South Africa are in the same boat is simply not true."[157]

Some, albeit hardly enough, Israelis have translated these thoughts into action. Anti–South African planks are an integral part of the platforms of several Israeli parties.[158] The Israel Labor Union, the Histadrut, has systematically shunned ties with the all-white South African Confederation of Labor. For a few years Israel had an anti-apartheid movement headed by Arthur Goldreich, one of the Rivonia defendants who managed to escape from South Africa and now makes his home in Israel. A Jerusalem printing house regularly translates volumes of suppressed literature from South Africa. Although the scope of these activities is narrow, no real debate has arisen around the principles that guide them. Explicit Israeli sentiments thus belie the proposition that links with South Africa are maintained because of empathy for the South African cause or because of a conscious plot to link the fate of these two states.[159] Under these circumstances, the verification of the conspiracy hypothesis demands further corroboration.

The alternative to this explanation is a third thesis, one that stresses a combination of ignorance, insensitivity, and indifference as the key to comprehending the perpetuation of this problematic alliance. "Israel's policies today are characterized not only by an insensitivity to moral and human issues, but also by a complete ignorance of what is happen-

ing in the real world."[160] Many Israelis simply do not possess the most
rudimentary knowledge on the state of their country's ties with South
Africa. Even fewer have more than a hazy notion of South African
policies and dispositions. And, most Israelis, much like citizens elsewhere, are ignorant of the prospects for and directions of change in
Southern Africa. Confronted with a morass of difficulties closer to
home, they are ill-equipped, this hypothesis contends, to query government policies.

Ignorance has, it is suggested, been compounded by a growing de-
sensitization to the issues and ramifications of Israel's South African
involvement. Under the Labor government, Israeli-South African relations started to undergo periodic review. These regular reassessments
were a reflection of the perceived need to weigh "a national abhorrence
of the racist philosophy and practice of apartheid" against pragmatic
advantages accruing to Israel from relations between the two countries.[161] In November 1976, barely six months after the Vorster visit,
Israel announced its intention of reviewing its links with South Africa.
This reassessment was slated to occur in two stages: first policy was
evaluated within the Foreign Ministry, and then a full-scale discussion
with the prime minister was scheduled to take place. After the rise of
the Likud coalition, it is not clear that the South Africa question has
been raised in cabinet meetings, although the Foreign Ministry continues to conduct reconsiderations at regular intervals. What has
changed in the past few years is the significance attached to the South
African question, and concomitantly, the stress placed on coming to
terms with the dilemmas entailed by this association. "The most dis-
turbing part of the new Israeli consciousness on South Africa, for those
who are concerned not only about Israel's image, but about Israeli
realities and Israel's future, is the lack of sensitivity to the issues
involved and the seriousness of the situation among so many Israelis."[162]

The indifference exhibited to the South African question, coupled
with the salience of other subjects, it may be suggested, has allowed
this topic to fade from the public eye. In these circumstances, no public
pressure has been exerted to coordinate the activities of the various
bodies involved in South African affairs. The individual entities engaged in activities in South Africa have simply continued to pursue
their own activities without any guidance or constraints. Often, some
policymakers are unaware of the actions of their peers in other government ministries. In effect, this hypothesis posits that the continuation
of Israel's South African connection is more a product of neglect than
of duplicity. It may be a nonpolicy rather than a reflection of conscious
choice. The South African relationship may have developed a momen-

tum that, without concerted efforts to define its purposes and scope, continues to advance on a trajectory of its own.[163]

None of these three hypotheses: the hurt-betrayal hypothesis, the similarity-empathy, conspiracy hypothesis, or the ignorance-indifference-inertia hypothesis can be conclusively confirmed at this juncture. Common to all three is the heavy emphasis placed on subjective factors. When instrumental reasons cannot be sustained, emotions appear to have replaced rationality as explanations for political behavior. This conclusion may not console Israel's friends nor reinforce Israel's critics, but it does point toward an explanation for a connection whose concrete reasons remain elusive.

Israel and South Africa: The Paradox Renewed

The ambiguity characterizing the reasons and explanations for Israel's ongoing association with South Africa does not alleviate the dilemma that Israeli policymakers must face when dealing with this topic. On the contrary, this analysis confirms and even magnifies some of the problematics attendant upon the continuation of present trends. The implications for Israel are not particularly reassuring.

In the first place, the international isolation experienced by Israel is not attenuated by any observable gains derived from the South African connection. If anything, this tie has now become a barrier to Israel's efforts to regain its standing in the international community. This obstacle is especially pronounced in the case of black Africa. The Egyptian peace treaty and the final withdrawal of Israel from Egyptian territories captured in the Six-Day War could provide an opportunity for the resumption of full diplomatic relations with African states. But African leaders feel that "the question of re-establishing diplomatic relations with Israel cannot be disposed of without taking into consideration Israel's strategic collaboration with apartheid South Africa."[164] The practical costs of maintaining ties with South Africa require further consideration.

Second, Israelis have yet to resolve the gap between their aversion to apartheid and their connection with South Africa. "How does one walk the narrow line between national need and national prostitution? . . . How does one reconcile the anti-Semitism of some members of the South African government and Israel's relations with that government? . . . Can this ambivalence be allowed to continue, and what will be the long-term cost for Israel? . . . What about morality and can morality withstand the logic of an expediency born out of Israel's need to survive?"[165] By furnishing undeserved sustenance to the South African regime, Israeli policy undermines the substance of that moral rectitude it seeks to instill in its citizenry.

Third, and from the Israeli viewpoint most perplexing, are the reverberations of Israeli policy in South Africa on the nature and development of an Israeli ethos. This subject mirrors in a nutshell the contradictions between Israeli society's egalitarianism and its discrimination, its tolerance and its exclusion, its universalism and its parochialism, its democracy and its authoritarianism, its militarism and its deep-seated commitment to peace, its ideals and its realities. At this historical confluence, the South African link unnecessarily complicates the choices facing Israel in the years to come, and delays the weighty task of the formulation of a new synthesis.

Israelis are currently engaged in a reassessment of the nature of their path. If there are very few ethical or pragmatic reasons for prolonging Israel's association with South Africa, it might be possible to replace this question at the forefront of the agenda of topics for reconsideration. Israel has very little to lose by reversing its South Africa policy. Such a shift might go a long way toward helping Israel redefine its self-image internally and internationally.

Israel's South African connection is morally, Jewishly, and instrumentally indefensible. But those truly concerned with the liberation of South Africa would do well to remember that even if the Israeli government can be dissuaded from pursuing its present policies, the impact of such a move on change in Southern Africa would be drastically less than if other, more powerful, states could be convinced to alter their course.

Notes

The author would like to acknowledge the invaluable research assistance of Tami Weinstein, Vivienne Burstein-Sher, and Tali Antebi; and to express thanks for the support of many colleagues and of the Harry S. Truman Research Institute of the Hebrew University of Jerusalem, which provided the facilities that made research for this paper possible.

1. "Speech by Ambassador of Israel, addressed to the Committee of Human Rights, on Israel's Position Regarding the Policy of Apartheid and Israel/South African Cooperation," Geneva, 16 February 1981. Similar statements have consistently been made by Israeli delegates in the past.

2. A good analysis of the 1975 vote may be found in Samuel Decalo, "Africa and the UN Anti-Zionism Resolution, Roots and Causes," *Cultures et Devellopment*, 8, no. 1 (1976): 89–117. For an African perspective on the significance of the UN for Israel, see: Peter Anyang'-Nyong'o, "The Impact of the Middle East Conflict in African Political Orientations and Behaviour," in *Settler Regimes in Africa and the Arab World: The Illusion of Endurance*, (Wilmette: The Medina University Press International, 1974), p. 195. ed. Ibrahim Abu-Lughod and Baha Abu-Luban.

3. United Nations General Assembly, Report of the Special Committee Against Apartheid, Supplement 22, 1976–1981. Also: "Report on the Relations between Israel and South Africa," in *Israel and South Africa: The Progression of a Relationship* ed,

Richard P. Stevens and Abdelwahab M. Elmessiri, rev. ed. (New Brunswick, N.J.: North American, 1977), pp. 202–22.

4. This became most apparent in the recent UN vote to place sanctions on Israel. For a more general analysis see Timothy M. Shaw, "Oil, Israel, and OAU: An Introduction to the Political Economy of Energy in Southern Africa," *Africa Today,* 23 no. 1 (1976): 15–26.

5. For the Soviet view: S. Astrakhov, "Alliance Between Tel-Aviv and Pretoria," *International Affairs* (Moscow) 8 (1977): 62–66.

6. Mark Segal, "South Africa Connections," *Jerusalem Post,* 29 August 1976.

7. This despite many efforts made recently by the South African government to woo U.S. Jews. For details see *South Africa Digest,* 10 March 1978, p. 11.

8. Bayard Rustin to Arthur Hertzberg, 27 August 1976.

9. This terminology is rampant. For an extreme example of the admixture of anti-Zionism and anti-Semitism see: Lindsay Barrett, "Isreal (sic) and Africa: Jewish Economic Interests," *Afriscope,* 8 no. 7 (1978): 14–16.

10. Israelis tend to assume that there must be a good reason for the government's stance vis-à-vis South Africa. This sentiment exists elsewhere as well, although few efforts have been made to substantiate it.

11. Prestate contacts, so belabored by Richard P. Stevens, "Smuts and Weizmann: A Study in South African Zionist Cooperation," in *Israel and South Africa,* Stevens and Elmessiri, ed. (also appeared in Abu-Lughod and Abu Lahan, *Settler Regimes,* pp. 173–86), did exist. Those that are pertinent to understanding the present situation will be elaborated upon in other parts of the paper.

12. And not Prime Minister, as many sources (apparently quoting each other) insist.

13. Highlighted by Yosef Goell, "Israel/South Africa: A View from Jerusalem," *Africa Report,* November–December 1980, pp. 18–22.

14. South Africa cut off the flow of Jewish funds to Israel at the time.

15. Reports of South African involvement in the 1973 war, despite a keen interest in events, was vigorously denied: *South Africa Digest,* 9 November 1973, p. 9.

16. Malawi, Lesotho, Swaziland, and Mauritius (which severed links in 1976).

17. This view came out in an editorial in *The Jerusalem Post,* 11 April 1976, and was echoed with few exceptions in the Israeli press.

18. One of the most thoughtful reviews of the visit was published by Benjamin Pogrund, "Israel's South Africa Ties," *Swasia* 3, no. 18 (May 1976). For further details see Azim Husain, "The West, South Africa, and Israel: A Strategic Tangle," *Third World Quarterly* 4 no. 1 (1982): 70.

19. *Maariv,* 16 September 1976.

20. *Maariv,* 19 May 1977; *Al Hamishmar,* 22 May 1977; *South Africa Digest,* 27 May 1977.

21. Many Labor party members expressed private dissatisfaction with the link. Of special note is Professor Shlomo Avineri's refusal to assume his post as director-general of the Ministry of Foreign Affairs until the Vorster visit ended and his reluctance to permit a strengthening of links during his tenure.

22. Unna was replaced by Joseph Harmelin, formerly head of Israel's security services. In the summer of 1981 Eliahu Lankin, a Jerusalem attorney, assumed the post. The present South African ambassador is Derek S. Frankin, formerly under-secretary in the South African Ministry of Foreign Affairs.

23. By far the most superior work on this topic is Gideon Shimoni, *Jews and Zionism: The South African Experience, 1910–1967* (Capetown: Oxford University Press, 1980).

24. For another view: "Afrikaner and Jew Show Route to Reconciliation," *To the Point International,* 12 December 1980. One of the most bizarre aspects of the Israeli connection to South Africa was the Vorster visit to the Holocaust Memorial at Yad Vashem.

25. Neville Rubin, "The Impact of Zionism and Israel on the Political Orientation and Behavior of South African Jews," in *Settler Regimes,* Abu-Lughod and Abu-Laban, ed. pp. 165–172; Leslie Rubin, "South African Jewry and Apartheid," *Africa Report,* February 1970, pp. 22–24 (and response by Henry Katzew, "South African Jews and Politics, Another View," pp. 22, 23).

26. Shimoni, *Jews and Zionism,* p. 304.

27. For a comparison with other contributions: between 1948–1966 receipts from South Africa totalled $38,757,000. 764,572,000 from U.S. Jewry. *Ibid,* p. 239.

28. Most recently Abba Eban, *South Africa Jewish Times,* 25 February 1981, p. 7.

29. My thanks to Gideon Shimoni for his clarification of these numbers.

30. The leader of South African Revisionists, Harry Hurwitz, was appointed personal advisor to Begin on external information, and lately, Minister to Washington, *To the Point International,* 6 March 1978, p. 9.

31. Quoted in *South Africa Jewish Times,* 3 September 1980, p. 11.

32. Anti-Semitic pamphlets are distributed regularly. A report on these incidents was published in *Maariv,* 20 July 1978.

33. Statement by South African minister of justice and police, Jimmy Kruger, *Jerusalem Post,* 23 November 1977.

34. Peter Medding's comments in Gideon Shimoni, "Jewish National Identification in the Diaspora: The South African Community" (Background Paper no. 2, prepared for the President's of Israel's Sixth International Seminar on World Jewry and the State of Israel, 1981), p. 17. Also: *Maariv,* 28 May 1975.

35. *Rand Daily Mail,* 8 July 1980. Contrast with: "South Africa's Jews: Widely Misunderstood Community," *To the Point International,* 20 September 1980.

36. Gideon Shimoni, "Jewish National Identification," maintains that the position of Jews in South Africa is partly a function of relations with Israel.

37. Hirsch Goodman, "Parallel Illusions," *Jerusalem Post Magazine,* 11 September 1981, pp. 5–6, did not grasp the point.

38. D. Ben-Gurion's defense of Israel's antiapartheid vote in the Knesset in 1961 is instructive. Details in Shimoni, *Jews and Zionism,* p. 321.

39. In 1975 the deputy minister of economic affairs visited Israel (*Maariv,* 20 August 1975). In August 1976, the South African minister of labor and mining came to Israel (*Jerusalem Post,* 3 August 1976). A high-level trade mission came in September 1976 (*Jerusalem Post,* 2 September 1976). In 1978 Owen Howoord came, and then met Israeli Finance Minister Simha Ehrlich in Belgrade (*Haaretz,* 25 September 1978). Israels Finance Ministers Y. Rabinowitz and S. Ehrlich were in South Africa in 1976 and 1978 respectively.

40. These details culled from the Israeli press, 1976–1981. It is sufficient to enter an Israeli supermarket to see the extent of the influx of South African goods.

41. *South Africa Digest,* 30 July 1976.

42. Peter Hellyer, "Israel and South Africa: The Racists Allied," in *Zionism, Imperialism and Racism,* ed. A. W. Kayyali, (London: Croom Heelm, 1979), pp. 288–89; Husain, "The West, South Africa, and Israel," p. 71.

43. *The Economist,* 5 November 1977, p. 91. Kunirum Osia, *Israel, South Africa and Black Africa: A Study of the Primacy of the Politics of Expediency* (Washington: University Press of America, 1981), pp. 25–26. Other suppliers include the United States and Australia.

44. *Maariv,* 1 June 1978. Full details have appeared in the *Jerusalem Post,* 1976–1981.

45. Rosalynde Ainslee, "Israel and South Africa: An Unlikely Alliance?", U.N. Department of Political and Security Council Affairs, Centre Against Apartheid, Document 20/1981 (July 1981), presents very full details.

46. Computed from table in Ethan Nadelman, "Israel and Black Africa: A Rapprochement?" *Journal of Modern African Studies* 19, no. 2 (1981): 191.

47. *South Africa Digest,* 26 October 1973, p. 4.

48. Benjamin Beit-Hallahmi, "South Africa and Israel's Strategy of Survival," *New Outlook,* 20, no. 3 (1977): 56, provides information on the hydroelectric project. The railroad deal is detailed in "Israel and South Africa: New Cooperation," *Africa Confidential* 18, no. 12 (1977): 5.

49. *South Africa Jewish Times,* 24 October 1979; *Maariv,* 13 June 1978.

50. *Jerusalem Post,* 4 August 1976. In November 1981 a delegation of forty industrialists visited Israel.

51. Victor Low, "Israel and South Africa," Jerusalem 1982; Dr. Low kindly allowed the author to peruse a draft of his paper prior to publication.

52. *Jerusalem Post,* 30 December 1976.

53. A trade survey showed that Israelis could invest in forty-six products in South Africa. *Zionist Record,* 8 August 1980. Ads appear frequently in the Israeli press. This past month a symposium was held in Tel-Aviv to attract Israeli investment to South Africa, *South Africa Digest,* 12 February 1982, p. 5.

54. "South Africa: The Israeli Connection," *Africa Confidential,* August 1978, pp. 5–6. An accord to avoid double taxation was signed in the same year, *Haaretz,* 13 February 1978.

55. This fronting process is well known. References to it may be found in the Israeli press: *Haaretz,* 3 February 1978; *Maariv,* 13 February 1978; *Jerusalem Post,* 23 March 1978. For another view see: "New Israel-South Africa Ties," *Arab Palestinian Resistance*9, no. 3 (1976): 82–87.

56. Kenneth Adelman, "Israel/South Africa: The Club of Pariahs," *Africa Report,* November–December 1980, pp. 8–11.

57. Figures supplied by Israel Ministry of Commerce and Industry. These figures do not include diamonds and military transfers. Nigeria remains Israel's largest trading partner in black Africa.

58. For the West, Husain, "The West, South Africa, and Israel," p. 47. For Africa, the detailed accounts in "Africa's Trade with South Africa," *Afriscope* July 1978, pp. 22–26; and Moshe Dechter, "South Africa and Black Africa: A Report on growing Trade Relations" (New York, American Jewish Congress, 1976).

59. Raised recently to 10 percent, *Haaretz,* 18 February 1982.

60. "Israel to Invest in Homelands," *New African,* April 1977.

61. *Maariv,* 27 July 1979; *Haaretz,* 15 May 1979.

62. One example is a pamphlet entitled: "The Jewish Heritage in South Africa," published by the South African Tourist Corporation.

63. *South Africa Digest,* 24 October 1980, p. 19.

64. *Yediot Aharonot,* 20 March 1978.

65. These visits were arranged by the South Africa Zionist Federation, *Jerusalem Post,* 6 August 1974.

66.*Haaretz,* 16 June 1977, gives a rundown of these exchanges.

67. Details in *South Africa Digest,* 7 July 1978. An Israeli, Avi Ostrovsky, conducts the only multiracial orchestra in South Africa.

68. Extremely harsh denunciations in: Omar Ibrahim, "Israel-South Africa Entente," *Mainstream* 5 no. 8 (23 October 1976).

69. These athletes recently appeared on the international lists of sports people banned from international competition.

70. *Maariv,* 24 January 1979.

71. Again, based on various press items, 1976–81.

72. The South African government arranges lectures and tours for invitees, covers all expenses, and often offers a free tour for wives.

73. Among those who have gone under these auspices are Yitzhak Rabin, Mordechai Gur, Ezer Weizman, Ephraim Katzir, and Hirsh Goodman.

74. Details of these visits appear in the *South Africa Jewish Times.*

75. Peter Hellyer, "Israel and South Africa: A Strengthening Alliance," *Arab Dawn* 58 (March 1980): 11–12; also, *Maariv,* 6 November 1977.

76. Bernard Magubane, "Israel and South Africa: The Nature of the Unholy Alliance," Paper presented at the United Nations Seminar on the Palestinian Question, Arusha, July 1980, pp. 17–18.

77. *The Economist,* 10 November 1977, p. 9; echoed by Ainslee, "Israel and South Africa," esp. p. 16.

78. Husain, "The West, South Africa, and Israel."

79. A particularly antagonistic portrayal may be found in Africa Research Group, "David and Goliath Collaborate in Africa," *Leviathan,* September 1969, pp. 22–26.

80. Recent events may indicate the fading of such a reservation in the past several months. Of special note is the signing of the (now delayed) strategic agreement between Israel and the United States in late 1981.

81. *Maariv,* 25 August 1978.

82. *Haaretz,* 3 February 1977.

83. Ainslee, "Israel and South Africa," highlights this contention.

84. "Newly Emerging World: Putting It Together," *To The Point International*, 19 May 1978, pp. 9–12.

85. Highlighted in the *Economist*, 5 November 1977. For an American viewpoint: Rita Hauser," Israel, South Africa, and the West," *The Washington Quarterly* 2, no. 3 (1979): 75–82.

86. For more information on Israel's position in the Horn of Africa, see: Shlomo Slonim, "New Scramble for Africa," *Midstream* 23, no. 9 (1977): 30–35; and Perer Schwab, "Israel's Weakened Position on the Horn of Africa," *New Outlook* 21, no. 2 (1978): 21–25.

87. Robert S. Jaster, "South Africa's Narrowing Security Options," *Adelphi Papers* 159 (Spring 1980). Also see *Foreign Report* 1510 (2 November 1977): 1–2.

88. *Haaretz*, 5 September 1977.

89. *Maariv*, 6 August 1976.

90. *Maariv*, 28 August 1978, quoting from foreign sources.

91. The *Economist*, 5 November 1977, repeated in many sources.

92. Osia, *Israel, South Africa and Black Africa*, p. 3; Stevens and Elmessiri, *Israel and South Africa*, p. 67.

93. This at the insistence of the United States, since the Kfir fighters are made with American engines, and require U.S. government approval for their reexportation; *Haaretz*, 13 August 1975 and 20 June 1978 (quoting *Aviation Week*). Also: *To The Point International*, 2 March 1979, p. 15.

94. Moshe Dechter, "The Arms Traffic with South Africa," *Midstream* 23, no. 2 (1977): 14–25.

95. Osia, *Israel, South Africa and Black Africa*, pp. 64–69. Dechter, *ibid*, claims that Jordan sold South Africa $17.9 million of short Tiger surface-to-air systems and Centurion tanks, pp. 22–23.

96. Permanent Representative of Israel to the United Nations Committee established under Security Council 421, 14 September 1979.

97. Ainslee, "Israel and South Africa," pp. 13–14; J. G. Calloway, "Israel and South Africa: Unity in Isolation," *Middle East International* 79 (January 1978): pp. 19–20. Ariel Sharon has not helped to alleviate these rumors by his recent statements that South Africa needs more modern weapons, *New York Times*, 14 December 1981; *Haaretz*, 15 December 1981.

98. Jaster, "South Africa's Options."

99. *Maariv*, 9 July 1975, quoting the *Guardian* correspondent in South Africa.

100. Israeli denial in *International Herald Tribune*, 3 June 1976.

101. *Maariv*, 23 August 1976, quoting *Guardian* correspondent in Lusaka. Also see E. C. Chibwe, *Afro-Arab Relations in the New World Order* (London: Julian Friedman, 1976), p. 23.

102. A. Elmessiri, "Israel and South Africa: A Link Matures," in *Israel and South Africa*, ed. Stevens and Elmessiri, p. 76; Y. Kachine, "L'Alliance des Sioniste et des Racistes," *Remarques Africaines* 15, no. 421 (1973): 8–9.

103. The best source continues to be Zdenek Cervenka and Barbara Rogers, *The Nuclear Axis: Secret Collaboration between West Germany and South Africa* (New York: New York Times Books, 1978).

104. Tami Hultman and Reed Kramer, "Pretoria's Nuclear Trump Card," *Afriscope*, September 1977, pp. 41–48. For an analysis of British assistance, see Dan Smith, "South Africa's Nuclear Capability," World Campaign Against Military and Nuclear Collaboration with South Africa, London, February 1981.

105. J. E. Spence, "South Africa: The Nuclear Option," *African Affairs* 53, no. 321 (1981): 442–44.

106. Robert Manning and Stephen Talbot, "American Cover-Up on Israeli Bomb," *Middle East* 68 (June 1980): 8–12; and Smith, "South Africa's Nuclear Capability," p. 19.

107. David K. Willis, "On the Trail of the A-Bomb Makers: How South Africa and Israel are Maneuvering for the Bomb," *Christian Science Monitor*, 3 December 1981.

108. Cited in Smith, "South Africa's Nuclear Capability," p. 16, but appears throughout the literature.

109. Manning and Talbot, "American Cover-Up," p. 12.

110. *Maariv,* 28 October 1978.

111. The most detailed evidence in Manning and Talbot, "American Cover-Up." Also see Hellyer, "Israel and South Africa," p. 1; and Husain, "South Africa, Israel and the West," pp. 58–60.

112. Some have claimed that validation was problematic because the explosion came from a neutron bomb; Manning and Talbot, "The American Cover-Up," p. 8.

113. *Jerusalem Post,* 20 March 1980. Raviv's credentials were withdrawn.

114. Hellyer, "Israel and South Africa," p. 11.

115. Many other rumors exist. A most recent report states that Israel, South Africa, and Taiwan are developing nuclear warheads with U.S. assistance; Barbara Rogers, "The Nuclear Threat from South Africa," *Africa,* no. 113 (January 1981), pp. 45–47.

116. For a good summary see Robert E. Harkavy, "Spectre of a Middle East Holocaust: The Strategic and Diplomatic Implications of the Israeli Nuclear Weapons Program," Ph.D. diss., University of Denver Graduate School of International Studies, 1980.

117. Alan Dowty, "Nuclear Proliferation: The Israeli Case," *International Studies Quarterly* 22, no. 1 (March 1978): 82 n. 5; P. R. Chari, "The Israeli Nuclear Option: Living Dangerously," *International Studies* 16, no. 5 (1977): 346.

118. Harakvy, "Spectre of a Middle East Holocaust," pp. 26–27.

119. Rogers and Cervenka, *The Nuclear Axis,* pp. 311–24.

120. Especially in view of the growing concern in Africa about the possibility of an alteration of the continent's nuclear-free status; B. Akporade Clark, Preface in Smith, "South Africa's Nuclear Capability."

121. Virtually every smallest detail of links has been documented with care. Underlying these efforts is often the questionable assumption that conclusions may be drawn merely from demonstrating interaction.

122. Statement by Andrew Young during a visit to Tanzania, quoted in Low, "Israel and South Africa," p. 17.

123. Adelman, "The Club of Pariahs," p. 4.

124. Michael Wade, "Bypassing Africa—And History," *New Outlook* 19, no. 7 (1976): 23–27; Naomi Chazan, "Israel's Short-Sighted Policy in South Africa," *Jerusalem Post,* 12 April 1976.

125. Osia, *Israel, South Africa, and Black Africa,* p. 100, reiterates this conclusion forcefully.

126. For details see: Leopold Laufer, *Israel and the Developing Countries: New Approaches to Cooperation* (New York: Twentieth Century Fund, 1967); Z. Y. Hershing, ed., *Israel-Africa Cooperation Research Project, Progress Report* (Tel-Aviv: Department of Developing Countries, Tel-Aviv University, 1970); Shimon Amir, *Israel's Development Cooperation with Africa, Asia and Latin America* (New York: Praeger, 1974).

127. Best overall compilation of studies on this period may be found in: Michael Curtis and Susan Aurelia Gitelson, eds. *Israel and the Third World* (New Brunswick, N.J.: Transaction Books, 1976). Elliot P. Skinner, "African States and Israel: Uneasy Relations in a World of Crisis," *Journal of African Studies* 2 (1975): 7, highlights the need to study the Jewish contribution to African liberation movements.

128. Boumedienne's statement, as quoted in Ali Mazrui, "Black Africa and the Arab Israel Conflict," *Middle East International,* 87 (September 1978), p. 14, is instructive.

129. Nehemia Levtzion, "The Friend and the Sister: Africa between Israel and the Arabs" (Jerusalem: Institute of Asian and African Studies, 1973). Also Skinner, "African States and Israel," p. 2.

130. Varying explanations have been forwarded. The best known is Susan Aurelia Gitelson, "Israel's African Setback in Perspective: In Cuntis and Gitelson, *Israel and the Third World,* pp. 182–99. Probably the most subtle analysis may be found in Aryeh Oded, "Africa between the Arabs and Israel," *Hamizrah Hahadash* 25, no. 3 (1975): 183–209; and Robert Vineberg, "The Rupture of Diplomatic Relations between Africa and Israel" (M.A. thesis, Department of Political Science, McGill University, 1977).

131. World Jewish Congress, African and Asian Media Survey, *African and Asian Attitudes on the Middle East Conflict* (New York: Department of African and Asian Studies, 1974).

132. Yoel Marcus, "The Ugly African," *Haaretz,* 9 January 1973, is one example. At the same time some very sensitive pieces appeared, the most prominent being, Yehoshua Rash, "Africa, Won't You Remember?" *Al Hamishmar,* 1 November 1974.

133. Israel Institute for Applied Social Research and the Institute of Communication of the Hebrew University of Jerusalem, "Foreign Relations of Israel with African States in the Eyes of the Public," January 1974.

134. An exception is Yuval Elitzur, *Maariv,* 21 March 1974.

135. One of the worst examples is Yosef Lapid, "For South Africa I Won't Equivocate," *Maariv,* 14 March 1979.

136. Gideon Shimoni stated this most forcefully in a recent conversation.

137. Susan Gitelson, "First Afro-Arab Summit in Cairo, March 1977," mimeographed. For details on Afro-Arab cooperation, see: Victor J. Le Vine and Timothy W. Luke, *The Arab-African Connection: Political and Economic Realities* (Boulder, Colo.: Westview Press, 1979); Hartmut Neitzel and Renate Notzel, *Africa and the Arab States: Documentation on the Development of Political and Economic Relations since 1973* (Hamburg: Institute of African Studies, African Documentation Center, 1979); Aryeh Oded, "Slaves and Oil: The Arab Image in Black Africa," *The Weiner Library Bulletin* 27, no. 32 (1974): 34–47.

138. On the improvement of nonformal relations, see Naomi Chazan, "Israel in Africa," *Jerusalem Quarterly* 18 (Winter 1981): 29–44; and Avi Gil, "Israel's Quiet Relations with Black Africa," *Jewish Observer and Middle East Review* 31, no. 2 (1977): 3–4.

139. Vincent B. K. Khapoya, "Africa and Israel in the Period of the Severance of Diplomatic Relations (Paper presented at the African Studies Association Meetings, Philadelphia, October 1980), recently reiterated by Nigerian sources, *Maariv,* 19 February 1982.

140. An excellent analysis of this may be found in E. Lotem, "Israel-Africa Relations in the Eyes of the Press," *International Problems* 14, nos. 3–4 (Fall 1975): 33–54.

141. Osia, *Israel, South Africa and Black Africa,* pp. 14–21.

142. Famous quote from *Die Burger,* 29 May 1968.

143. "Afrikaner and Jew have much in common," *South Africa Jewish Times,* 22 April 1981.

144. *Yediot Aharonot,* 16 August 1973, quoted in Cervenka and Rogers, *The Nuclear Axis,* p. 311.

145. *The Citizen,* 27 July 1981.

146. *South Africa Digest,* 20 November 1981, p. 6. One assumes that the survey polled white South Africans.

147. "Emerging New World."

148. It is possible to compile a long list of Israeli journalists who have visited South Africa in this way. Certain press people, who might write critical articles, have not been given visas.

149. *South Africa Jewish Times,* 15 August 1979.

150. Peter Hellyer, "Israel and South Africa," in Kayyali, passim.

151. Mabugane, "Israel and South Africa;" Richard Stevens, "Israel and South Africa: A Comparative Study in Racism and Settler Colonialism," in Kayyali, pp. 265–87; A. Kalman, "Israel and South Africa Unite Against Black Liberation," *African Communist* 1, no. 68 (1977): 60–68.

152. The title of Kayyali, *Zionism, Imperialism and Racism,* is indicative.

153. Alfred T. Moleah, "Israel/South Africa: The Special Relationship," *Africa Report,* November-December 1980, p. 12.

154. Nehemia Levtzion, "The Comparison Between Israel and South Africa," *Miguan* (1976), summarizes this position well.

155. Dov Barnir, *Al Hamishmar,* 3 September 1976.

156. Aryeh Palgi, "No Cooperation with the Second Massada," *Al Hamismar,* 7 September 1977.

157. *Maariv,* 3 November 1977.

158. Sheli, The Israel Civil Rights Movement, and Shinui. The Labor Party has been silent on this matter formally.

159. Beit-Hallahmi, "South Africa and Israel's Strategy of Survival," p. 57, already sees signs of Israelis beginning to believe these claims.

160. Ibid., p. 56; echoed by Wade, "Bypassing and Africa—And History."

161. Goell, "A View from Jerusalem," p. 18.

162. Beit-Hallahmi, "South Africa and Israel's Strategy of Survival," p. 57.

163. This view has been propounded by some observers. Recent conversations with Israelis involved in the South African venture tend to bear out the proposition that frequently the right hand is unaware of what the left hand is doing.

164. Imobigbe, "Israeli-Egyptian Treaty," p. 12, also Nadelmann, "Israel and Black Africa," p. 214. Sadat was reported to have asked Begin to sever diplomatic relations with South Africa in order to facilitate the resumption of relations with Africa, *Al Hamishmar,* 1 January 1978. Sharon's visit to South Africa after a journey to several African states in November 1981 was understandably not well received in Africa.

165. Goodman, "Parallel Illusions," p. 6.

Reflections on Two Isolated Peoples

Matthew Holden, Jr.

Introduction

Afro-Americans and American Jews are isolated peoples. Each constitutes a community, a shared moral order. Each is in natural estrangement from an overwhelming majority by which it is encircled. To the Jews, the majority is "Gentile"; to the Afro-Americans, the majority is "white." In the public policy arena, the borderland where all groups must sometimes meet, the two groups converge and diverge and create intense intercourse.

A common purpose has been assumed between these two peoples. Afro-Americans and Jews who write or speak about common problems seem to expect, or to believe that they should have, sympathy from the other. Yet sympathy is not easily forthcoming. Richard Neustadt's brilliant lectures on crises in Anglo-American relations contain this strongly suggestive passage:

> To make the matter plain [the pattern of conflict] is woven from four strands: muddled perceptions, stifled communications, disappointed expectations, paranoid reactions. In turn, each "friend" misreads the other, each is reticent with the other, each is surprised by the other, each replies in kind.[1]

Each side tends to believe that the other should accept itself in its own terms, and tends to regard failure as if due to willful perversity. The genuine need, however, is not sympathy, but empathy. It is not the sense of emotional identification with the other side and what it desires, but the comprehension (which may or may not imply approval) that causes each side to think, feel, or act in a particular way.

This indicates a need to determine where we are, and how we got here. We may, at least, try to get *some* of the muddled quality out of our perceptions.² The relationships between Afro-Americans and Jews, that are now described by the word "alliance" or "coalition," were much more complex than any one word can suggest.

Sixty years ago, Afro-Americans and American Jews, through some persons who claimed leadership roles within these groups, first met in tentative association. Before that, the *communities* had almost nothing to do with each other. Of course, it is an essential fact that a variety of *persons who were Jewish* played critical roles in various phases of the long, and still unfulfilled, struggle. But these persons played personal roles. Either they were not involved in Jewish communal leadership or, in any case, did not participate in the black struggle, *in their communal roles*. Some time just above fifty years ago, this tentative association became a little less uncertain. Some leaders in Jewish institutions, and not merely Jewish individuals of particular principle, began to show a form of commitment that seemed unlikely to be renounced.

Thirty years ago, perhaps, the idea of a firm Afro-American–Jewish coalition had become standard doctrine. Honored much in assertion, and sometimes in practice, the ideal held that social progress— especially in civil rights and racial equality—would receive the support of leaders in both communities, and that those leaders would not be challenged seriously from within. Yet, the old "coalition" has "collapsed," but not in the sense that Afro-Americans and Jews do not work together. Rather, it can no longer be assumed that Afro-American and Jewish leaders will wish to work together. Nor can it be assumed that those who do wish to work together will, even if they try, be able to carry their respective constituencies with them.

I do not claim to offer a solution here. But it may be that we should first consider how the relationship appears to have come about, and what might appear to be some key considerations in the popular culture of each group. The way may be open hereafter to see how leadership structures on either side can reconcile the divergent needs.

The Rest of the Country as the Framework

To be a "minority" is to have less power than someone else, whether one outnumbers them numerically or not. A minority group has, therefore, a natural incentive to seek rapprochement with the most powerful groups that it can find. The principle has specific application.

Both Afro-Americans and Jews sought to ally themselves with political strength, whenever they could. Prior to the Franklin D. Roosevelt administration, natural pressures moved Jews and Afro-Americans in different directions. In the time of Grover Cleveland, the Democratic party was predominantly Southern. But Northern Democrats sought to achieve a share of the black vote, and President Cleveland seemed no more inclined to drive blacks out of politics than did his Republican counterparts of the time.[3] Nonetheless the last powerful centers of support for blacks were among some, but clearly not all, conservative congressional Republicans. When these conservatives lost their fight, in 1890, to establish a federal elections bill (the Voting Rights Act of its time), the black electorate in the South deteriorated, Republican presidential politics turned from the time of Theodore Roosevelt and Taft toward a competition for white votes in the South. In the majority of the election years, this nascent "Southern strategy" has guided Republican presidential politics.[4]

By the time the Democrats returned to the White House, in the Wilson administration, blacks were at a worse disadvantage than they had been at any time since the Civil War. They were no longer of value to the Republicans and totally rejected by the national Democrats. Lawrence Grossman puts the point very well! "No matter how satisfactory their relations with Negroes in their own states, Northern Democrats, dominated by political considerations, would allow themselves to be dominated by Southern white racists until the 1900's and 1940's, when new conditions and new attitudes transformed both the party and the nation."[5] In the new Wilson administration, blacks had no standing. The new Democratic Congress showed, even in the political symbolism of new legislative proposals, a commitment to white supremacy that had not been similarly apparent for twenty or thirty years. Democrats introduced measures to require segregation on trains moving in interstate commerce, to forbid interracial marriages in the District of Columbia, and to preclude the enlistment of blacks in the military services.

The position of Jews was rather different. Not only did they have at least some standing in both parties! They also found a particular responsiveness in President Wilson,[6] who never met Brandeis before 1917, but quickly accepted him as adviser and friend.[7] When Wilson nominated Brandeis to the Supreme Court he withstood nearly all the most respected leadership of the American bar to get him confirmed.[8]

When Wilson appointed Henry Morgenthau, Sr., ambassador to Turkey, within those domain Palestine then lay, he put him under no strictures of neutrality about Jewish interests; nor under any obligation to prove that he was doing nothing special for Jews. "Remember," said Wilson to Morgenthau, "that anything you can do to improve the lot of your co-religionists is an act that will reflect credit upon America, and you may count on the full power of the Administration to back you up."[9] The president was accessible at the Paris Peace Conference to Jewish private advisers; he was a supporter of minority rights in the treaties for the emergent East European states; and he was open to safeguarding Jewish interest in Palestine.[10] Wilson, was both perceptive about Jewish needs and responsive to this Southern wing, especially its strategic concern for white supremacy. I do not claim to know what Jews thought of this. But it would have been incredible had they jeopardized their own good fortune.

It was, thus, only natural and practical that the two groups should have had little to do with each other. In the first decades of this century, the main structures of opinion and power presented massive resistance to fair treatment for Jews or even simple human decency to Afro-Americans. The friends of blacks, or those who on any pragmatic ground were ready to offer the smallest measure of relief, who had any political influence, were on the conservative end of national politics. Some were even thought not to be particularly sympathetic to broad social reform, or to Jews. (The conservatives' shift toward alliance with the white supremacists deserves an analysis that I cannot here provide.)[11] The friends of Jewry covered a wider spectrum, but for the most part they did not include people with much sympathy for the claims of Afro-Americans.

The ultimate convergence of Jewish and Afro-American leadership reflected the change in national politics produced by Franklin D. Roosevelt, but the embryonic relationship anticipated the New Deal by almost a decade. Murder was midwife to this fragile child—murder called lynching!

It is impossible to comprehend the civil rights movement, without an appreciation of the earliest right-to-life movement in the United States: the right of already born people to remain alive as against the right of some other person to take life on any casual pretext. Whatever its roots in Southern culture, lynching had become a means of white control over blacks in the South. It may be true that the crime had declined sharply in the late nineteenth century, as W. J. Cash alleges.[12] But the American Establishment had not yet concluded that lynching was unacceptable in civilized society. Ida B. Wells, a journalist of the period, was forced out of Memphis, where she edited a little paper, for her vigorous editorial protest against lynching. Her subsequent crusade across the United States and Europe aroused considerable scorn from so respectable a journal as the *New York Times*.[13] Nevertheless, somewhere in the country, and mainly in the South, blacks were being lynched at the rate of one per week as late as 1922.[14]

Antilynching, as a national issue eliciting the support of the respectable, was sharply crystallized in the early days of the NAACP. In that crystallization the Association played an active role.[15] The long campaign, frustrating and stalemated in the 1920s,[16] was revived in 1933 and carried on through 1937,[17] and was a subject of additional debate after World War II.

This political history is only for context here. Let us return to the specific theme of the Afro-American relationship to Jewish leadership, or Jewish relationship to Afro-American leadership. In 1915, Leo Frank, a New York Jew, was managing a factory in Georgia. He was accused of having raped and murdered a woman employee, convicted, and sentenced to die.[18] The atmosphere was dominated by mobs.

Louis Marshall, the lawyer of great repute and president of the American Jewish Committee for seventeen years (1912–29),[19] tried to get the conviction reversed. The Supreme Court said no, with Justice Holmes and Justice Hughes in dissent. If a state preserved the forms of a fair trial, the Court said, it could not go behind to inquire into the spirit of the trial (*Frank* v. *Mangum,* 237 U.S. 509 [1915]). When Frank's sentence was subsequently commuted to life, he was taken from the jail and lynched.

Four years later, in 1919, some Arkansas sharecroppers attempted to unionize against their landlords. The result was a gunfight. Blacks and whites were killed! Certain members of the union were charged with murder. Four years after that, the NAACP won the case for them in the Supreme Court (*Moore* v. *Dempsey,* 261 U.S. 89 [1923])[20] The Court, with the dissenter in *Frank* v. *Magnum* now writing for the majority, held that a mob-dominated trial deprives a defendant of due process of law.

Walter White says: "Louis Marshall wrote me a warm letter of congratulation in which he said of the position which he had taken unsuccessfully in the Frank case, that 'the stone the builders rejected has become the cornerstone of the temple.' He enclosed a check as 'a thank offering' and volunteered his legal services without cost to the NAACP, which he gave to the end of his life."[21] *Marshall's appearance here is the first I can find of an active role by a leader of the German Jewish establishment.*

Eugene Levy, the biographer of James Weldon Johnson, says that Marshall "eagerly" accepted an invitation to join the NAACP Board around 1925.

Cyrus Adler, says, in the first reference I can find to blacks in the first twenty-five years of the *American Jewish Year Book,* that Marshall had believed there was "a special duty on white people of the United States to protect and aid this people. . . ."[22] The NAACP's 1929 *Annual Report* also refers, with appreciation, to the services of Marshall. If one has any idea of the ordinary workings of the world, it is probable that the interest that Marshall developed—going back to the Moore decision six years before—was one useful step in linking NAACP leadership to some other parts of the American public elite. The extension of the network from Marshall is suggested by the replacements. Herbert Lehman, then lieutenant governor of New York, was elected to the Board of Directors to succeed Marshall. Felix Frankfurter and James Marshall, son of Louis Marshall, were both brought onto the Legal Committee.

James Weldon Johnson later said, at the funeral of Louis Marshall, "I have been asked to serve as an honorary pallbearer—Mr. Marshall had been one of the most active and valuable members of the Legal Committee of the Association. . . . I chatted with Mr. Rosenwald and with Judge Benjamin Cardozo, the only ones I knew personally. Mr. Rosenwald took the trouble to introduce me to several. He gave me a flattering introduction to Alfred E. Smith. Mr. Smith regarded me for a moment with what appeared like cool curiousity. . . ."[24]

Felix Frankfurter came onto the Legal Committee in 1929, and in 1931 told Walter White to keep his eye on "a young man named [William H.] Hastie who will graduate in June from the Harvard Law School—he is one of the finest students who has ever studied at Harvard during my time."[25] Hastie, in turn, the intellectual mentor of Thurgood Marshall at the Howard Law School, has probably been the all-round most diversified role model for black attorneys since then.

Louis Marshall's son-in-law was executive director of the Federation of Jewish Charities in Philadelphia. This man, Jacob Billikopf, was the link whereby William Rosenwald, son of Julius, became interested in making certain special contributions to the NAACP.[26] The matching pledges came from several other sources, including Lehman, S. S. Fels, the Warburgs, and Edsel Ford.

Over the years, from the 1920s to the end of World War II, there were three threads in the formation of the "coalition" of Afro-American and Jewish leaders on civil rights issues: (1) a change in national politics that gave both leadership groups somewhat greater incentive to work together; (2) an evolving pattern of black civil rights activity, from the lynching issues through the poll tax, school litigation, voting litigation, segregation; and (3) economic participation issues.

The "rest of the country" was the framework in which these nascent relationships can first be seen. The United States as a whole, as a system of power, provided few avenues of redress for Afro-Americans, and substantial—though still limited—avenues of redress for Jews. The convergence of Afro-Americans and Jews, politically, was partly a function of a strong and perceived interest in the protection of physical life, against lynching. The convergence was also a function of changes in the national political relationships that began to overcome the almost automatic conflict that would earlier have been found between Jews and blacks, if only because the allies of one were necessarily the opponents of the other.

On the Emergence of the Alliance of Leaders

The concern that can be perceived was at the leadership level when blacks who claimed leadership within their community, and Jews who claimed leadership within their community made tentative contact in the 1920s. The fruition, which emerged on a larger scale, was the result of a historical accident that occurred by the happenstance inclusion of both leadership groups within the Democratic New Deal "coalition."

Jews had already begun to lose, prior to the New Deal, some of their Republican attachments.[27] Afro-Americans, on the other hand, had shown a desire to be free of their one-party Republican attachment, at least since the 1880s. Even in the South, there were those who supported Democrats as their interests dictated. Bishop Henry McNeal Turner, the African Methodist Episcopal bishop of Georgia, supported a Democratic gubernatorial candidate who opposed lynching in 1892.[28] In the North, there were a variety of hardheaded fishes-and-loaves politicians who worked with the Democrats. These practical politicians, like their Jewish counterparts, did not claim the ethnic leadership. Those who did claim ethnic leadership, and who backed Wilson in 1912 (as did Bishop Alexander Walters,[29] and W. E. B. Du Bois) soon found themselves embarrassed by the severity of the Wilson administration.[30]

In 1928, Walter White, the then up-and-coming assistant secretary of the NAACP, who was on leave in France, was urged to come home quickly. It seems that Al Smith wanted help in pulling in the black vote in the North, but, pleading fear of Southern retribution, refused to make any express appeal to the interests that blacks thought of as theirs. Smith reportedly later said he made a mistake in that regard.[31] From the Wilson years, through the first election of Franklin D. Roosevelt, Democratic presidential candidates rigorously observed the rules laid down by their Southern colleagues. Politics was treated as a white man's affair.

Thus an interesting paradox is worthy of consideration. If political party leadership does not make significant gestures toward an interest group until it can see the likelihood of substantial votes, and if the interest group does not provide its votes until it has received a significant gesture, how does the pattern change? In this instance, the change arose from external circumstances. The Depression installed Franklin D. Roosevelt and the Democratic party in power. Racial appeal had nothing to do with it. But the economic benefits that resulted from the first Roosevelt administration, and the administration's relative willingness to admit that blacks attained the basic level of humaness, gave some Afro-Americans a degree of confidence. That confidence led blacks to vote for Franklin D. Roosevelt when he ran the second time in 1936. Once black voters began to move in the direction of the Democratic party, Democrats had increased incentive to secure and retain their allegiance.[32] The fact that Jewish electoral support was also gravitating toward Franklin D. Roosevelt put both these groups within the framework of the New Deal "coalition." The inclusion of the leadership of both groups within the New Deal coalition imposed constraints that gave them both incentives to cooperate with each other to some greater extent than before.

By 1948, with Harry Truman's advisers (Clark Clifford, etc.) urging the President that his reelection and the Democratic party's security depended on pulling both Jews and blacks securely into his camp, the Afro-American-Jewish "coalition" was virtually complete, even though it was never quite anticipated. Its articulation was as much after-the-fact as anticipatory, and was strengthened by the needs of the leadership elements in both groups to maintain as good relations as possible with the administration. The coalition took on a life of its own during the period when civil rights issues, as publicly debated, could be understood by each group as manifestly in its interest. In this context, one can see the coalition rather clearly. It was as much implicit as explicit. But it was real. On issues involving votes, Afro-Americans and Jews could vaguely find themselves going in the same direction. Those who led Jewish communal organizations, or the Afro-American civil rights and racial advancement organizations, could act more or less collaboratively, with little or no expectation that their internal critics would be able to undermine them because of that collaborative action. This could all be done with only a vague sense of commonality on the part of "average" people, and without any need to challenge deep-seated feelings in the popular culture.

This involved a definite change. As of the 1930s, the Jewish community had very little apparent interest in the existence of unofficial apartheid[33] for Afro-Americans. In a tough world, each person or group may reasonably do what its information at the time, judged by its own experience and fears, indicates is in its own interest. All through the 1920s, what had once appeared a reasonable civil toleration for Jews in Germany deteriorated, until in 1933 it came to a full collapse. It was only reasonable that the American Jewish community should have been preoccupied with this ominous shift. Jewish leadership focused on matters of primary concern to Jews.

The transition to a wider frame of reference was more or less complete by the latter part of the 1940s. There had been three major steps. The tentative collaboration, gradually expanding, between the NAACP leadership and the German-Jewish leadership, beginning in the 1920s, was the first step. The shift in American political currents, unexpectedly pulling both Jews and Afro-Americans into the New Deal framework, was the second, and this was heightened by the electoral necessities of Harry S. Truman as he approached 1948. The expansion of the Jewish concern about racism per se, a direct response to Hitler, was the third step.[34]

The Jewish part of the alliance first emerged from the old German-Jewish elite, with its emphasis on quiet diplomacy, and from its vehicle, the American Jewish Committee. The Committee did not, in fact, overtly identify its interests with black civil rights until after World War II. But it had been created in 1906, with its professed charter "to prevent the infringement of the civil and religious rights of Jews, and to alleviate the consequences of persecution."[35]

From this motive grew the embryo of Afro-American–Jewish cooperation. The emphasis should be placed properly. In 1946, the American Jewish Committee could move into the area of racial equality, which had not previously drawn its efforts, by emphasizing fair practices legislation. It should be noted that the Committee, for the first time, was drawn to an institutional interest in the fundamental citizenship interest of the right to vote (e.g., the anti–poll tax question) and the fundamental human interest of the right to life (e.g., the antilynching question) that had preoccupied black leadership for more than fifty years.

It may be that in tracing the evolution of the relationship, I might be judged as emphasizing without sufficient warrant the old German-Jewish leadership. Certainly people who played key leadership roles in other Jewish circles were to be found. The great Rabbi Stephen S. Wise, who virtually dominated the American Jewish Congress for many years, was an original member of the National Negro Committee, the body that convened the founding conference of the NAACP.[36] Yet it is notable that the material that shows with whom the black people interacted hardly mentions Rabbi Wise or his associates.

The time also came when the American Jewish Congress played a crucial and open role in the civil rights issues. The Congress, in contrast to the Committee, was at the time notably more populistic. Once they were involved with civil rights issues, they were also more aggressive, urging their members to take on community-level projects against discrimination. They also appeared prominently on the side of the NAACP, when Southern states (in the 1950s) sought legal means to drive the organization out of existence. Indeed, the time came when the Committee, the Congress, and the Anti-Defamation League were all bureaucratized, led by professionals who interpreted their instructions broadly, and pulled their lay leadership into close ties with the black civil rights movement.

The black civil rights leadership's ties were established to participate with the Jewish community, which was rich and powerful and held high public prestige. The old German-Jewish elite was inevitably on the defensive. Its own leadership, based on money and access to high places, was challenged by a leadership relying more on numbers and public opinion. Its stand on Zionism was increasingly a handicap as was its dissociation from values derived from the Jewish popular (East European) culture. This last would ultimately prove a source of weakness, for once the needs of the Jewish community and the needs of the black community began to diverge, other Jewish leadership—having no interest in coalition—could emerge to exploit, rather than ameliorate, that divergence.

Schism in the leadership ranks also proved a source of the weakness in the linkages between Afro-American and Jewish politics in the United States today. The process of extreme ethnocentrism has, by now, reached the point where Jewish politicians, at least vis-à-vis Afro-Americans, express themes deep in the popular culture, some of which are not held, or would not be asserted, by a Jewish leadership that undertook to work with Afro-American leadership. If my understanding of what many discerning consider the obvious is correct, the Jewish leadership that sees a point in working with Afro-Americans has lost the decisive influence among its constituency to spokespersons evincing equally sincere and serious but different intentions. Advocates of the premise that the vital interest of blacks and Jews is one essential whole, composed of many parts separating the observant from the nonobservant, are under pressure from competitors who believe the parts are in sum greater than the whole—some of whom may be elective officials—prepared to adopt (and/or to be perceived as one countenances) anti-black race-specific postures. The belief that in promoting or creating this image politicians naturally draw upon the positive resources and strength of the popular culture triggers a reinforcement mechanism, the consequences of which cause and effect action are the multiplication of disvalues that are declared values equated with virtues. Popular culture, as the standard of excellence rather than the host of the parochial, confusing the commonplace with common sense occasions a role reversal that precipitates what Max Weber apparently did not contemplate: the triumph of politics over bureaucracy—that is (in this specific instance), the relative decline of those who have vested interest in cooperation with blacks in the face of those who are greatly benefited by evoking fears and needs in the popular culture.

In view of the way the relationship came into being, it is also comprehensible that two other sources of confusion are present. The first is the paradox that Jewish group activity, which always has a group reference, is defended in the name of the principle of individualism. Conversely, black activity, which was always highly oriented to the individual black person, is defended today in the name of the group.

Yet the debate is artificial because, now and in the past, communications have tended to be stifled.

If one put oneself back in the position of the NAACP, for instance, acquiring new—and apparently powerful—supporters in the 1920s and 1930s, who would inquire too closely into ultimate meanings? Hardly a treaty or a statute could be drafted without some ambiguity. Why, then, should these people have been different? If one put oneself in the position of Jewish leaders, finding occasion to make this new alliance, who would inquire too much into where it would lead twenty or thirty years from then.

There were, at the time, major public and private structures of discrimination that worked against the well-being of Jews and of Afro-Americans. The evolution of a joint pattern of action, articulated in the language of individual rights, was a means to begin to break through those structures. Only by merging forces did Afro-Americans and Jews seem likely to have the effect they needed, at any time in the foreseeable future. The leadership that articulated "Afro-Americans" and "Jewish" positions could each do so in the same words, though there might have been ultimate differences.

As events have evolved in more recent times, these differences have come to be important. Moreover, they have become more important because of a second factor. The culture, economics, structure of power, and dynamic processes of each group are seen in a somewhat confused way, by the other, leading to demands and expectations that cannot be either disappointed or troublesome. The "facts" are not easy to see, nor to interpret. The simplest words and phrases, or those that may appear at first glance the simplest, may mask cargoes of volatile meaning.[37]

Let me choose a straightforward example. It is very doubtful that either group has a good comprehension of the leadership structure on the other side, and what that leadership structure really is capable of achieving. I suggest that when, in the past, Jewish leadership had all it could do to cope with its own European problems, the black leaders on the other side of the relationship must have had little latitude, or organizational capacity, to know much about the Jewish situation.

Implicit in my reliance on the idea of a popular culture is the belief that neither community is monolithic. Leaders do not control communities, and people do not accept policies or tactics merely because they are proposed. If Jewish and Afro-American leaders do not readily accommodate, each to the other, sheer perversity is not the source of the trouble. It may be that they see what needs to be done, but cannot easily do it. Or it may be that they really do not see the same things.

Yet intelligent people formulate positions as if obstinacy or perversity were the key. When a Jewish leader demands that Afro-Americans "deal with" growing anti-Semitism, he is making a very dubious claim. Leave aside the question of whether he is not mistaken, and whether the scale of anti-Semitism is small in black communities. If anti-Semitism were widespread, which I think it is not, then it would deserve careful attention from black leaders. Yet it does them injustice to imply that all they need do is decide something and "deal with" it. Given the forces at work to produce centrifugal effects in that community, what might they do?

Under Continual Assault

In recent times, affirmative action is the most divisive domestic problem concerning both Afro-Americans and Jews. Affirmative action is, of course, under severe criticism from many parts of the white population—including many who genuinely favor racial progress, and genuinely find affirmative-action methods morally untenable. However, American Jewish intellectuals appear to have taken a uniquely prominent role in opposing affirmative action as policy and as principle. Similarly, some of the Jewish communal organizations, which at one time identified themselves with civil rights, have also been notably vigorous in opposing various affirmative action measures.[38] Their lawyers have been found filing papers—asserting party status or *amicus* status—in law cases relating to higher education, to political representation of blacks, and to hiring and promotion. Their lobbyists are to be found involving themselves in the legislative process.

It is thus a quiet warfare, where usual friends become sometime adversaries. (Of course, we must qualify such statements to allow for recognition of Jewish support of affirmative action, which deserves more attention. However, since it is not the focus of the public dispute, it shall be bypassed here.)

On the other hand, most blacks who write, speak, or assert leadership roles also assert the legitimacy, utility, and, some, the necessity, of affirmative action.[39]

Why is the cleavage so sharp? Why is Jewish opposition to affirmative action so intense? It is, of course, true that present positions of advantage are at stake. Patently, the public school system, the university system, and public employment of the City of New York confer an advantage upon present employees—who are predominantly Jewish—and a new set of rules that would confer a benefit upon new potential employees would be resisted. But this is not enough. If American Jews sometimes fail to grasp the reality of Afro-Americans' historical experience, as it affects contemporary understanding, so it may be that Afro-Americans fail to grasp what the Jews' historical experience means to them. We would do well to understand, if we also believe, this: *American Jews derive from their experience a feeling of being under continual assault.*

Consider Jews as an isolated and subordinated people in Eastern Europe, before World War I. Poland, Romania, and Hungary were forced into the adoption of minority rights in the settlement after World War I. The governments of these countries violated or repudiated these guarantees systematically, within five to ten years. Jews were driven from their occupations, and excluded from universities, not *only* by informal harassment, but by the formal adoption of laws prescribing the number, and fixing the maximum number, of Jews that might be students or professors.[40]

Eastern Europe was swept by the windstorm, Germany by the firestorm. The economist Calvin Hoover published a book, *Germany Enters the Third Reich,* in 1933. Since Hitler took office as chancellor on January 30, 1933, this is a virtually contemporaneous account. According to Hoover, these changes took place immediately, long before the grisley events that have become infamous. Page upon page recites special restrictions that were placed upon Jewish enrollment in universities, on Jewish judges in the courts, and even on Jewish pathologists working upon German cadavers! What must the 1920s have been to yield this result![41]

Nothing in American Jewish experience would seem like these European experiences. Yet one cannot be blind to aspects of American culture that have at least some conceptual similarity. In academic life, people pride themselves on rising above vulgar prejudice. Yet it is possible to find experiences that might not, in principle, be different from what vulgar prejudice might dictate. A. Lawrence Lowell was one of the most original and innovative students of politics that this country has yet to produce. He was an educational reformer of considerable determination. But he was also a defender of a social order that has now gone. As president of Harvard, in the 1920s he sought to impose enrollment limits on Jewish students at Harvard. His biographer says that Jewish enrollment had gone from 7 percent of Harvard College to more than 21 percent in the first two decades of this century.[42] Lowell, arguing for assimilation, maintained that the increase in Jews would drive other students elsewhere, and that Jews interested in assimilation would also then go elsewhere.[43] Lowell was defeated. Though the maintenance of Harvard on assimilationist principles called for a limit on Jewish enrollment,[44] one would have to be a dullard not to see that the very presentation of such a rule would give the Jewish community matter to ponder for a long time.

Kazin repeats the theme as he speaks of Lionel Trilling:

The first Jew in recorded history to get tenure in a Columbia English Department as crowded with three-Anglican names as the House of Bishops. . . . We have room for only one Jew (the English chairman had told Clifton Fadiman) . . . and we have chosen Mr. Trilling.[45]

Jewish sensitivities to the ominous note of "too many Jews" are not dulled by knowledge that Jews, also, from time to time must accede. Laurence Steinhart, ambassador to Turkey during World War II, found himself with less freedom than Morgenthau had during Wilson's years. Ambassador Steinhart felt obliged to recommend to his superiors that non-Jews be assigned to strategic positions in the embassy. The Turks were concerned that their country seemed to have become the one country to which the naming of a Jewish ambassador seemed automatic, the practice having been initiated with Theodore Roosevelt's appointment of Oscar Straus. Moreover, in those times, the Nazis were propagandizing heavily, seeking to enforce the idea that the United States was using Turkey as a vehicle for Jewish emigration to the Middle East. (This matter was not made clearer by the ambassador's presumptive political ambitions that were frustrated in the end by a judgment, made by some of the Jewish community, that he had not sufficiently identified with Jewish welfare at the time).[46]

These vignettes show how it is that within the Jewish experience, even the American Jewish experience, there is the real possibility of attack. American Jews have achieved high positions and respect, but they feel that they cannot afford to let themselves believe in their own good fortune, even when it is apparent. They also have some reason to fear that then present position may be eroded to a degree that would leave them imperiled. Other white groups perceive, from time to time, social discrimination and prejudice. But few, if any, express the sense that they are potentially exposed to some severe penalty in the future, that their present good fortune may be reversed.[47]

Affirmative action is seen in this perspective by a writer who describes it as "another illustration of governmental actions which are free of intended anti-Semitism but endanger Jews."[48] The concern evokes a character in one of Philip Roth's stories, I think *Goodbye, Columbus.* The character repeatedly asks: Is it good for the Jews or bad for the Jews? The question is legitimate. But is it not also a celebration of doctrinal individualism? It reflects what would be called, in Parsonian sociological forms, particularistic concern with the group, as distinguished from some universalistic rule for the human species. The historical detour helps us to find a comprehensible reason, if not an agreeable reason, in the recurrent Jewish opposition to affirmative action. Ultimately, it may be that this course of action is what should, normally, be predicted if little cognizance is given to the fact of a sense of continual assault. The failure to evaluate the sense of assault as a basis for Jewish action leaves mystery, where sense would otherwise exist. Whether the sense of continual assault justifies the course of action that Jewish leadership follows is another matter.

Under Continuous Assault

If blacks fail to perceive continual assault, and the political-cultural consequence it produces, American Jews seem to fail to perceive that Afro-Americans are also under continuous assault. The term *racism* has so many emotive connotations that it may be useful to let it stand aside. Its meaning can be stated differently. Within American culture, there has been a recurring question *among educated people* as to whether a black person has the capability of a white. There has long been a receptivity to the belief that blacks taken as a whole, are less likely to have the capabilities that white persons would have. There is a recurrent propensity to explain the subordinate position of blacks as the inferior position, and to explain the inferior position as the position of the inferior person. (On this, as on so many things, Hamilton and Jefferson seemed to disagree. Hamilton, of aristocratic persuasion, seemed to say that "blacks' 'natural facilities are probably as good as ours' "[49] while Jefferson, the democratic dogmatist, continually returned to an assertion of natural inferiority.)[50]

The roots of this cultural receptivity to the concept of black inadequacy are deep, profound, complicated, and originating in a complex relationship of religion, science, and power in historical experience. In fact, the issue continued to represent itself in new forms as if there were a continual cultural-social search for means to verify the hypothesis of inferiority. This issue most recently presented itself in the arguments (evoked by Shockley, Jensen, etc.) as to whether the capacity for abstraction was equivalent between black and white. The hypothesis at a given moment may be either genetic or cultural, and they change from time to time. Each time a particular hypothesis as to black limitations is discarded, or called into question, some new hypothesis is advanced with similar effect. These hypotheses, assimilated to current practice at any given moment, become further instruments of assault.

The assault is profoundly cultural and psychological. People desire not only practical, material objectives or what the late Harold Lasswell called "welfare" values. They also desire "deference" values "that consist in being taken into consideration [in the acts of others and of the self]."[51]

The withholding of moral and intellectual respect from the black population is perhaps the most pervasive form of assault.

Consider movie and television entertainment. It is "just entertainment," not to be taken seriously, and thus those who criticize it "lack a sense of humor."

Yet is this so?

Entertainment has always been not merely a means of relief from boredom, but a means as well of reasserting old values or establishing new ones. Why else did Shakespeare's plays have to pass the Lord Chamberlain? Why else is Shylock deemed objectionable even in present-day American high school drama? In this light, consider the assault that entertainment makes upon black America daily.

Three illustrations.

Within the past two years, CBS presented a television movie, "Jimmie B. and Andre," which carried the designation "based upon" a true story. The central thread was a close relationship between a white man (American of Greek descent) and a black boy, whom he virtually took in off the streets, and made a part of his own family. In the movie, a series of other lessons were taught, with no sense of perspective: (1) women on welfare evidently send their children out to work, and spend the cash on dope; (2) they allow their dope peddler friends to come into their own homes and beat up their own children; (3) when they die, their relatives' sole interest is in support payments that they can get for the children; (4) local black clergy have no role in this except to encourage people to put money into the collection plate, and to support weak white officials (in this case, the judge); (5) the judge, presented with the maltreatment of the youngster, could cynically rule for an unworthy relative, with the intervention of the black pastor who can help him at the polls; and (6) justice is done only through the rough means of white police officers—in Detroit!—who exercise the freedom to decide whom they will beat and how often, in order to get the truth so that they can obtain retribution in behalf of the little boy. It is not possible, given the limits of public information, to know how the movie treated the factual material that was its basis. But it is possible to know that no one would have any better understanding of the world of black Detroit after having seen that movie, and that those with no knowledge would have been profoundly misinstructed.

Some years ago, James Earl Jones and Dianne Carroll were cast in *Claudine.* From this movie, one would have derived the moral instruction that the world was too tough and Dianne Carroll (as the mother) simply gave up. The burden of the movie is that the struggle for improvement is too great, and by implication that the civil rights struggle was pointless. The children could be left to shift for themselves, at least overnight, under care of the teenage daughter, while the mother would go off for the night with her garbage-truck-driver boyfriend, carrying her best shoes in her hand, with the admonition of the teenage daughter in her ears: Don't get pregnant.

Perhaps the most debilitating is *The Jeffersons*. The pure type of American success story is the smart man, possibly lacking polish, who starts from nothing and becomes rich. After all, if everything turns on getting well educated first, then there is very little hope. Such a person learns, of course, what other people have learned—in the end money is often a great equalizer, and it is more likely to confer a very great advantage if there is a very great amount. George Jefferson's understanding of the principle is definite. But his understanding is used to picture him as a figure of ridicule, respected neither by his associates, his wife, his housemaid, nor—surely!—by the audience that watches his antics. Bill Hitchcock, in *The Crash of '79*, uses his money the same way, but is merely deemed sophisticated.

The problem of moral and intellectual respect is a key consideration in black politics. Yet transactions that involve blacks and their allies show it to be a specially troublesome problem.[52] It has been so in dealings with trade unions, with Democratic liberals, and even inside the White House in the most recent administration. If communications between allies are often stifled, as Neustadt says of Britain and America, that point can particularly be made as to communications between Jews and Afro-Americans.

Whatever else may be true, the sense of discomfort (indeed, disagreement!), that some interpretations of the Jewish–Afro-American relationship must induce is seldom clear in exposition. Consider the following sentence: "It would be no exaggeration to suggest that the '40s and '50s represented the 'Jewish phase' of the civil rights movement."[53]

The black civil rights struggle was simply the assertion of claims of equality of citizenship, and of resistance to the insistent pressures of white supremacy.[54] This struggle had fluctuated, but had never ceased since the beginning of the century. The main Jewish communal agencies for the first time committed a major share of their resources to the Afro-American civil rights struggle, in the 1940s and 1950s, thus bringing to fruition what had begun in the 1920s and 1930s.[55] Jewish public opinion, well into the 1970s, was notably supportive of civil rights. And the Jewish communal agencies, having committed their resources, played crucial roles. It would be difficult to overestimate the credit that, in context of the whole country, would be due.

If this were the point of the cited sentence, one would have no basis for reservation. But this evidently would not capture what Friedman means. "According to James Q. Wilson's *Negro Politics*," says Friedman, "blacks and black organizations played a minor role in these early battles."[56]

Upon review, this summation of Wilson's study *may* be correct, though it appears rather imprecise, and doubtfully correct. *Negro Politics,* a pioneering study, based upon a doctoral dissertation, took its data from Chicago and New York, primarily in the years after World War II. It is doubtful whether this book *could have been* adequate to support a generalization about the role of "blacks and black organizations in . . . early [civil rights] battles."[57] In addition, the summary is at variance with what is a major point in the book. Much of the analysis involves a comparison of "voluntary" organizations (e.g., the Urban League or the NAACP) with the professional politicians in the local party organizations. The voluntary organizations were interpreted by Wilson as much more likely to put forth civil rights goals of a "status" type (e.g., fair employment practices legislation). The professional politicians were more likely to pursue "welfare" goals (e.g., divisible benefits that could be assigned to individual persons).[58] If Wilson said, and I cannot find this statement upon reviewing *Negro Politics,* that the black organizations played a "minor" role in the civil rights (status) battles, this would have been inconsistent, with the design of the book.

I would argue, as the discussion of antilynching would indicate, that it would also have been inconsistent with the historical record.

The issue here is not simply a tedious dispute about historiography or about the interpretation of data in political science and sociology. While that would be interesting in itself, for scholarship, Friedman's article is not principally an exercise in scholarship. It is, rather, a policy paper. Its express purpose, by title, is to articulate *New Directions for American Jews.* It is, also by its own internal assertion, a critique of the 1981–82 Joint Program Plan of the National Community Relations Advisory Council.[59] My *inference* is that the article is part of a debate, the scale and context of which I cannot assess, within Jewish leadership circles, as to their further posture regarding the black community and black-related issues.

My further inference is that the article expresses disagreement with Jewish leaders who seek to reestablish, or to maintain, strong ties with Afro-American leadership. The author expresses no discomfort, to speak of, with the Plan until it turns to "domestic and social issues."

The Plan he said, noted that "rising indices of black anti-Semitism had 'created concerns and anxiety among Jews' "[60]:

> The Plan went on to examine the causes of deterioration of the old alliance, including the shift of the Black struggle from the South to the North and "a growing sense of kinship among some blacks with people of the Third World."[60]

It would appear, at least in my interpretation, that he finds the Plan's analysis unsatisfactory in this respect!

> Yet in an attempt, perhaps, to display even-handedness or to demonstrate continued Jewish identification with the plight of the poor, the Plan went on to place a major share of the responsibility for recent tensions on the shoulders of the Jews themselves.[61]

It is not self-evident, at least to an outsider, why the even-handedness is inherently bad. The implication appears to be, however, that the frictions arose solely from factors in the black community. Presumably, the function of this formulation is to defend the view that requires attention to be turned away from black-related issues. It would be futile—not to say illogical—to argue that any community should, or could, act contrary to its own perceived best interests. If this is the conclusion that contemporary Jews reach, no outside observer will be able to alter the judgments that follow.

However, the formulation that Jews have "done enough," because they have in the past defined and overcome the civil rights barriers in "their" phase of the movement, appears to rest upon very weak ground. Moreover, it could contribute to further deterioration. To the extent that, in a time of stress built upon realistic conflict, Jewish action is predicated in terms necessarily offensive to Afro-American interests *and self-images,* the opportunities for cooperation will be lessened rather than reduced.

I began this section with a commentary upon continuous assault. The extended discussion of civil rights history is in response to a formulation that participates in the assault. But I should move on to the more general point that there are important issues, domestic and foreign, that involve the potential reciprocation of assault.

The Reciprocation of Assault

It would appear that we now have a circumstance where both Afro-American and Jewish leaders face the prospect of reciprocal assault, each upon the vital interests and respect symbols of the other.

Domestic Questions

There is some profound difference of opinion and interest as to what should be sought in domestic American policy. Jewish leadership has shown a tendency, recently, to line up strongly on matters that necessarily involve the most profound forms of assault. In effect, and without intent, Jewish leadership has tended to find that its interests are served by advocating positions that rest upon measures closely aligned to racial stratification.

This has its manifestations in one matter that might have been thought egalitarian: standardized testing. But, in present-day terms, standardized testing is one of the more important means of assault upon black claims and potentialities. Let me say explicitly that standardized testing is not, per se, a bad thing. The question is: who is testing whom, to what purpose or end?

Controversies about testing and test results are not principally about "aptitudes," those aptitudes being more often mere expressions of previous training. Nor are they questions about "intelligence." They are instead questions about how to allocate social resources or to assign social roles, and thus become questions about the basis for policies of stratification.

Testing, per se, is a reasonable means to determine useful knowledge. But the usefulness of the knowledge reflects prior social decisions that can, in many circumstances, be part of the pattern of continuous assault.[62]

If one perceives continuous assault, and takes account of institutionalized disadvantage inherited from older decisions, then optimism about the assurance and rate of movement away from racial stratification is necessarily tempered. This accentuates a point of difference between some Afro-American understandings and the understandings of at least some commentators in Jewish leadership circles.

One view expressed in Jewish circles appears to mean that in the absence of specific legal requirements for discrimination, or legally expressed sanction for private discriminatory agreements, the exercise of public authority is not legitimate. That I take to be the meaning of the following passage:

> The justice for Jews and other minorities in the civil rights laws was not that the laws mandated relief for Jews or other specified groups—they didn't—but that they prohibited racial or religious discrimination. With considerations of race or religion eliminated, the bigot's target was removed, or at least blurred.[63]

It is better to recognize, realistically, what is at stake in the formulation of what "justice . . . in the civil rights laws" meant. If we follow that quoted, then it follows that the purpose was to achieve a legal formulation that would allow, by purely private action, the relief of the burdens then experienced. The theoretical basis for this view has been stated elsewhere in the advocacy of "equality of opportunity" in contrast to "equality of results." But the complete denial of the relevance of "results" is an arid formalism. "Opportunity" is not "equal" if, over time, one participant is virtually guaranteed to lose all the time to another party. It is not different from the principle that "due process" has been denied, even if the trial is technically correct, by virtue of a coercive atmosphere. That was the point at stake in the *Frank* case and the *Dempsey* case, the common juncture of the first active Black-Jewish collaboration.[64]

The practical situation is highly pertinent. The overall assessment of social and economic status would indicate that, in most parts of the economy, Jews in 1982 would be relatively well-off, if specific and adverse discriminatory measures were avoided. If blacks use a particularistic standard (is it good for *us* or bad for *us?*), they would justifiably reach a different answer.

The paraphernalia of unofficial apartheid have been removed, to a degree that might be regarded as surprising. In that respect the "bigot's target [has been] blurred." But mere blurring of the bigot's target was never the sole purpose. The purpose is, in fact, to achieve a reasonable opportunity for the actual exercise of citizenship rights, in the broadest sense of that term, with the prospect that the next generation or two will not retrogress into, or stagnate in, an inferior position.

Occupational diversity is substantial. There are relatively few occupations in which it is apparent that blacks will not be hired. From increased occupational choice comes the increased chances for the "working class Respectables" and for the expanded black middle class. These two subgroups of the black population are, in the immediate future, the source of hope, and their atrophy the source of danger. The black middle class, particularly, is taken as an indicator that so much progress has been made, that race is no longer a significant factor in everyday existence, to the extent that it should warrant public policy attention.[65]

The peril of the black middle class, which will necessarily have to be the class in which the capital deficiency is ultimately repaired, is that it presently lacks the resources to stabilize itself as a class. (Class is intergenerational, and if one lacks the capability to assure that one's dumb children—not one's smart children—will be able to hold to the position, then one's class position is insecure.)

The reason is that the black middle class depends upon the public sector, or upon the nonprofit sector. Its members may have high earnings. But they are largely people who came to high earnings from a very low economic base. The ratio between their earnings and their holdings in capital is dangerously low. Their presence in public sector/nonprofit sector activities is directly responsive to prior limitations in the job market, when relatively few of them could get into the entry levels in the private sector. But since this public/nonprofit sector is the most squeezed by decline in the economy, it is reasonably certain that a proportion of the black middle class will experience downward mobility, as they earlier experienced upward mobility.

In the private sector, the black middle class is simply a recent arrival. Young lawyers in white law firms, still at the associate stage, are very much at risk. It is apparent that, in addition to their personal strengths or limitations, the extent to which firms are prosperous overall will influence their ability to succeed. Similar considerations apply to a wide variety of other occupations and situations, such as junior executives in industry and university tenure. In addition, the private sector has adopted "merit" hiring criteria more extensively than might have been predicted. But there is still some evidence that rates of hiring, of promotion, of discipline, and of firing remains disparate.

If the purpose of the change in law is to be realized, then it would be necessary to adopt supplemental means appropriate to the factual circumstances of the affected population, in this case the black population. In this sense, it is legitimate to adopt restitutive, reparational, or corrective activity.

In this context, the debates about general principles may be useless. The problem is for the Jewish leadership to be able to recognize what it is asking Afro-American leadership to accept: simply stagnation, leading to retrogression. It is also for black leadership to recognize what it might, under some conditions, be asking Jewish leadership to accept: actual retrenchment from present positions of advantage, in the interest of improving the black position. It is not constructive, in any situation, to formulate a question to which the other party can only render a hostile answer. The problem, in these domestic issues, is first to move away from the dogmatism that presently characterizes debate, and to see what opportunities may exist.

International Questions

The domestic issues are troublesome. The world politics issues are dangerous. The demands of world politics upon the United States, structure to a very profound degree, the latitudes within which domestic policy changes can be made. This is true in a very broad sense, because of the impact of economic, mineral, and strategic concerns on a global basis.

The issues of world politics also have specific relevance, however, to the problem of reciprocal assault.

The overseas connection has, I think, had a more profound significance in the Jewish popular culture than in the Afro-American popular culture, for a long time and until recently. Perhaps it still has. Ever since Jews have been a significant force in American politics, they have sought to secure the diplomatic power of the United States in support of their fellow Jews abroad. Further, the question of the treatment of Jews in Europe after World War I, and of the settlement as it would affect Palestine, were both of great importance. In the contemporary situation, the critical issue is Israel. The defense and survival of Israel is the key issue for American Jews, and for those whom they would treat as friends.

The belief is present among some members of the Afro-American intellectual community, that the Jewish community demands of Afro-Americans' automatic agreement as to whatever may be its views on Israel.

The process is reflected in two accounts made privately, though in my presence. The Jewish community of a Southern city was asserted, but not shown, to have sent word to a black university president, in that city, that they would seek to preclude future contributions to his institution. The reason is that Jesse Jackson had been given the freedom of the campus. Not only do we all respond adversely to threat, but, in this particular case, the threat involved a small, financially imperilled, historically significant institution. What dynamic should we expect in the circumstances indicated? In the other account, a major scholar of world reputation, was reported to have been informed that the Jewish community was "reevaluating" its relationship to him, though the precise nature of his relationship to the matters affecting Israel was not clear to me.

Blacks perceive, to a certain extent, correctly or not, that Jewish critics oppose not only their views on particular questions of foreign policy, but also their very right to hold and assert such views at all. This view would appear exaggerated.

In particular, Jewish political analysis and tactics appear to incorporate a sharp conception of *primary* interests. Thus, the American Jewish Committee, in days past, could absorb black civil rights interests when it could assimilate them to "issues of primary concern to Jews." Jews do oppose any political or intellectual act that appears to threaten Israel. And they have, it would seem, been disconcerted by black expressions on Middle East issues *not before understood as a black primary interest,* particularly when those expressions seemed in opposition to Israel.

The matter was surely crystallized by the events associated with Ambassador Young's meeting with PLO personnel in 1979. Nothing makes it untenable on its face, although credible contrary interpretations can also be formulated. Most black commentators, I expect, would think Young to have been engaged in a tentative exploration, with the expectation that he would be "the fall guy" if it did not work out well.

The point can surely be argued, since Ambassador Wolf had been engaged in a series of discussions in Vienna. But it cannot be proved or disproved on public evidence. The fact is that Ambassador Young had developed a domestic political posture that made him highly vulnerable. His open expression of personal views put him in perfect alignment with the wish for defiance that is so strong in black culture. But it simultaneously put him out of alignment with the measured style normally demanded in the broad American culture for a man in his role. Nearly any controversial event might have provided the final straw. That this precipitous event did happen in relation to Israel was random, fortuitous. The entire subsequent reaction had little to do with American blacks' perceptions of Israel or of Jews. Once Ambassador Young, as both the most visible and, some thought, most powerful, black man in politics came to this crossroads, it was but predictable that there would be an enormous rallying-round.

If, of course, blacks perceived the Jewish community to be overwhelmingly powerful, then it would also be predictable that some of the criticism would be directed against the Jewish community. The issue does not appear to me to depend on the question of the defense of Israel. Most of black leadership, and most of the black intellectual community, appears not to regard that as in question. It is, of course, not possible or honest to disguise that some anti-Israel propositions do enter the black political debate.

These matters should not be overgeneralized. It may be that black political leadership, and the black intellectual community, have paid little attention to some anti-Israel articulations, or have infrequently articulated their own opposition to these views. But it should not be disguised from the rest of the world that the majority of black leadership—NAACP, National Urban League, Congressional Black Caucus, major religious denominations, major fraternities and sororities, professional associations, etc.—have not adopted these doubtful views. Moreover, some have expressly rejectd such views, with no apparent cost, which implies that in the overall black constituency, there is no demand for such anti-Israel views.

The episode provides some lessons, however, as to Jewish perceptions. Israel becomes the ultimate value, and in behalf of that ultimate value American Jews have adopted an extraordinary self-restraint. Virtually all Israeli policies and practices are treated *as if* to evaluate or criticize them would, in fact, call Israel itself into question.

If Jews of the diaspora have accepted this restraint upon themselves, it is to be expected that Jewish beliefs about black attitudes toward Israel will also be intense. This is a source of conflict.

The point of contention that threatens to be very dangerous is South Africa. It is not clear to me what degree of unanimity Israeli leaders have on their relationship to South Africa. Nor is it clear to me what degree of support American Jews are prepared to give to a pro-Republic of South Africa policy, if that should be the direction in which Israel turns. South Africa must be understood in the context of historic black leadership concerns about Africa, in that of the reemergent black identification with the symbolism of Africa since World War II, and with the emergence of apartheid in South Africa since the War.

Afro-American leadership was, in the years between World War I and the end of World War II, particularly interested in the fate and status of three independent countries: Ethiopia, Liberia, and Haiti. The revived and expanded interest in all Africa after World War II, and the extension of the Afro-American interest in "roots," has changed the relationship qualitatively. The point in dispute emerges to the extent that there is a repprochment between Israel and the Republic of South Africa. The relationship between Israel and the Republic of South Africa is not the focus of this paper. However, certain elements are evident. In the African continent, the Republic maintains itself by a sophisticated combination of economic and military power, an ability to act coercively far beyond its boundaries. What the future may hold I do not purport to analyze. But the ramifications are manifold for the rest of Africa, and for American policy in Africa. To the extent that Israel's interests are also engaged, the domestic interaction between Jews and Afro-Americans in United States politics, because of American policy in Africa, becomes a more troublesome prospect than anything yet faced.

Conclusion

I return to the Neustadt themes. Muddled perceptions and stifled communications, he points out, are pervasive, from which it follows that disappointed expectations also are pervasive.

> Yet relatively speaking, the fourth strand is a rarity. Paranoid reactions do not always or inevitably stem from disappointment. . . . Misperceptions evidently make for crisis in proportion to the intimacy of relations. Hazards are proportionate to the degree of friendship. Indifference and hostility may not breed paranoia; friendship.[66]

One may not accept this entire formulation. Otherwise, we should have trouble explaining the suspicion-paranoia that exists between Greeks and Turks or between the Soviet Union and the United States. But it is suggestive. It builds on common experience. We are the most angry when we think we have been betrayed or let down, by those upon whom we expected to depend or in whom we trusted.

The issues between Jews and Afro-Americans today elicit such volatile feelings and reactions as to remind one of the passage from Matthew Arnold's "Dover Beach":

And we are here as on a darkling plain
Swept with confused alarms of struggle and flight,
Where ignorant armies clash by night.

There is bitterness enough for all to drink, and mutual recrimination destroys the judgment. If we would work through the issues, we must study not only the issues themselves, but each other. In a certain sense, Jews need to study Afro-Americans, Afro-Americans to study Jews, and both to study—with as much objectivity as may be possible— larger dynamics of human action. Each needs to get into the mind and the skin, so to speak, of the other. American Jews are a brilliantly successful people, whose daily existence is clouded over by a pall of never-ending fear. Will the ancient enemy, anti-Semitism, come in some new form and take away the most recent successes?

In these latter days, the Jews' fear seems to drive that community to ally itself with those whose purpose is to reconstruct an older order of racial stratification, in slightly new fashion.

Afro-Americans are a brilliantly surviving people, their demise being prematurely predicated for two hundred years, but their daily existence is shadowed by a never-ending frustration; will the ancient enemy, racism in its most intense form, never cease to block even the narrowest paths, so that what appears to be progress may prove real and not mirages? And the Afro-Americans' compelling needs seem to drive them to seek real goals that cannot but activate the Jewish fear further.

"Communication" is not a panacea. In a pure zero-sum game, no communication is possible to resolve the conflict. If, of course, we were to assume that a relationship now exists between Afro-Americans and Jews, this discussion would be pointless. Instead, in this setting, we assume real conflicts that may, in some degree, be moderated or managed and real interests that, in some degree, be found convergent.

The future of constructive action depends upon a deeper understanding of the vital images and interests in each group. If that is to happen, each side must avoid false perspectives that lead to damage of the psychic or physical necessities of either (or in either) group.

Whenever the popular cultures of any two groups meet, the likelihood of conflict is great. One of the functions of responsible leadership, political or intellectual, is to help clarify values in the popular culture, values in the rest of the world, and sheer practical necessity, so as to identify what may be constructive paths.

It may be that, in some sense, the modern communications era has done to ethnic-communal leadership what it appears to have done in the larger political arena. It may have eroded the capability of leadership to act by enhancing the appeal of instant-drama communications. Thus it may be that one of the factors in intense Afro-American–Jewish friction is not merely difference of interest, which must have been at least as great in the past. It may also be that the simultaneous projection of political leaders rooted in the popular culture, into the highest governmental posts, and the necessities of telecommunications and instant-drama appeal, reduces the time frame within which reasonable consideration can be given to the necessities of living in peace with each other.

The question is whether the leadership, in each community, has even the will to seek constructive choices or not. And, even more, in a time when leadership is at a discount, can the structure and the culture of each community make it possible to do so? If the question chills, so must a negative answer to any believer in a political order encompassing as valid principles the market economy, democracy, constitutionalism, and pluralism. In the American case, those principles may require adjustment to each other, but none can be sacrificed.

Notes

1. Richard E. Nuestadt, *Alliance Politics* (New York: Columbia University Press, 1970), p. 56.

2. "Some" deserves emphasis for there is no aspect of American society, so far as I can tell, about which there is more misinformation than race relations. Nor is there any aspect about which we all insist, more determinedly, in holding to our preconceptions.

3. Lawrence Grossman, *The Democratic Party and the Negro: Northern and National Politics, 1898–1892* (Urbana: University of Illinois Press, 1976), notably pp. 60–142.

4. The Dewey campaigns appear to me deviant from the Republican norm since then. The first fruits are apparent in the Eisenhower years, but it is only with the Goldwater campaign that the GOP set out almost explicitly to be the white party in the south. It has gone farther since.

5. Grossman, *The Democratic Party and the Negro*, p. 171.

6. My colleague Henry J. Abraham, in preliminary comments on this paper, says that Theodore Roosevelt and William Howard Taft were similarly sympathetic.

7. Alpheus T. Mason, *Brandeis: A Free Man's Life* (New York: Viking, 1946), pp. 375–408.

8. Among those most opposed to Brandeis was Moorefield Storey, whose important role in the history of the NAACP, and in particular in the NAACP's effort to bring major national leaders into a campaign against lynching, is recited in Charles Flint Kellogg, *NAACP* (Baltimore: Johns Hopkins University Press, 1967), vol. 1.

9. Isaiah Friedman, *Germany, Turkey, and Zionism* (Oxford: Clarendon Press, 1977), p. 194.

10. Seth P. Tillman, *Anglo-American Relations at the Paris Peace Conference of 1919* (Princeton, N.J.: Princeton University Press, 1961), pp. 225–28.

11. My initial exploration into this theme is in *The Divisible Republic,* part 2, essay 4 (New York: Abelard-Schuman, 1973).

12. W. J. Cash, *The Mind of the South* New York: Vintage Books, 1941), pp. 45, 116–20 and 306–11.

13. Alfreda M. Duster, ed., *Crusade for Justice, Autobiography of Ida B. Wells* (Chicago: University of Chicago Press, 1970).

14. I calculated from figures in Florence Murray, ed., *The Negro Handbook, 1942* (New York: Wendell Malliet & Company, 1942), p. 52.

15. Kellogg, *NAACP,* vol. I.

16. James Weldon Johnson, Secretary of the NAACP (1921–30), details the Association's intense involvement with this issue, and the preparation and presentation of the Dyer Anti-Lynching Bill in Congress between 1919 and 1923 in *Along This Way* (New York: Viking, Compass Edition, 1968), pp. 362–74. Walter White, Johnson's successor (and Roy Wilkin's immediate predecessor) pays graceful tribute: "It was Jim's skillful hand which guided the efforts for passage of federal legislation against lynching during the twenties. . . . We were able to secure passage of the Dyer Bill by the House of Representatives, but invariably the bill would meet its death in the Senate because of filibusters. . . ." (Walter White, *A Man Called White* [New York: Viking Press, 1948], p. 42).

17. White, *A Man Called White,* p. 42 and passim; Eugene Levy, *James Weldon Johnson: Black Leader, Black Voice* (Chicago: University of Chicago Press, 1979); and, in particular, NAACP, *24th Annual Report for 1933* (New York, 1934), pp. 22 and generally.

18. For a recent journalistic account of the Frank case, see *Washington Post,* 18 March 1982.

19. Howard Morley Sachar, *Course of Modern Jewish History* (Cleveland: A Dotte Book, 1963), p. 521. "Marshall [had] extraordinary prestige and standing among his fellow Jews. Israel Zangwill once jestingly remarked that American Jewry lived under Marshall Law; someone else called Marshall, Louis XIX."

20. Mary White Ovington, *The Walls Came Tumbling Down* (New York: Harcourt, Brace and Company, 1947), pp. 154–63.

21. White, *A Man Called White,* p. 53.

22. *American Jewish Year Book* 26 (1930): 30.

23. NAACP, *23rd Annual Report for 1929* (New York, 1930), pp. 57–58.

24. Johnson, *Along This Way,* p. 407.

25. White, A Man Called White, p. 156.

26. *NAACP 24th Annual Report for 1930,* p. 55.

27. Lawrence H. Fuchs, *The Political Behavior of American Jews* (Glencoe, Ill.: Free Press, 1956).

28. Grossman, *The Democratic Party and the Negro,* p. 167. Turner was highly militant, a political pragmatist, and an advocate of recolonization in Africa. In the end, disillusioned with the United States, he left and died in Canada.

29. Bishop of the African Methodist Episcopal Zion Church, the third largest black denomination.

30. Holden, *The Divisible Republic,* part 2, pp. 95–97.

31. White, *A Man Called White,* pp. 99–101.

32. I have not examined the relevant statistics, but I would assume this pattern must have been reflected in the 1934 election results. I base this inference on the fact that the first black *Democratic* Congressman, Arthur W. Mitchell, was a relatively new Chicagoan who, in 1934, defeated Oscar O. DePriest, an old-time, though, highly militant and "absolutely fearless" black Republican who was also rather conservative, and anti-New Deal (Maurine Christopher, *Black Americans in Congress* [New York: Thomas Y. Crowell, 1978], pp. 174–75). The term "absolutely fearless" was applied to Congressman DePriest by Congressman William L. Dawson in a conversation with me when I was both a graduate student and a precinct captain's assistant in the Second Ward of Chicago about 1953.

33. Let me emphasize that the term "unofficial apartheid" is not hyperbolic. I have discussed it in some detail in *The Divisible Republic* (New York: Abelard-Schuman, 1973), part 2. Municipal *racial* zoning was attempted before World War I and declared unconstitutional in *Buchanan* v. *Warley,* six years before the Supreme Court held zoning as a general practice to be constitutional *(Euclid* v. *Ambler Realty),* but cities still tried racial zoning as of the 1930s (as Richmond, Virginia did). All this was years before the

Malan government came to power in South Africa in 1948 and initiated the process leading to the Group Areas Act in that country. Moreover, the extent of other things understood to be "off limits" to blacks, even in the North after World War II, was so great as to warrant the designation: job categories, residential areas, by private agreement among builders, brokers, and bankers, faculty clubs for Northern universities, dormitories at Northern universities, etc.

34. I may point out that the most critical research regarding prejudice and discrimination, was sponsored either by the social science arm of the American Jewish Committee or the social science arm of the American Jewish Congress, in the years after World War II.

35. Charter of American Jewish Committee, 1906.

36. Kellogg, *NAACP.*

37. Stuart C. Gilman, "Alternate Life-Worlds for Blacks and Whites: A Research Note," *Ethnicity* 5 (1978): 14–19 contains some ideas that are helpful on this point.

38. This chapter is being revised as the Voting Rights Act issues appear to be approaching their climax in May 1982. It should be observed that, in the minds of some knowledgeable black observers, one of the reasons for the "proportional representation" agitation is not its likelihood in VRA cases. Rather, the purported desire is that strong antiproportional representation language should be included in this statute, as a precedent for its inclusion in other legislative enactments in other matters such as employment discrimination. This is not something, however, that I have verified, although it does not seem prima facie ridiculous as an interpretation.

39. As Jewish opposition is not uniform, neither is Afro-American support, but that aspect also cannot be examined here.

40. Howard M. Sachar, *The Course of Modern Jewish History* (Cleveland: A Delta Book, 1963), pp. 360, 362–4, 366.

41. Fiction is not history, but Hoover gives one the sense that there is much veracity about Arthur R. G. Solmssen, *A Princess in Berlin* (New York: Ballantine Books, 1980).

42. The episode is discussed in Henry A. Yeomans, *Abbott Lawrence Lowell* (Cambridge: Harvard University Press, 1948), pp. 209–18. It is also mentioned briefly in Sachar, *Course of Modern Jewish History,* p. 341.

43. One might note that a great deal of sociological research on the integration of residential areas in the 1950s and later is based on the same concept. In housing it is called "tipping point."

44. Lowell was also interested in the creation of dormitories in which all students would live, in contrast to the private facilities that then existed, and had been active in this question when he was still a faculty member. His biographer attributes his interest to his belief in the educational validity of overcoming class and ethnic distinctions among students, including his opposition to the asserted "Little Jerusalems" as certain predominantly Jewish residences were called. However, note one interesting feature: when freshman residence halls were made compulsory, somehow the black students did not apply for the first ten years, and when a black student did apply, was refused on the grounds that no one should be "forced" to associate with a student of another race in the dormitories. This was a live question at nearly the same as was the question of Jewish enrollment limitations. (Yeomans, *Lowell,* pp. 75–77.) Stephen R. Fox (*The Guardian of Boston: William Monroe Trotter* [New York: Atheneum, 1970], 261–3) discusses this episode in relation to Trotter, a pioneer civil rights advocate who was also a Harvard alumnus.

45. Alfred Kazin, *New York Jew,* New York: Alfred A. Knopf, 1978, 40–41.

46. Barry Rubin, "Ambassador Laurence A. Steinhart: The Perils of a Jewish Diplomat," *American Jewish History* 70:3 (March 1981), 331–46.

47. In this regard, Jews are more similar to blacks than they are to virtually every other group.

48. Nathan Perlmutter, "The Instinct of Self-Defense," *Present Tense* (8, no. 3 (Spring 1981): 39.

49. Jefferson to John Jay, 14 March 1779, printed in *Slaves and Masters,* 1567–1854, with an Introduction by Charles H. Wesley (Chicago, Ill.: Encyclopedia Brittanica Educational Publishers, 1969), p. 414.

50. Winthrop D. Jordan, *White Over Black* (Baltimore: Penguin Books, 1968), pp. 435–44; George M. Fredrickson, *The Black Image in the White Mind* (New York: Harper Torchbooks, 1972); and John Chester Miller, *The Wolf by the Ears: Thomas Jefferson and Slavery* (New York: Free Press, 1977), pp. 46–59.

51. Harold D. Lasswell and Abraham Kaplan, *Power and Society: A Framework for Inquiry,* New Haven: Yale University Press, 1950, 55–56.

52. This is most likely to be a problem in dealing with allies who hold a strong position (and therefore are aware of what they are doing for one), and is almost a nonissue in dealing with adversaries or those who are so distant (as most contemporary Republican leadership is) that one simply does not exist on their horizon.

53. Murray Friedman, "New Directions for American Jews," *Commentary* (January 1982), p. 40.

54. August A. Meir, *Negro Thought in America, 1880–1915* (Ann Arbor: University of Michigan Press, 1963).

55. The discussion of the relationship between black leadership and Jewish leadership from the early 1920s onward is illuminating throughout Meir's excellent *Negro Thought in America.*

56. Meier, *Negro Thought in America,* 41.

57. Wilson himself is meticulous in identifying his method of inquiry, his primary concentration on Chicago, and the extent to which he thinks his Chicago conclusions are broadly generalizable (*Negro Politics* [Glencoe, N.Y.: Free Press of Glencoe, 1960], pp. 9–11).

58. These and other, matters were discussed intently at a panel where Wilson was the main paper presenter, at the American Political Science Association in New York in 1960. The panelists included the late John A. Morsell, then assistant director of the NAACP, Herbert Garfinkel, Paul Pfretzschner, and myself (the late Jack Isakoff and Maurice Klain may also have been on the panel). A letter that I subsequently wrote Wilson is indicative.

59. My understanding is that the National Jewish Community Relations *Advisory* Council (emphasis mine) is an umbrella organization encompassing the American Jewish Committee, the American Jewish Congress, the Anti-Defamation League, and local Jewish agencies from a number of cities. There is no counterpart black organization, though the Black Leadership Forum may have some potential similarities. In *The Divisible Republic,* part 1, pp. 172–73, I put forward some ideas as to an "Afro-American general council" that would have some overall advisory and deliberate function, but the idea has thus far been persuasive to few people. Maybe its time has passed.

60. Friedman, "New Directions for American Jews," *Commentary,* January 1982, p. 40.

61. Holden, *The Divisible Republic,* 172–73.

62. For example, testing of active duty personnel in the armed services, on matters that clearly must reflect previous high school education (or its lack), can then be interpreted back as a commentary on the adequacy of one set of military personnel or another (*Washington Post,* Sunday, 21 February 1982; and criticism of the *Post* in *Washington North Star,* 9 April 1982).

63. Perlmutter, *Instant of Self-Defence.*

64. Notes 14–15 above.

65. On the "working class Respectables," whom I regard as the core without whom progress is not possible, I have no more to say here, but must reserve consideration to another time. However, cf., Holden, *The Divisible Republic,* part 1, pp. 29–30.

66. Neustadt, *Alliance Politics,* pp. 71–72.

DATE DUE			

Jews ... 193494